Adult
Intergenerational
Relations

Vern L. Bengtson, PhD, is AARP/University Professor of Gerontology and Sociology at the Andrus Gerontology Center of the University of Southern California, and past President of the Gerontological Society of America. He directs the 23-year-old "Longitudinal Study of Three-Generation Families" at USC. Among his most recent publications are *The Changing Generations* (with Andrew Achenbaum), and *Intergenerational Linkages: Hidden Connections in American Society* (with Robert Harootyan), also published by Springer Publishing Co.

K. Warner Schaie, PhD, is the Evan Pugh Professor of Human Development and Psychology and Director of the Gerontology Center at the Pennsylvania State University. He has previously held professional appointments at the University of Nebraska, West Virginia University, and the University of Southern California. Dr. Schaie received his BA from the University of California–Berkeley, and his MS and PhD degrees from the University of Washington, all in psychology. He is the author or editor of 22 books and over 150 journal articles and chapters related to the study of human aging. Dr. Schaie is the recipient of the Distinguished Scientific Contributions Award of the American Psychological Association and of the Robert W. Kleemeier Award for Distinguished Research Contributions from the Gerontological Society of America.

Linda M. Burton, PhD, is Professor of Family Studies and Sociology at the Pennsylvania State University. She has been a Brookdale National Fellow, Spencer Foundation Fellow, and Fellow at the Center for Advanced Study in The Behavioral Sciences, Stanford University. Dr. Burton received her BS, MA, and PhD degrees from the University of Southern California. She has authored journal articles and chapters related to intergenerational family process and the life-course of African-American families. Her current research examines the relationship between neighborhood context, multigenerational family structure, teenage childbearing, and the family role responsibilities of elderly African-American women.

Adult Intergenerational Relations

Effects of Societal Change

▲ ● ■

Vern L. Bengtson, PhD
K. Warner Schaie, PhD
Linda M. Burton, PhD

Editors

Springer Publishing Company

Copyright © 1995 by Springer Publishing Company, Inc.

Springer Publishing Company, Inc.
536 Broadway
New York, NY 10012

Cover design by Tom Yabut
Production Editor: Joyce Noulas

95 96 97 98 99 / 5 4 3 2 1

Library of Congress Cataloging-in-Publication Data

Adult intergenerational relations : effects of societal change / Vern
   L. Bengtson, K. Warner Schaie, Linda Burton, editors.
        p.   cm.
    Includes bibliographical references and index.
    ISBN 0-8261-8560-6
      1. Aging.   2. Intergenerational relations.   I. Bengtson, Vern L.
   II. Schaie, K. Warner (Klaus Warner), 1928   III. Burton, Linda.
   HQ1061.A35   1994
   305.26 – dc20   94-17759
                                                                 CIP

Printed in the United States of America

Contents

v

Contributors

Linda M. Chatters, PhD
Institute of Social Research
University of Michigan
Ann Arbor, MI 48106

Rand D. Conger, PhD
Iowa State University
Department of Sociology
Ames, IA 50011

Glen H. Elder, Jr., PhD
Department of Sociology
University of North Carolina
Chapel Hill, NC 27516

Janice I. Farkas, PhD
Population Research Institute
The Pennsylvania State University
University Park, PA 16802

Du Feng
Andrus Gerontology Center
University of Southern California
Los Angeles, CA 90089

Christine L. Fry, PhD
Department of Anthropology
Loyola University of Chicago
Chicago, IL 60626

Roseann Giarrusso, PhD
Andrus Gerontology Center
University of Southern California
Los Angeles, CA 90089

John C. Henretta, PhD
Department of Sociology
University of Florida
Gainesville, FL 32611

Christopher Hertzog, PhD
School of Psychology
Georgia Institute of Technology
Atlanta, GA 30332

Dennis P. Hogan, PhD
Department of Sociology
The Pennsylvania State University
University Park, PA 16802

Rukmalie Jayakody, MSW
Institute for Social Research
University of Michigan
Ann Arbor, MI 48106

Matthew Jendian
Andrus Gerontology Center
University of Southern California
Los Angeles, CA 90089

David I. Kertzer, PhD
Dupee University Professor
Department of Anthropology
Brown University
Providence, RI 02912

Martin Kohli, PhD
Institut für Soziologie
Freien Universität-Berlin
D-1000 Berlin
Germany

Victor W. Marshall, PhD
Center for Studies of Aging
Toronto, ON M5S 2G8
Canada

Susan Morgan, PhD
Institute on Aging
The Florida State University
Tallahassee, FL 32306

John Myles, PhD
Institute on Aging
The Florida State University
Tallahassee, FL 32306

Alice S. Rossi, PhD
Department of Sociology
University of Massachusetts–Amherst
Amherst, MA 01003

Laura Rudkin, PhD
Carolina Population Center
University of North Carolina
Chapel Hill, NC 27516

Carmi Schooler, PhD
National Institute of Health
Bethesda, MD 20892

Bi-Ling Shieh
Andrus Gerontology Center
University of Southern California
Los Angeles, CA 90089

Michael Stallings, PhD
Andrus Gerontology Center
University of Southern California
Los Angeles, CA 90089

Judith Treas, PhD
Department of Sociology
University of California, Irvine
Irvine, CA 92717

Peter Uhlenberg, PhD
Department of Sociology
University of North Carolina
Chapel Hill, NC 27514

Sherry L. Willis, PhD
Dept. of Human Development
   and Family Studies
The Pennsylvania State University
University Park, PA 16802

Preface

This is the seventh volume in a series on the broad topic of "Societal Impact on Aging." The first five volumes were published by Erlbaum Associates under the series title of "Social Structure and Aging." The present volume is the second published under the Springer Publishing Company imprint. It is the edited proceedings of a conference held at the Pennsylvania State University, October 17–19, 1992.

The series of conferences originated from the deliberations of a subcommittee of the Committee on Life Course Perspectives of the Social Science Research Council chaired by Matilda White Riley in the early 1980s. That subcommittee was charged with developing an agenda and mechanisms that would serve to encourage communication between scientists who study societal structures that might affect the aging of individuals and those scientists who are concerned with the possible effects of contextual influences on individual aging. The committee proposed a series of conferences that would systematically explore the interfaces between social structures and behavior, and in particular to identify mechanisms through which society influences adult development. When the second editor was named director of the Penn State Gerontology Center, he was able to program the implementation of this conference program as one of the center's major activities.

The six previous volumes in this series have dealt with the societal impact on aging in psychological processes (Schaie & Schooler, 1989); age structuring in comparative perspective (Kertzer & Schaie, 1989); self-directedness and efficacy over the life span (Rodin, Schooler, & Schaie, 1990); aging, health behav-

iors, and health outcomes (Schaie, Blazer, & House, 1992); caregiving in families (Zarit, Pearlin, & Schaie, 1993); and societal impact on aging in historical
perspective (Schaie & Achenbaum, 1993). The present volume was designed to
examine how societal changes in major social institutions and structures have
impacted intergenerational relationships across the adult life span.

The strategy for each of these volumes has been to commission six reviews
on three major topics by established subject-matter specialists who have credibil-
ity in aging research. We then invited two formal discussants for each chapter—
usually one drawn from the writer's discipline and one from a neighboring discipline. This format seems to provide a suitable antidote against the perpetuation
of parochial orthodoxies as well as to make certain that questions are raised with
respect to the validity of iconoclastic departures in new directions.

To focus the conference, the editors chose three topics of broad interest to
gerontologists. Social and behavioral scientists with a demonstrated track record
were then selected and asked to interact with those interested in theory building
within a multidisciplinary context.

The volume begins with an examination of what we currently know about
the status of intergenerational relationships. This is accomplished in two ways.
First, the demography of changing intergenerational relationships is described
for the general American scene. Next, a case history of changing relationships is
presented by a detailed case study of intergenerational continuity and change in
a rural setting.

The second topic in this volume deals with the cross-cultural issues in intergenerational relationships. These include a case study of intergenerational
support in childrearing with adolescent childbearers in African-American families, and a review of kinship and individuation in American, African, and Chinese elderly.

The third topic includes reports and reflections from two major longitudinal
studies of intergenerational relationships. The first comes from the Seattle Longitudinal Study. It is psychological in nature and deals with perceptions of family environments both within and across successive generations. The second,
from the University of Southern California three-generations study, assesses the
impact of recently conducted follow-up studies on the continuing viability of the
"intergenerational stake" hypothesis. Because one of the discussants took serious
exceptions with the conclusions reached, a rejoinder by the authors of the original chapter is also included.

We are grateful for the financial support of the conference that led to this
volume that was provided by conference grant AG 09787-02 from the National
Institute on Aging, and by additional support from the College of Health and
Human Development of the Pennsylvania State University. We are also grateful

to Barbara Impellitteri and Barbara Labinski for handling the conference logistics, and to Anna Shuey for coordinating the manuscript preparation.

K. Warner Schaie

REFERENCES

Kertzer, D., & Schaie, K. W. (1989). *Age structuring in comparative perspective*. Hillsdale, NJ: Erlbaum.

Rodin, J., Schooler, C., & Schaie, K. W. (1991). *Self-directedness and efficacy: Causes and effects throughout the life course*. Hillsdale, NJ: Erlbaum.

Schaie, K. W., & Achenbaum, W. A. (1993). *Societal impact on aging: Historical perspectives*. New York: Springer.

Schaie, K. W., House, J., & Blazer, D. (1992). *Aging, health behaviors, and health outcomes*. Hillsdale, NJ: Erlbaum.

Schaie, K. W., & Schooler, C. (1989). *Social structure and aging: Psychological processes*. Hillsdale, NJ: Erlbaum.

Zarit, S. H., Pearlin, L., & Schaie, K. W. (1993). *Social structure and caregiving: Family and cross-national perspectives*. Hillsdale, NJ: Erlbaum.

CHAPTER 1

The Demography of Changing Intergenerational Relationships

Janice I. Farkas
Dennis P. Hogan

The shift from a high-mortality/high-fertility society to a low-mortality/low-fertility society impacts family structure by altering the frequency of numbers and types of family members, as well as changing the amount of time spent in various family roles (Bengtson et al., 1990; Goldman, 1986; Watkins et al., 1987). Assuming that mortality and fertility trends continue, it would be expected that, even though the number of living generations in families will increase, the absolute number of living relatives will decrease (Crimmins, 1986), particularly certain types of relatives (children, grandchildren, siblings, aunts, uncles, cousins, and nieces and nephews).

By itself, a decrease in mortality has the potential to increase the amount of time spent in family roles such as child, parent, and spouse. Increased longevity increases the number of living generations in family structures. But decreases in fertility also influence time spent in family roles. For instance, with fertility de-

The research reported here was supported by NICHD Grant No. 1 R01 HD26070, the Population Research Institute's NICHD Population Center Grant, and by the Public Health Service National Institute on Aging Training Grant 5 T32 AG60048. We thank Mariah D. R. Evans and Jonathan Kelley for familiarizing us with the data set analyzed in this chapter and providing us with access to the data files. We also thank Kristen Brocking for her research assistance.

creases come decreased time spent as a parent of young children. Fertility patterns also determine the number of members born into families.

Because of these countervailing trends, changes in family structure that have resulted from a demographic transition are best examined when the simultaneous changes in mortality and fertility are considered together. The simultaneous decrease in mortality and decrease in fertility should result in a "verticalization" of family structure (Bengtson et al., 1990). That is, as the number of living generations in a family increases because of increased longevity, the number of family members *within* each generation decreases as a result of low fertility. Thus, it should be increasingly common for families in aging societies to have three or four, even five, living generations (Goldman, 1986).

Gender differences in the effects of demographic changes on family structure are important to consider, particularly higher male mortality at older ages. This phenomenon results in women having a higher probability of surviving a spouse and more years as a parent. Gender differences in marriage patterns also play a role in determining family structure in later life because elderly men are more likely to be married than elderly women, in part because they have a greater likelihood of remarriage than women (Bengtson et al., 1990).

Demographic transitions and subsequent changes in family structure have implications for kin contact and for reliance on kin for assistance in time of need. Because changes in mortality and fertility, as well as marriage patterns, directly determine family structure, they also determine the number and types of generational kin available to call on for support. Recently, theorists have developed models linking forms of kin networks to variations within and between societies in reproductive behavior, the care of children, and the care of dependent elderly (Lancaster & Lancaster, 1987; Turke, 1989). In high-fertility societies, extended kin networks disperse the costs of childbearing. Extended kin networks permit the enhancement of reproductive potential as older children and the aged assist in the nurturance of children (siblings and grandchildren, respectively) who share their genetic heritage.

In more modern societies, social and economic resources are procured outside the family. Persons who limit their family size attain greater educational and socioeconomic success and therefore can invest more heavily in their children's socioeconomic success. To focus their investment on fewer children, modern parents must reduce their investments in extended kin. The parents, in turn, will have less access to assistance from extended kin, thereby increasing the cost of their own children and promoting a further reduction in fertility. The disappearance of sibling-provided child care accelerates this process.

In small-family societies, the parents' central concern is concentrating resources to ensure their children's social and economic success. Because children represent the major focus of the parents' reproductive heritage, parental investment in these children is expected to continue well into adulthood and to accelerate with the birth of grandchildren. Evolutionary theory suggests that parental investment will be diluted when a larger number of children compete for resources and will be more heavily concentrated on children who bear grandchildren. These hypotheses about intergenerational exchange in a small-family society are supported empirically by a recent analysis of assistance in American families (Eggebeen & Hogan, 1990).

The full implications of the demographic transition and of dramatic shifts in the family structure are only now becoming apparent, so much of the information we have about these changes and their implications for kin contact and the use of kin support is based on demographic simulation models. But these models are not necessarily rooted in the actual demographic circumstances faced by any population historically, nor have they been designed to address variations associated with national differences in demographic history and state-imposed structure of the life course (Mayer & Schoepflin, 1989). To understand the implications of the demographic transition to an aging society for the structure of kin lineages over the life course, and for kin relations (contact and assistance) in these different situations, we analyze newly available data for the United States, Australia, and five European nations. This cross-country comparison provides an opportunity to go beyond these simulation models to consider generational relations in several industrialized societies with aging populations. The data permit us to assess differences between the nations, by gender, and between age groups. These data unfortunately are cross-sectional, precluding the empirical examination of changes in generational relations for actual cohorts over their life course. Because this is a one-time cross-sectional survey, we do not have data on change in the kin networks of these societies.

Based on simulation models of the consequences of demographic change for kin networks, we expect that families in these countries will have a very vertical family structure with many adults experiencing several adult generations in their lineage. We expect that the presence of each additional type of adult lineage member (grandparent, parent, child, and grandchild) will be associated with increased contact and reliance on generational kin. We expect that a lineage with more generations present also will be associated with enhanced generational relations, as members of the lineage promote contact with others in the generational line. Evolutionary theory would also suggest such a process since investment (contact and support) would be more likely to occur in lineages where descendants are present. Alternatively, evolutionary theory also leads to the hypothesis that the focus of parental resources on children may compete with and thus reduce contact and assistance to parents and grandparents. We anticipate that older persons, being socialized at a point in historical time when family assistance was more emphasized, will be more likely to rely on kin for support, except in situations in which they lack necessary kin. Finally, because the aging process is so different for men and women, with older men more often having a surviving spouse on which to rely, we will emphasize gender differentials in kin relations.

DATA AND METHODS

The data come from the International Social Survey Program (ISSP), a set of cross-national annual social surveys. In 1986 and 1987, as a supplement to their respective national social surveys, each of the participating countries conducted a module on the topic of social networks and social support developed for the ISSP. The seven participating countries for this module are Australia, Austria, West Germany, Great Britain, Hungary, Italy, and the United States. The social support module contains questions about the availability of, and contact, with adult relatives and friends, as well as questions identifying the person the respondent would expect to rely on for help in certain situations. The seven countries' surveys were based on interviews with random national samples of persons ages 18 and older.[1] Sample sizes range from 1,020 in Italy to 2,791 in Germany. Pooling these surveys together we have a total of 10,661 respondents, 54% of whom are women, 65% of whom are currently married, and 28% who are aged 55 and older.

The measures of kin structure we use were designed to capture key dimensions of kinship (lineage position, number of generations in the lineage) within the constraints imposed by the need to have measures that could be defined with the survey data collected in all of the nations.[2] These include four dummy variables indicating whether a person has an adult child, an adult grandchild, a living parent, and a living grandparent. There are sixteen possible combinations of these generational kin, but less than half are experienced with any frequency (see Table 1.1). Therefore, we have constructed a seven-category variable to summarize lineage position and number of generations in the lineage. We first examine variations in kinship structure across nations, by age group and gender.

This is followed by a multivariate analysis of contact with and reliance on assistance from these generational kin. The dependent variables consist of measures of contact with and expected reliance on these generational kin for assistance.[3] The measure of contact is intended to measure the number of generations with whom a respondent is in frequent regular contact (a visit, letter, or phone call). This variable can range from 0 for those with no contact with any person in their generational line over the past year to 24 for a person in daily contact with a grandparent, parent, adult child, and adult grandchild.[4] Expected reliance on kin is measured by a composite measure designed to evaluate the de-

TABLE 1.1. Percent of Persons in Each Generational Position within Their Lineage by Age (Pooled Samples)

GENERATIONAL STRUCTURE	AGE				POOLED SAMPLE	
	18-24	25-44	45-64	65+	%	N
One Generation	**0.6**	**5.6**	**9.3**	**15.9**	**7.4**	**752**
Respondent Only	0.6	5.6	9.3	15.9	7.4	752
Two Generations – Youngest	**27.4**	**52.1**	**8.3**	**1.2**	**29.1**	**2955**
Parent Alive	27.0	51.7	8.2	1.0	28.9	2930
Grandparent Alive	0.4	0.4	0.1	0.1	0.2	25
Two Generations – Oldest	**0.1**	**2.6**	**41.9**	**31.7**	**17.4**	**1763**
Child Alive	0.1	2.5	41.6	30.5	17.1	1733
Grandchild Alive	0.0	0.1	0.3	1.2	0.3	30
Three Generations – Youngest	**69.7**	**28.5**	**0.3**	**0.1**	**22.3**	**2256**
Grandparent & Parent Alive	69.7	28.5	0.3	0.1	22.3	2256
Three Generations – Oldest	**0.0**	**0.1**	**7.3**	**46.8**	**8.7**	**884**
Child & Grandchild Alive	0.0	0.1	7.3	46.8	8.7	884
Three Generations – Middle	**0.6**	**9.4**	**29.1**	**1.9**	**12.7**	**1279**
Parent & Child Alive	0.1	8.5	28.6	1.7	12.1	1218
Parent & Grandchild Alive	0.4	0.8	0.4	0.1	0.5	52
Grandparent & Child Alive	0.0	0.0	0.2	0.1	0.1	9
Grandparent & Grandchild Alive	0.0	0.0	0.0	0.0	0.0	0
Four Generations – Middle	**1.6**	**1.8**	**3.7**	**2.4**	**2.4**	**242**
Grandparent, Parent & Child Alive	0.1	1.1	0.8	0.1	0.7	75
Grandparent, Child & Grandchild Alive	0.0	0.0	0.1	0.1	0.0	4
Parent, Child & Grandchild Alive	0.0	0.1	2.6	2.4	1.1	112
Grandparent, Parent & Grandchild Alive	1.5	0.4	0.1	0.1	0.4	44
Grandparent, Parent, Child & Grandchild Alive	0.0	0.1	0.1	0.1	0.1	7

N=10131
Note: The percentages may not sum to 100 due to rounding. Some categories with responses that seem structurally infeasible are most likely respondent error or that the surveys also included step and adopted children when inquiring about respondent's adult children.

gree of reliance on kin for support across different types of situations in which help may be needed. There are six questions that ask whom the respondent would choose for help in different hypothetical situations. The lead-in statement and questions are as follows:

"Now we'd like to ask you about some problems that can happen to anyone."

1. "First, there are some household and garden jobs you really can't do alone—for example, you may need someone to hold a ladder, or to help you move furniture."
2. "Suppose you had the flu and you had to stay in bed for a few days, and needed help around the home, with shopping and so on."
3. "Suppose you needed to borrow a large sum of money."
4. "Suppose you were very upset about a problem with your husband, wife, or partner, and haven't been able to sort it out with them."
5. "Now suppose you felt just a bit down or depressed, and you wanted to talk about it."
6. "And now suppose you needed advice about an important change in your life—for example, about a job, or moving to another part of the country."

For each of these questions, respondents provided their first and second choice for help. The response categories include no one, spouse or partner, mother, father, daughter, son, sister, brother, other relative, closest friend, other friend, neighbor, someone you work with, and various formal support systems that vary by question, such as social services, a paid helper, a doctor, a clergy member, an employer, or a financial institution. To arrive at the composite measure, for each type of situation answers are coded 1 if generational kin were chosen for either the first or second choice, and 0 otherwise. Thus, the composite measure of kin reliance ranges from a minimum of 0 to a maximum of 6.

The independent variables for the multivariate analyses include variables that capture position in the age stratification system (dummy variables for age group and gender), the social stratification system (education),[5] and social structure (country of residence). The respondent's family situation is gauged by marital status (currently married, previously married, or never married), and the measures of generational kin.

KIN STRUCTURE

We begin by describing the availability of kin in each of these populations. Very few people lack kin entirely (only 0.34% of the pooled samples). These persons are single, and disproportionately are old (75%), female (86%), and live in Germany (50%). Most persons in these urban industrial societies have some kin, with fully 93% having one or more generational kin. The percentage of persons lacking any generational kin varies considerably by age and gender. Less than 6% of persons under age 44 lack any adult generational kin (because of surviving parents and grandparents). Ten percent of men age 55 and older have no generational kin, along with 12% of women ages 55 to 64 and 19% of those age 65 and older. Thus, persons without generational kin tend to be older (48% are age 55 and older), unmarried (55%), and female (58%). Over the past several decades many young persons have delayed or foregone marriage and parenthood (especially in Germany, Austria, and northern Italy). As these cohorts reach old age, these societies can expect to see an increase in older persons without generational kin. In the United States where childlessness is less common and where lineages tend to be large (a legacy of the baby boom) projections suggest little increase in the numbers of persons without generational kin (Himes, 1992).[6]

Table 1.1 provides a systematic analysis of age differences in the number of available kin by generational lineages and generational position for the pooled samples. Although these data lack the longitudinal detail necessary to portray the changing generational positions of persons over their life course, the distribution of persons in each age group by their lineage structure illustrates this process. The age pattern of these data (and the life course pattern implicit in them) is not surprising. The high survivorship to older ages for both sexes is apparent in the relatively few persons who report a "missing" generation (e.g., a grandparent with an adult grandchild without a surviving child).

What is surprising to us is the very small percentage of persons in a complex lineage at any age. Only seven persons in the pooled sample (or about 1%) reported that they have surviving grandparent, parent, child, and grandchild (corresponding to a six-generation lineage, if the presence of a generation under 18 is assumed). Even at ages 45 to 64 when a multigenerational lineage is most common, only 3% of persons report they are part of a four-generation adult lineage (corresponding to five generations, assuming minors in the lineage). Three-generation adult lineages are common in these societies, most typically assuming the form of surviving parent and adult child for persons ages 45 to 54, and then reemerging as a child, adult grandchild lineage for persons age 65 and older (49% of women 65 and older). The verticalization of the family structure is, as the research reviewed earlier suggests, an important historical shift, though the mental images this literature calls forth are perhaps more dramatic than the facts warrant.

What also is surprising is the substantial proportion of persons who report belonging to a two-generational adult lineage structure. Of the pooled sample, 46% had only one adult in their lineage (two-generation lineage). The most common experience for a person under age 44 in a two-generation lineage was to have parents who remained living. Those individuals age 45 and over were more likely to have an adult child as their only surviving vertical kin. Thus, at any given time nearly half of all persons belong to two-generation adult lineages rather than the three-, four-, or more generation lineage structures often predicted for aging societies. However, true life-course data probably would show that many more adults experience complex lineage structures for at least *part* of their life.

The multinomial logit regression results in Table 1.2 predict the likelihood of a person being in a multigenerational lineage structure by country of origin, gender, age, education, and marital status. European populations differed substantially from that in the United States in their generational lineages. There is less likelihood that a person residing in Australia, West Germany, Great Britain, and Hungary has no lineage, is the youngest in a two- or three-generation adult lineage, or is a member of a four-multigeneration lineage (compared with the likelihood of being the middle kin member in a three-generation lineage tier). However, persons in these countries were *more* likely (compared with Americans) to be the oldest kin member in a two-generation lineage (relative to being the middle kin member in a three-generation lineage).

Educational attainment also decreases the likelihood of being in most multigenerational lineages relative to lower educated adults. Women are more likely than men to be the eldest member of a two-generation lineage or to be a member of a four-multigeneration lineage. Unsurprisingly, older persons are more apt to either have no living vertical kin or to be the elder person in multigenerational lineages.

KIN CONTACT

Preliminary tabulations showed that only 10% of persons with surviving kin in their lineage have no contact with these kin. Persons in two-adult-generation lineages were the most likely generational linkage to contact their surviving parent or surviving grandparent with slightly more than 90% engaging in weekly contact. However, only 29% of persons with only a surviving child or a grandchild had no weekly contact. Noncontact was low for persons in either the middle or youngest position in complex lineages. Only 3% of the youngest individuals in a complex adult lineage reported no kin contact. At the other end of the complex lineage continuum grandparents had the highest level of noncontact (more than 21%). We found that individuals in the most complex adult generational lin-

TABLE 1.2. Multinomial Logit Regression Model. Comparative Analysis of Respondent's Position in Generational Structure by Number of Generations (Odds Ratio)

Variable	Respondent Only (none)	Two Generation youngest (P or GP Alive)	Two Generation oldest (Chld or GChld Alive)	Three Generation youngest (P & GP Alive)	Three Generation oldest (Chld & GChld Alive)	Four or more middle (P, Child, & GChld Alive)
Country						
Australia	0.294***	0.281***	1.764***	0.134***	0.632*	0.208***
West Germany	0.425***	0.391***	1.307***	0.206***	0.231***	0.073***
Great Britain	0.338***	0.208***	1.864***	0.092***	0.289***	0.125***
Italy	0.907	0.656***	1.403***	0.462***	1.897***	0.970
Austria	0.733	1.425	0.689	1.566	0.864	1.108
Hungary	0.430***	0.288***	1.094	0.162***	1.092	0.608***
United States	---	---	---	---	---	---
Gender (1 = male)	0.943	1.009	1.387***	0.770***	0.940	0.606***
Age						
Age 18-24	3.568***	133.284***	0.089*	611.693***	.000	18.251***
Age 25-44	1.856***	15.470***	0.197***	14.071***	0.028***	1.133
Age 45-64	---	---	---	---	---	---
Age 65+	25.510***	2.007*	10.933***	0.209	76.923***	8.184***
Educational Attainment						
Low Level	---	---	---	---	---	---
Middle Level	0.753*	0.930	0.796*	0.904	0.474***	0.775
High Level	0.715***	1.291**	0.766**	1.348***	0.251***	0.509***
Marital Status						
Married	---	---	---	---	---	---
Previously married	0.337***	0.245***	0.896	0.299***	0.299***	0.312***
Never Married	0.459***	0.307***	1.917***	0.151***	0.431***	0.259***

Notes: Significance level: * 0.05, ** 0.01, *** 0.001.
Key to abbreviations: P is parent, Chld is child, GP is grandparent, and GChld is grandchild.

TABLE 1.3. Comparison of Complete and Reduced Models for Kin Contact and Reliance on Kin

	F Test	Degrees of Freedom
Models of Kin Contact		
Model 1 vs. Model 2	1885.106***	4,9771
Model 2 vs. Model 3	15.820***	4,9767
Model 3 vs. Model 4	0.000	2,9765
Models of Reliance on Kin		
Model 1 vs. Model 2	28.568***	4,9759
Model 2 vs. Model 3	17.255***	4,9755
Model 3 vs. Model 4	0.000	2,9753

Notes: Significance levels: * 0.05, ** 0.01, *** 0.001

In Model 1 the variables are distance, country, gender, age, marital Status and educational attainment. Model 2 includes all the variables in Model 1 *plus* the type of surviving kin (e.g., parent, child, grandparent, or grandchild).
Model 3 includes all the variable in Model 2 *plus* the count of the surviving kin.
Model 4 includes all the variables in Model 3 *plus* the generational structure (e.g., three generations, youngest).

eages (which provided greatest opportunity for additional and frequent contact) seldom contacted more than two vertical generations—usually a parent and child. The average level of contact of 6.06 illustrates that the average person has regular contact with only a single other person in their adult generational lineage. Persons in a three-generation lineage also had low levels of contact, only 7.28 on average.

To determine whether the presence of each additional type of adult lineage member or the complexity of generational structure is what increases kin contact in these aging societies (controlling for proximity to parents and children), we estimated a series of Ordinary Least Squares (OLS) regression models for level of frequent kin contact.[7] The first model estimated the effect that country of residence had on kin contact. In the next model, we explored whether type of surviving kin was significant and the third model included the count for each type of surviving kin. The fourth model estimated included the generational structure and respondent's position in the lineage. Surprisingly, the complexity of generational structure taking into account presence of each type of generational kin did not significantly affect kin contact or reliance on kin (Table 1.3).[8]

Kin contact differs between populations in European countries and the United States (Table 1.4). Persons residing in the United States contact kin significantly more frequently than persons in most other Westernized countries studied (when controlling for parent's and children's proximity). Differences in the level of contact by country of residency become less pronounced with the

TABLE 1.4.   Ordinary Least Squares Regression Coefficients for models of Total Contact with Kin

Variable	Model 1	Model 2	Model 3
Surviving Vertical Kin			
Parent (1=Living)		4.268***	4.297***
Child (1=Yes)		5.114***	5.001***
Grandparent (1=Living)		1.401***	0.848***
Grandchild (1=Yes)		0.729***	0.701***
Number of Vertical Kin			
Count of Parents			-0.016
Count of Children			0.064**
Count of Grandparents			0.353***
Count of Grandchildren			-0.009
Distance			
Parents	-0.306***	-0.384***	-0.385***
Children	-0.464***	-0.372***	-0.374***
Country			
Australia	-0.815***	-0.460***	-0.428***
West Germany	-0.260**	0.069	0.112
Great Britain	-0.503***	-0.255***	-0.221**
Italy	0.102	0.207*	0.267**
Austria	-0.338**	0.027	0.074
Hungary	-0.296**	-0.098	-0.059
United States	---	---	---
Gender (1 = male)	-0.416***	-0.272***	-0.272***
Age			
Age 18-24	-0.396***	0.526***	0.475***
Age 25-44	-1.394***	-0.106	-0.060
Age 45-64	---	---	---
Age 65+	-0.835***	0.050	0.612
Marital Status			
Married	---	---	---
Previously married	0.033	0.045	0.046
Never Married	0.319***	0.660***	0.648***
Educational Attainment			
Low Level	---	---	---
Middle Level	0.116	0.077	0.087
Highest Level	0.107	0.207***	0.220***
Intercept	8.719***	1.853***	1.768***
R^2	0.179	0.534	0.537

Notes: Significance levels: * 0.05, ** 0.01, *** 0.001

addition of surviving vertical kin, but Australia and Great Britain continued to show significantly lower contact with kin when compared with the United States. Italians showed the highest degree of kin interaction when compared with the United States. However, West Germany, Austria, and Hungary have levels of kin contact similar to persons in the United States.

Contact with kin varies across age groups. Younger adults have less contact with kin than do middle-aged adults but are in more frequent contact with kin when presence of vertical kin is added to the model. However, aging adults (older than age 65) have less contact with their kin than do midlife adults. This attenuated contact for the oldest adults weakens with the addition of controls for type of surviving vertical kin. After considering availability of kin, older persons contacted kin as frequently as midlife adults.

Frequent contact with kin is more dependent on the *type* of surviving adult kin than the number of available vertical tiers of generational adult kin. Unsurprisingly, having an adult child or a parent has more impact on kin contact than the survival of an aging grandparent or an adult grandchild. Kin contact was also positively related to number of children and grandparents. More surprising is that the number of generations in the lineage was less important to kin contact than the type of kin surviving (see Table 1.3).

In additional analysis (see Figure 1.1), we found that persons with a surviving parent were more frequently in contact with their adult children than persons without a parent.[9] We also found that persons with both an adult child and at least one living parent had more frequent contact with both of these kin compared with persons with an adult child only or a parent only. This suggests the key role that the middle generation plays in interlinking the generations. It also is possible that the middle generation is responding to parental pressure to maintain contact with descendants.

Women contact kin more frequently than men in all nations. This tendency persisted when controlling for availability of adult kin, lineage position and generational structure, and age. Increased educational attainment also increases the likelihood of contacting kin. Persons with the highest educational attainment were those most likely to visit, call, or write their kin.

We next tested for several interactions to determine whether those patterns of kin contact were different in the United States compared with other nations (see Table 1.5). Older Americans are no more likely to have frequent contact with kin than older persons in other nations (see Table 1.5). The presence of a surviving parent increases frequent kin contact more in the United States than in other nations, as does having a grandchild. An adult child has the same effect on kin contact in the United States as in other nations. While having a grandparent

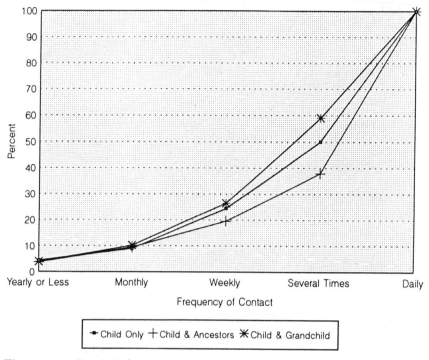

Figure 1.1   Parent's frequency of contact with adult children by lineage in cumulative percentages.

survive increases frequent contact with kin among Americans, the effect is relatively small compared with that in other nations.

KIN ASSISTANCE

Next we explored the effects that number and type of adult lineage members had on seeking assistance from kin. Few persons, just more than 10%, felt they would not solicit assistance from a parent, child, or other relative. Of the remaining sample, nearly 40% would ask help from kin in times of need for three out of the six problems they were asked about.

The type of adult lineage members available significantly affects whether a person would seek assistance from kin in times of need (Table 1.6).[10] Older adults with children were more likely to rely on kin assistance. It appears individuals often turn to their grandparents, when available, for some type of assistance. Grandparents only infrequently seek assistance from grandchildren, when

TABLE 1.5. Ordinary Least Squares Regression Coefficients for
Interaction Models of Kin Contact and Reliance on Kin for Assistance

Variable	Kin Contact		Reliance on Kin	
	Model 1	Model 2	Model 1	Model 2
Surviving Vertical Kin				
Parent (1=Living)	4.269***	4.196***	0.301***	0.282**
Child (1=Yes)	5.115***	5.093***	0.671***	0.684***
Grandparent (1=Living)	1.404***	1.477***	0.289***	0.286***
Grandchild (1=Yes)	0.724***	0.623***	0.183**	0.211***
Interaction Variables				
Parent*United States		0.488***		0.206
Child*United States		0.044		-0.081
Grandparent*United States		-0.474***		-0.004
Grandchild*United States		0.705***		-0.194
Distance				
Parents	-0.383***	-0.385***	-0.168***	-0.169***
Children	-0.372***	-0.374***	-0.198***	-0.197***
Country				
Australia	-0.424***	-0.136	0.065	0.214
West Germany	0.107	0.391	0.142*	0.293
Great Britain	-0.217**	0.068	0.198**	0.347*
Italy	0.245**	0.545**	0.273***	0.420**
Austria	0.067	0.354	0.482***	0.630***
Hungary	-0.062	0.219	0.580***	0.741***
United States	---	---	---	---
Gender (1 = male)	-0.272***	-0.269***	-0.271***	-0.271***
Age				
Age 18-24	0.523***	0.514***	0.530***	0.535***
Age 25-44	-0.106	-0.100	-0.079	-0.077
Age 45-64	---	---	---	---
Age 65+	0.015	0.045	0.589***	0.537***
Interaction Variable				
Age 65+*United States	0.218		-0.411***	
Marital Status				
Married	---	---	---	---
Previously married	0.047	0.037	0.130**	0.134**
Never Married	0.660***	0.652***	-0.049	-0.049
Educational Attainment				
Low Level	---	---	---	---
Middle Level	0.078	0.075	-0.175***	-0.175***
Highest Level	0.207***	0.200***	-0.333***	-0.332***
Intercept	1.817***	1.591***	3.995***	3.854***
R^2	0.534	0.545	0.147	0.147

Notes: Significance levels: * 0.05, ** 0.01, *** 0.001

TABLE 1.6. Ordinary Least Squares Regression Coefficients for Models of Reliance on Kin for Assistance (n = 9872)

Variable	Model 1	Model 2	Model 3
Surviving Vertical Kin			
Parent (1=Living)		0.302***	-0.006
Child (1=Yes)		0.672***	0.509***
Grandparent (1=Living)		0.296***	0.130
Grandchild (1=Yes)		0.174**	0.204*
Number of Vertical Kin			
Count of Parents			0.255***
Count of Children			0.108***
Count of Grandparents			0.075*
Count of Grandchildren			-0.024
Distance			
Parents	-0.161***	-0.167***	-0.167***
Children	-0.210***	-0.199***	0.191***
Country			
Australia	0.089	0.131*	0.155*
West Germany	0.144**	0.212***	0.260***
Great Britain	0.220***	0.268***	0.300***
Italy	0.320***	0.342***	0.397***
Austria	0.500***	0.555***	0.614***
Hungary	0.619***	0.655***	0.708***
United States	---	---	---
Gender (1 = male)	-0.287***	-0.270***	-0.268***
Age			
Age 18-24	0.318***	0.525***	0.472***
Age 25-44	-0.361***	-0.078	-0.074
Age 45-64	---	---	---
Age 65+	0.524***	0.524***	0.537***
Marital Status			
Married	---	---	---
Previously married	0.148**	0.133**	0.130**
Never Married	-0.092	-0.045	-0.061
Educational Attainment			
Low Level	---	---	---
Middle Level	-0.177***	-0.171***	-0.165***
Highest Level	-0.363***	-0.334***	-0.335***
Intercept	4.764***	3.928***	3.778***
R^2	0.136	0.146	0.152

Notes: Significance levels: * 0.05, ** 0.01, *** 0.001

there are available children. Most likely, grandparents seek kin assistance from grandchildren when adult children are not available to assist them or when they need assistance in addition to that which their adult children can provide. Having more than one living parent and more than one child also increased the likelihood of relying on kin in times of need.

We find that older adults, those age 65 and older, expect to rely on kin assistance more frequently than do middle-aged adults when controlling for kin available. Younger adults also would rely on kin more frequently.

Women expect to solicit help from kin more frequently than do men regardless of marital status and generational composition. Divorced or widowed persons are also more reliant on kin for assistance in times of need. Adults with less education expect to rely on kin for help more often than adults of higher education levels.

Although they have higher rates of contact with kin, Americans expect to rely on kin assistance less frequently than do their counterparts in Europe and Australia. This is especially true for American adults in the oldest age category (see Table 1.5). The type of kin surviving impacts significantly on the likelihood of depending on kin assistance, but this effect does not differ between the United States and other nations.

CONCLUSIONS

To a large extent each of the seven counties we studied has passed through the demographic transition transforming it to an aging society. Differences in kin contact and reliance on kin between Americans and other aging Westernized societies are pervasive, although our most noteworthy finding is the continuity of contact with kin and, to a lesser extent reliance on kin. Americans have more contact with kin than other groups, but this is more a result of the availability of kin than any difference in family size. American elderly have frequent kin contact, but they expect to rely on kin assistance less when compared with elderly in other countries.

National patterns of extended generational lineages did not emerge to the extent popular accounts had led us to expect. Regardless of the conclusions based on simulation modeling techniques, at any given time few adults have membership in an adult generational lineage of more than two or three adult links. It is likely that for most persons a multigenerational lineage typically characterizes only a small portion of the life course, if it is experienced at all. Furthermore, membership in a multigenerational lineage does not enhance levels of kin contact, or reliance on kin, other than by measuring the number of kin available. This suggests that even if multigenerational lineages were to become the norm in the future, it would have little impact on kin contact and assistance for aging persons. Rather than the length of the lineage, the size of the kin group—especially closely related kin—is the key to understanding historical changes and national differences in kin relations.

NOTES

[1] For purposes of comparability, we exclude 16- and 17-year-olds sampled in the Austrian study.

[2] The biggest constraint is that the survey asked only about the existence of adult kin; we cannot tell if young children, young grandchildren, or great-grandchildren are present in the lineage of any respondent. Nor can we tell if there is a surviving great-grandparent. This limits our ability to specify precisely the number of living generations—as opposed to the number of living adult generations—in the lineage. But the adult members of the lineage are those in whom we are most interested because the verticalization of the kin structure refers, after all, to the survival of adult generational kin.

[3] Again we are somewhat limited by the data collected. We have information about contact (telephone or letter, visiting) with each of the four possible generational relations. We have data on expected reliance on kin for assistance directly for parents and for children, and for "other kin" (including grandparents and grandchildren). The "other kin" group excludes brothers and sisters who were asked about specifically.

[4] This obviously is a function of the number of generations alive; part of this analysis involves assessing the strength of this relationship.

[5] Education systems vary in noncomparable ways across the nations. The education variable here is coded to indicate the relative education (low, middle, high) of a person in their nation.

[6] Kinlessness appears to be more a product of government actions that had a negative impact on kin survivorship (e.g., wartime death) than anything else. Future uses of American military personnel will, for many families, risk the life of an only son or daughter, increasing the likelihood that armed conflict will leave some older persons without generational kin.

[7] Respondents that reported having "no vertical generational kin" were omitted from the remaining analysis.

[8] Models were also estimated to determine the influence that number of specific kin (e.g., number of grandparents) and the multigenerational membership had on total contact with and reliance on kin. The addition of the explanatory variables did not significantly increase the R^2 for these models ($p < .05$). Therefore we report information only on the most parsimonious models.

[9] Additional analysis of mother's contact with adult children and of the father's contact with adult children, separately, revealed the same pattern of contact. The highest level of

kin contact was for mothers or fathers with a child and ancestors. The lowest level of contact was observed for those with a child and grandchild.

[10]Models were estimated to determine if the number of kin available increased the explanatory strength of reliance on kin. Inclusion of number of living parents, children, grandparents, and grandchildren did not significantly increase the R^2.

REFERENCES

Bengtson, V., Rosenthal, C., & Burton, L. (1990). Families and aging: Diversity and heterogeneity. In R. H. Binstock and L. K. George (Eds.), *Handbook of aging and the social sciences* (3rd ed., pp. 263–287). San Diego, CA: Academic Press.

Bumpass, L. L., (1990). What's happening to the family? Interactions between demographic and institutional change. *Demography, 27*, 483–498.

Crimmins, E. M. (1986). The social impact of recent and prospective mortality decline among older americans. *Sociology and Social Research, 70*, 192–199.

Eggebeen, D. J., & Hogan, D. P. (1990). Giving between generations in American families. *Human Nature, 1*, 211–232.

Gibson, G. (1972). Kin family network: Overheralded structure in past conceptualizations of family functioning. *Journal of Marriage and the Family, 34*, 13–34.

Goldman, N. (1986). Effects of mortality levels on kinship. In *Consequences of mortality trends and differentials*. New York: United Nations.

Himes, C. L. (1992). Future caregivers: Projected family structures of older persons. *Journal of Gerontology: Social Sciences, 47*, S17–26.

Hogan, D. P. (1987). Demographic trends in human fertility and parenting across the lifespan. In J. B. Lancaster et al. (Eds.), *Parenting across the lifespan: Biosocial dimensions*. New York: Aldine.

Hogan, D. P., & Spencer, L. (1993). Kin structure and assistance in aging societies. In G. L. Maddox (Ed.), *Annual review of gerontology* (pp.169–186). New York: Springer.

Lancaster, J. B., & Lancaster, C. S. (1987). The watershed: Change in parental investment and family formation strategies in the course of human evolution. In J. B. Lancaster, J. Altmann, A. S. Rossi, & L. R. Sherrod. (Eds.), *Parenting Across the Lifespan: Biosocial Dimensions*, New York: Aldine.

Mayer, K. U., & Schoepflin, U. (1989). The state and the life course. *Annual Review of Sociology, 15*, 189–209.

Preston, S. H. (1984). Children and the elderly: Divergent paths for america's dependents. *Demography, 21*, 435–457.

Troll, L. E. (1988). New thoughts on old families. *The Gerontologist, 28*, 586–591.

Troll, L. E., Miller, S. J., & Atchley, R. J. (1979). *Families in later life*. Belmont, CA: Wadsworth.

Turke, P. W. (1989). Evolution and the demand for children. *Population and Development Review, 15*, 61–90.

Watkins, S. C., Menken, J. A., & Bongaarts, J. (1987). Demographic foundations of family change. *American Sociological Review, 52*, 346–358.

Commentary:
Demographic Influences on Intergenerational Relationships

Peter Uhlenberg

B ecause demographic processes (births, deaths, marriages, and divorces) create and destroy intergenerational relationships, it is obvious that changes in demographic behavior will alter the structure of intergenerational relationships in a population. However, the effects of various demographic changes on kinship structure are not so obvious that one should trust casual or "commonsense" statements about the effects of historical changes. One systematic approach to studying the relationship between demographic behavior and intergenerational kinship structure uses simulation models. These models allow one experimentally to study how the distribution of kin of different types varies under differing demographic regimes. Although clearly useful, this approach has two significant limitations in explicating actual historical change. First, historical changes seldom occur in a smooth and orderly fashion. This makes it difficult to use simulation models to capture the effects of past changes at particular periods. Second, a simulation model can shed no light on the meaning or significance of the various intergenerational relationships that exist in a population.

An alternative approach to studying effects of demographic change on intergenerational relationships relies on collecting and analyzing survey data from a population. These data can deal both with the existence of various relationships and the meaning of these relationships in the lives of individuals. If comparable data are collected from a population at several different periods, one could describe change in kinship structure and relate this change to observed historical change in demographic behavior. Not surprisingly, such data with any richness of detail are difficult to find. Lacking adequate time-series data, the study by Farkas and Hogan makes use of cross-sectional data collected in seven countries. By looking at Western countries around 1986 to 1987, they argue that these data provide a picture of kin structure for countries that essentially have completed the demographic transition. It is important to note, however, that these data do not permit one to address questions about the implications of demographic change. No information is presented on kin structure at earlier (or later) stages of development.

LINEAGE DEPTH

An important finding of Farkas and Hogan is the small proportion of persons at any age in any of the seven countries that is in a lineage of great depth. Although it is commonly asserted that "four- or even five-generation" families are becoming common, empirical data show that relatively few individuals are members of lineages that exceed three generations. In their pooled sample of more than 10,000 individuals, only 2.4% are in lineage of four or more generations of adults. (And the 2.4% is an exaggeration because there is some obvious misreporting in the data in Table 1.1. There are persons under age 24 recorded as having children and grandchildren who are older than 18). Because they do not have information on kin who are younger than 18 years old, a complete picture of generational depth is not available from these data. But a sample in the Boston area found that more than 80% of all adults were in lineages of three or fewer generations, and more were in two-generation lineages than were in four- or five-generation ones (Rossi & Rossi, 1990). No doubt the average lineage depth has increased as more people have survived to older ages, but empirical evidence helps us to avoid overemphasizing structures that are rare (the five-generation family).

Not only do Farkas and Hogan report that few adults have adult kin belonging to more than two other generations, but also they find that having more generations present in the lineage has little consequence for level of contact or exchange of assistance. As other researchers have found (Rossi & Rossi, 1990), the intergenerational link of greatest importance is between parents and children. As one moves to more peripheral kin, levels of contact and assistance fall off rapidly. For the elderly, this suggests that changes in number of grandchildren and great-grandchildren are likely to be less consequential than changes in the number of living children. Are significant changes occurring in the supply of adult children available to older persons?

Some researchers (Bengtson, Rosenthal, & Burton, 1990; George & Gold, 1991) have too quickly concluded that the low fertility in the United States (and other Western countries) in recent decades means that the elderly now have fewer children available. There are two problems with such assertions. First, they fail to specify the timing of changes in the supply of children that the elderly have. Second, they do not assess how many children are needed to provide the elderly with adequate contact and support.

Because childbearing often occurs in women who are under age 35, the effects of decreasing fertility on parent-child relationships in later life will not be felt until 30 or 40 years later. Indeed, because the young-old tend to have low rates of dependency, the crucial stage of life for relying on children for assistance is after age 80. Thus, the drop in fertility in the United States after 1965 will not have a major impact on the status of the elderly for several more decades. Further, it is important to assess the extent to which the decrease in fertility produced an increase in proportion of women who were childless or who had just one child. The most critical distinction in number of children for the elderly is between any or none, and the second most important contrast is between one and two or more. To the extent that fertility declines are associated with movement from large- to moderate-sized families, the changes are not overly consequential for parent-child relationships in later life.

Several demographers have examined the past and future distribution of older women by number of living children they have (Chen & Morgan, 1991; Himes, 1992; Preston, 1992). Focusing on the oldest-old population (85 +), concerns expressed about the increasingly short supply of children for dependent older persons appears misplaced. The highest proportion of very old women without children or with just one child occurs in the early 1990s, when the cohorts born around 1900 are at this stage of life. About one fourth of these women were childless, and another fourth had just one child. Over the next several decades the parents of the baby boom will occupy the oldest ages in the population. The proportion of women over age 85 with two or more surviving children is projected to increase from less than half in 1995 to about 70% by 2015. Later on, as parents of the baby bust reach the oldest ages, the proportion with zero or one child will increase. However, projections up to 2050 show the proportions with either zero or one child never reaching the levels of the early 1990s.

DISTANCE

In analyzing effects of country and generational structure on frequency of contact with kin, this study uses regression models that control for geographic distance between parents and children. Distance is an important control variable when examining effects of other variables because numerous studies have demonstrated that distance is a strong predictor of level of kin interaction. But it would be interesting to elaborate on differences across countries in the geographical dispersion of kin. For example, the study reports that Americans have relatively high levels of contact with kin compared with individuals in most Western countries. But this result controls for the possible effects of proximity. If kin networks are more dispersed in the United States than in other countries, it is possible that actual levels of contact in the United States are lower.

Another question related to proximity is whether geographical distance between parents and their adult children has been increasing over time. Have ties between the generations been attenuated by the increasing mobility of the population? Most researchers who comment on this issue assume that mobility has been increasing. For example, Dewit, Wister, and Burch (1988) write:

> The rise in geographic mobility among young adults . . . threatens to restrict access of older persons in the maintenance of supportive ties. (p. 57)

However plausible this assumption of increasing geographic mobility over time may seem, it is dangerous to make this assumption without considering available evidence. Three types of information cast doubt on the assumption of increased dispersion of kin over time. First, data from the Current Population Survey on annual mobility rates of the U.S. population, which have been collected since the 1950s, do not show an upward trend. A recent report states:

> The rates of moving during the 1980s were not much different from the 1970s, but were considerably lower than during the 1950s and 1960s, when 20 percent or more of the population moved every year. (U.S. Bureau of the Census, 1991)

Second, a variety of surveys going back to 1962 all come to the same conclusion — about 75% of parents older than age 65 have a child living within a 25-mile radius of them (Hoyert, 1990). Third, comparing data on percentage of the population living outside of their state of birth from censuses since 1910 does not suggest a trend toward increasing interstate movement among American adults (Uhlenberg, 1993). Thus, while distance is an important factor affecting contact between kin, it is doubtful that kin are now more dispersed than in the past. In addition, improved communication and transportation technology over time may have reduced the significance of distance as an impediment to intergenerational contact.

LIFE COURSE AND INTERGENERATIONAL RELATIONSHIPS

In discussing reliance on kin for support, Farkas and Hogan note that rates are higher among young and old adults than among those in the middle. Because one party in a relationship receiving help implies that the other party is providing assistance, one might ask whether many adults in the middle are providing support to both their children and their parents. This notion of a "sandwich generation" or "women caught in the middle" has received a great deal of attention in recent years, both from journalists and researchers. Although this chapter does not address the prevalence of middle-aged women providing care for both dependent parents and children, it may be worth noting that this is not a common occurrence.

Both simulation studies (Boyd & Treas, 1989) and empirical studies (Rosenthal, Matthews, & Marshall, 1989; Spitze & Logan, 1990) conclude that few women face the challenge of providing care for parents and children simultaneously. Reasons why competing demands to two different generations seldom occur at the same time are not difficult to uncover. First, only about a third of all women are expected to ever provide long-term care for a dependent parent (Rosenthal, Matthews, & Marshall, 1989). Many do not have parents who experience long-term dependency, and many with disabled parents are not primary caregivers for these parents. Second, the time at which parents are most likely to be in need of assistance tends to occur after one's responsibility for active parenting of children is past. Using data from the 1984 Long-Term Care Survey and the 1984 Current Population Survey, Stone and Kemper (1989) find that only 0.5% of all women younger than age 65 were caught in the middle of caring for members of both older and younger generations. Of those who were in this position, only one third were primary caregivers for a dependent parent. Although relatively few women (or men) may experience the much discussed burden of caring for members of two generations simultaneously, increasing longevity certainly does increase the odds that a person will experience a period of life in which old parents are in need of assistance.

CONCLUSIONS

The chapter by Farkas and Hogan does not advance our understanding of the role of demographic change in altering intergenerational relationships. Indeed, given its use of cross-sectional data from one point in time it cannot speak to the issue of change. But it does make several useful contributions and should stimulate further research on this topic.

Most important is the effort to provide a cross-national perspective on the topic of intergenerational relationships. Little comparative work has been done, and this is a beginning. Intriguing differences are found between the seven countries. For example, why is reliance on kin for assistance relatively low in the United States? One might have predicted that reliance on kin is inversely related to the strength of the social welfare state. But findings in this study do not support such a conclusion. The challenge for other researchers is to push comparative research on questions like this further.

A second useful result is the descriptive work on the distribution of individuals in various life-course stages by lineage type. Although it is not intrinsically difficult to collect information on kinship lineages, it is surprising how little data we have on this topic. The paucity of empirical data has encouraged a misconception to develop that four- and five-generation families are becoming common under modern demographic conditions. As we gain a more accurate perspective on actual generational depth, additional work will need to track more carefully how lineages change for individuals as they move through the life course. And the question of what difference it makes whether one has kin of more distant generations alive also needs further exploration.

Finally, as existing survey data on kin contact and reliance on kin are analyzed, it becomes obvious that further studies will need to collect richer data. In particular, more attention should be given to collecting information on intergenerational relationships over longer periods of the life course. This does not necessarily require longitudinal studies. A cross-sectional study could collect retrospective data on levels of contact and amounts of assistance provided to kin. Information of this type is much more satisfying than simple reports on the current situation of individuals. Are there transition points in the life course where contact or assistance tend to either increase or decrease? What are the consequences of changes in the nature of intergenerational relationships? As populations continue to age over the next several decades, a variety of issues related to intergenerational relationships of the elderly will become increasingly salient.

REFERENCES

Bengtson, V. L., Rosenthal, C., & Burton, L. (1990). Families and aging: Diversity and heterogeneity. In R. H. Binstock & L. K. George (Eds.), *Handbook of aging and the social sciences* (pp. 263–287). New York: Academic Press.

Boyd, S. L., & Treas, J. (1989). Family care of the elderly: A new look at "women in the middle." *Women's Studies Quarterly, 17*, 66–74.

Chen, R., & Morgan, S. P. (1991). Recent trends in the timing of first births in the United States. *Demography, 28*, 513–533.

Dewit, D. J., Wister, A. V., & Burch, T. K. (1988). Physical distance and social contact between elders and their adult children. *Research on Aging, 10*, 56–80.

George, L. K., & Gold, D. T. (1991). Life course perspectives on intergenerational and generational connections. *Marriage and Family Review, 16*, 67–88.

Himes, C. L. (1992). Future caregivers: Projected family structures of older persons. *Journal of Gerontology: Social Sciences, 47*, S17–26.

Hoyert, D. L. (1991). Financial and household exchanges between generations. *Research on Aging, 13*, 205–225.

Preston, S. H. (1992). Cohort succession and the future of the oldest old. In R. M. Suzman, D. P. Willis, & K. G. Manton (Eds.), *The oldest old* (pp. 50–57). New York: Oxford.

Rosenthal, D. J., Matthews, S. H., & Marshall, V. W. (1989). Is parent care normative? The experiences of a sample of middle-aged women. *Research on Aging, 11,* 244–260.

Rossi, A. S., & Rossi, P. H. (1990). *Of human bonding: Parent-child relations across the life course.* New York: Aldine.

Spitze, G., & Logan, J. (1990). More evidence on women (and men) in the middle. *Research on Aging, 12,* 182–198.

Stone, R. I., & Kemper, P. (1989). Spouse and children of disabled elders: How large a constituency for long-term care reform? *The Milbank Quarterly, 67,* 485–506.

Uhlenberg, P. (1993). Demographic change and kin relationships in later life. *Annual Review of Gerontology and Geriatrics, 13,* 219–238.

United States Bureau of the Census. (1991). Geographic mobility: March 1987 to March 1990. *Current population reports* (Series P-20, No. 456), p. 1. Washington, DC: Government Printing Office.

Commentary: Beanpole or Beanstalk? Comments on "The Demography of Changing Intergenerational Relations"

Judith Treas

Once upon a time, three sociologists—Vern Bengtson, Carolyn Rosenthal, and Linda Burton (1990)—planted some bean seeds in a chapter on families and aging. Noting the remarkable declines in fertility and mortality that had transpired, they inferred the emergence of a new type of North American family structure—a "beanpole family" impossible under earlier demographic regimes. Their point was that declining mortality meant more generations alive at any given time, but falling fertility would constrain the numbers within each generation. This "verticalization" of the family was the product of twin forces of intergenerational extension and intragenerational contraction.

Now these bean seeds were truly magical. The vivid imagery and staggering implications of a beanpole family seemed to turn their germ of an idea into a mighty beanstalk. Who, reading that chapter, did not find his or her imagination sailing skyward? The beanpole family was a provocative notion, and its tendrils have already worked their way into the vocabulary of family sociologists like myself. Of course, as with Jack's beanstalk, it was only a matter of time before someone on the ground took an empirical ax to the excesses of a useful concept. Enter Farkas and Hogan.

Their chapter on the demography of intergenerational relationships addresses one component of "verticalization"—the number of surviving adult generations in the family and the implications of this number for intergenerational

26

contact as well as for preferences for help providers. Intergenerational extension is important, but the beanpole story also includes the drama of intragenerational contraction. Hogan and Farkas focus on the trunk but not the branches of the beanpole family. A growing literature on siblings makes clear that brothers and sisters influence intergenerational relations—at least between parents and grown children (Treas & Lawton, in press). Having more siblings is typically associated with getting less help from parents, interacting less frequently with parents, and providing them with less help. Conversely, adults are more likely to rely on siblings when they have no parents and no children to turn to. Thus, we might have learned even more about intergenerational relations had Farkas and Hogan been able to address the beanpole assumption of declining sibling numbers.

In contrast with simulation studies that have estimated kin availability, the chapter by Farkas and Hogan relies on contemporary survey data from seven countries collected in 1986 and 1987 by ISSP. (Not the least of this chapter's contributions is as a model for use of the ISSP; the annual ISSP surveys are a rich source of comparative data on a host of topics, but they have been underused to date). The surveys asked about whether the respondent has a surviving adult child, grandchild, parent, or grandparent. A count of the adult generations living yields an empirical assessment of how pervasive intergenerational extension is in the lives of real people.

The results show that almost everyone (93%) can count on having some kin up or down the generational ladder. The issue, however, is whether families are beanpoles. The authors express surprise that only 1% of the pooled sample report five adult generations alive. Conforming to their accounting (which assumes another untallied generation of those age 18 or younger), we are talking about a six-generation family. This would surely not be a reasonable threshold for the beanpole phenomenon. Obviously, six-generation families are very rare; one would not be too surprised to see one featured on the cover of a tabloid at the supermarket check-out. Families with four adult generations are also rare, but 12.7% of all respondents do report three adult generations. In fact, 29.1% of middle-aged people report three adult generations with a possible child generation uncounted.

Is this a lot of generations? Do the numbers buttress the notion of a beanpole family or debunk it? Bengtson, Rosenthal, and Burton did not operationalize their concept for those who came later. The interpretation of the generation numbers in this chapter is in the eye of the beholder. The interest in the beanpole family undoubtedly stems from our assumptions that it represents a new phenomenon that family relations must accomodate. Hence, it would be useful to be able to contrast these contemporary figures—if only roughly—with estimates of generational kin availability in previous times.

Other sections of the chapter turn to the implications of intergenerational extension — namely, intergenerational contact and preferences for assistance. The contact variable is the number of generations with whom the respondent has weekly contact. It is important to keep this definition in mind because it counts the grandmother who sees her daughter and granddaughter once a week as having more frequent contact than the woman who sees her grown daughter daily. The definition emphasizes the diversity of generational contacts, not how much contact is had. This is a useful perspective on intergenerational relations, but one wonders whether a diversified portfolio of intergenerational relations really promises special payoffs in terms of, say, individual well-being.

The results of an OLS regression show that having surviving parents or children enhances kin contact more than having surviving grandparents or grandchildren. This finding calls for caution in extrapolating increased kin interaction proportional to any increase in beanpole lineages. Conversely, there is evidence of generational multiplier effects on kin contact. Those with parents still living have more contact with grown children than do those without surviving parents. Because family roles are often viewed as conflicting and competing with one another, this finding reminds us that family roles may complement one another. Being a parent and an adult child may actually introduce some economies of scale into family interaction.

All things considered, contact is predictably greater for the never married, for the better educated, and for women. In this pooled, cross-sectional, multivariate analysis, Americans have contact with more generations than do respondents in most other Western countries. These cross-national differences are interesting, and they beg for explanation. Controls for availability of lineal kin reduce the differentials between countries, but intriguing differences remain. For example, having a grandparent or grandchild alive increases kin contact more in the U.S. than elsewhere.

The last section of the chapter considers who respondents would turn to for help with various problems. Having surviving generations in the lineage does encourage a preference for kin assistance. Being young or old, female, previously married, and less educated increases the reliance on kin for help with problems, too. Several hypothetical problems in the helping scale (e.g., holding a ladder, helping around the house) favor those who are close at hand; thus, it is not surprising that proximity between the generations increases preferences for relying on kin. However, variables that tap kin availability, proximity, and respondent characteristics cannot eliminate country differentials in kin reliance.

In the end, Farkas and Hogan seem to caution against selling the cow to buy the seeds. Although the family with three adult generations is no longer a rarity for middle-aged people, generational extension seems not to characterize the experience of most individuals at most points in time. The evidence on the implications of multigenerational beanpole families is mixed. Perhaps because the parent-child relation is so strong, a proliferation of other lineal kin has a lesser effect on kin contact or family reliance.

REFERENCES:

Bengtson, V., Rosenthal, C., & Burton, L. (1990). Families in aging: Diversity and heterogeneity. In R. H. Binstock & L. K. George (Eds.), *The handbook of aging and the social sciences* (pp. 263–287). New York: Academic Press.

Treas, J., Lawton, L. (in press). Early and middle adulthood. In M. B. Sussman & S. V. Steinmetz (Eds.), *Handbook of marriage and the family*. New York: Plenum Publishing.

CHAPTER 2

Intergenerational Continuity and Change in Rural America

Glen H. Elder, Jr.
Laura Rudkin
Rand D. Conger

The historic decline of the farm population represents one of the most dramatic features of industrial and postindustrial change in the Western world. Slightly less than one third of Americans lived on farms at the beginning of the 1920s. This figure had declined by half at midcentury and by nine tenths up to the economic recession of the early 1980s (Bogue, 1985). Less than 3% of all Americans were living on farms in 1980.

Outmigration represents a major source of this decline, prompted in part by the accelerating impact of mechanization and other technological advancements, coupled with the declining profitability of farm production. How did outmigration from America's farms affect family ties, and especially relations between the generations? Using data from a multigeneration study in Iowa, we address this question by comparing the kin ties of farm-family offspring who are now living in farm and rural settings.

No state provides a more compelling example of a declining rural farm population than Iowa, a sparsely settled agricultural state that lost nearly 5% of its population across the farm crisis of the 1980s, more than any other state except

West Virginia. Prompted in part by mounting farm losses and the expanding size of farm units, the population of some rural counties declined by up to 20% during the decade as small communities witnessed the collapse of local businesses and a shrinking economic base. The farm-based sector of Iowa is now less than 15% of the state's population, but the lifestyle of farming continues to have broad appeal (Barlett, 1993; Mooney, 1988) with its interweave of work, family, and nature.

By the end of the 1980s, the Iowa landscape was littered with the casualties of the agricultural crisis. Seventy-five banks had closed, plus several hundred retail stores, and some 1,500 service stations (Conger & Elder, 1994). Businesses had boarded-up windows and "for-sale" signs in towns across the state. The construction industry was still down by 40% from the late 1970s. Good jobs were very difficult to find in the small towns. As a young mother (Shribman, 1991) put it, "It would be great to be able to stay here, but there's no opportunity. . . . When you watch businesses close, one by one by one, you have to start asking why you're staying."

In the midst of the farm crisis, a panel study of Iowa families (Conger & Elder, 1994) was launched to investigate the effects of the economic changes underway in the state of Iowa. Patterned after *Children of the Great Depression* (Elder, 1974), the proposal viewed the family, its strains, relationships, and adaptations, as a set of linkages between the socioeconomic decline in the region, and its effects on adults and children. The research plan called for a sample of rural households with two parents, a young adolescent, and a near sibling; a socially diverse sample with a substantial representation of farm and rural nonfarm households; and the collection of panel data including videotaped observations in the household, survey forms, and interviews. The parents (G2 generation) were asked a series of questions about relations with their own parents (G1 generation), both in the past and in the present. We draw on these data to investigate the intergenerational implications of a farm-reared generation that followed different paths, farm and nonfarm.

Following a successful pilot study, a research team carried out the first wave of data collection in the winter of 1989 with a sample of 451 households from eight counties in the north central region—just north of Des Moines and Ames, the home of Iowa State University and the location of the project at the Family Research Center. Seven of the eight counties had poverty rates above the state average of 11%, and most lost more than a tenth of their resident population over the 1980s.

Thirty percent of the families were involved in farming, and two thirds of these men defined themselves as primarily farmers. Their farms generally exceeded 350 acres, owned and rented, and most were devoted to grain and livestock operations. Thirteen percent of the study families had given up farming as a result of the farm crisis. The other families had not farmed, though some of the parents had grown up on farms.

Forty-four percent of the wives who grew up on farms are married to men who have farmed at one time or another. The typical husband and wife in the G2 generation were born just after World War II. They married for the first time in 1970 and have three children. Three out of five parents have some education beyond high school, and 40% of the men served in the military during the Vietnam era.

The median income level for the G2 generation in 1989 is $33,700, a figure that matches the median for American families of this size. Farm families generally had higher family incomes than other families at the end of the 1980s, much higher than families that had lost their farms and the nonfarm households. Economic pressures at the end of the decade led to more work hours and jobs for the G2 generation. More than three fourths of the wives were gainfully employed, usually on a full-time basis. This employment figure applies even to farm households; indeed, many of these families have resorted to off-farm employment to keep the farm going.

As noted earlier, the life history of farm-reared Iowans in the G2 generation records exits from farming at two life stages, among other possibilities: at the beginning of their adult careers and then some years later in response to the farm crisis. The first exit represents an intergenerational break in which a son or daughter does not follow the parents into a farming career either through occupational or marital choice. The second type of exit may also involve an intergenerational break with parents in terms of family continuity in farming, but it is distinctively a career break where men and women in farming leave the occupation for nonfarm employment.

Both of these exits have important implications for proximity to parents, frequency of contact, quality of relations with parents, and caregiving. In the first type of exit, the question for young men centers on their choice of farming or an alternative mode of employment. Among young women, the question concerns marriage and the forces that led some farmers' daughters to marry farmers or farmers-to-be and others to marry men not engaged in farming.

Other things being equal, we believe the path to family farming is likely to enhance emotional ties—both positive and negative—with parents and in-laws, and to lead to more caregiving for elderly parents. The emotional intensity of ties with parents in family farming most likely added to the intergenerational tensions associated with farm losses during the 1980s. We discuss these expectations in the next section, then review the measurements for the study, and turn to our findings.

FARMING, OUTMIGRATION, AND INTERGENERATIONAL TIES

The past quarter century has witnessed a remarkable advance toward greater understanding of family change, individual lives, and the experience of aging in American history (Hareven, 1987). As historical studies have spread across the social sciences, their findings have enlarged an appreciation for the complexity of these developmental processes (Elder, 1981). One aspect of this complexity centers on the interlocking nature of family economies, intergenerational relations, and the life course of aging, a core theme of this chapter. Change in the family economy initiates change in relations between the generations, both within and across family units, and thereby alters the pattern of aging.

Consider, for example, the diverse pathways associated with the family options of textile and heavy-metal workers within the course of industrialization. The economic options of the textile industry around 1900 called for a multiple earner strategy involving both old and young (Hareven, 1982). This strategy favored later marriage among daughters who provided a measure of economic support for parents. In the steel industry of Pennsylvania (Elder, 1981; Haines, 1979), wives and daughters were excluded from employment in the mills, a condition that favored gender inequality, the early marriage of daughters, and high fertility.

Rural Choices and Life Careers

In rural America, important intergenerational implications of change in the family economy are linked to the life choices made by the sons and daughters of farmers. Historically, the size of farm families ensured that a good many sons and daughters would be faced with the need to move away from home.

The choice of succeeding one's parents in farming and the agricultural lifestyle was typically an option for a young man, but not for a young woman. As Deborah Fink (1986) points out for the farm state of Iowa, "only men are recognized and supported as farmers" (p. 232). Rules of inheritance permitted the family land to be divided between brothers, with each plot supplemented by rented land. But some farmers were unusually successful in launching sons on land acquired recently through low-cost loans. Typically, the actual intergenerational transfer of land from father to son would not occur until late in the father's life, the mid-60s in the state of Iowa (Friedberger, 1988).

A farmer's sons who could not be placed on the home farm often faced the prospects of local or more distant employment. The job would usually be non-farm and would require a change in residence. In terms of proximity, the new residence might be as close as the nearby town or crossroads, or as distant as the far reaches of the hinterland. In either case, the transition away from farming produced greater geographic distance from parents and most likely reduced the frequency of contact over what it would have been had the son remained on the farm (Lee, 1988). In this manner, entry into farm or nonfarm employment carries implications for intergenerational relations and continuity, particularly for relative exposure to the demandingness, negativity, and needs of aged parents.

The life choices of young women who grew up on farms in the Midwest generally entailed a change in residence through marriage and employment. Some women enter farming through marriage to a local farmer or to the promising son of a local farmer. Others enter the world of nonfarm priorities through marriage or employment. Little is known about the forces that led some daughters into farming through marriage, and others into nonfarm employment and eventual marriage to a town resident.

Opportunity and motivation are known to play an important role in the probability of a farmer's son's entry into farming (Lyson, 1984), and both factors are relevant to the marital choices of daughters. For young men, the opportunity to enter farming is greatest when the father is a full-time owner and operator of a farm. Evidence of this influence (Elder, Robertson, & Conger, forthcoming) suggests that the positive economic prospects of potential farm husbands are likely to be a marital attraction for daughters from farm families, as indicated by high economic and educational status.

Opportunity also has much to do with the relative prosperity of the historical time in which the Iowa men and women came to their decisions. Their parents grew up on farms during very difficult times, the 1920s and 1930s, and entered farming as the demand for agricultural products soared during World War II and the postwar era. Family farming continued to prosper during the early years of the G2 generation (second generation) and their young adulthood, the 1960s and 1970s. Conditions changed radically with the collapse of land values in the 1980s, and more than 1 out of 10 farmers in the sample had left farming by the 1990s.

A primary aspect of motivation that bears on life choices, including that of outmigration, concerns the quality of childhood relations with parents. Building on the precursors of extreme social mobility (Lipset & Bendix, 1959), such as felt parent rejection and family tensions, we view family experiences of this kind as a prime determinant of decisions to leave the farmstead for marriage and employment in nonfarm communities. Family tensions, conflicts, and feelings of rejection increase the attractiveness of leaving home.

Careers and Intergenerational Relations

As members of each new generation left family farms for a future elsewhere, they experienced a series of changes that distinguished their world from that of the young who entered farming by marriage or occupational choice. Residential and occupational changes set in motion changes in community life and its imperatives. Education received greater priority in urban communities up to the modern age of agriculture and agribusiness. Education is stressed now in both worlds, rural and urban.

No doubt consumption priorities have changed in the lives of farm-reared men and women who moved to nonfarm communities. Historically, family-based farming subordinated personal consumption to the priorities of successful family farming and its way of life. Barlett (1993, p. 248) concludes that the depression-like farm crisis of the 1980s "reinforced a return to lower aspirations for family living standards and a reassessment of farm practices." As one Iowa farmer put it, the crisis underscored the familiar if austere merits of a "non-consumptive life" (Friedberger, 1989, p. 165). Another large-scale farmer in the Iowa study who wanted his sons to consider farming (and would not say anything about it) laid out the harsh realities: for one, "they have got to learn to do without a lot of the material things if they want to farm."

From the standpoint of ties with parents and participation in their care, the transition from farm to nonfarm employment may shift personal priorities away from "other care to personal care." Collective family interests are reinforced by the interdependencies of material resources and labor in family farming. Even farm children acquire a sense of being counted on for their contributions to the collective welfare. By comparison, nonfarm endeavors more strongly favor the pursuit of individual goals in the marketplace.

These differences are presumably most readily observed when farm families are compared with families in metropolitan areas and may be elusive when the nonfarm comparison involves communities of 2,000 or fewer. Nevertheless, the collective themes of farm family life remain a compelling contrast for intergenerational relations and care.

Conventional wisdom has assumed that intergenerational bonds are strongest in rural families. Indeed William Goode's (1963) " 'classical family of Western nostalgia' is believed by many to be alive and well and living on the farm – or perhaps, more generally, in the countryside" (Lee, 1989, p. 1). The popular image of farm family life features close ties and supportive relations across the generations, though surprisingly little empirical evidence shows any difference between the kinship ties and caregiving of urban and rural families in the United States (Lee, 1988, 1989). Part of the reason for such inconclusive differences may stem from the heterogeneous categories in the comparison.

Typically rural families at different life stages are compared with urban families. However, the population of rural families includes full-time farm operators on large farms, part-time farm families, subsistence farm families, and the rural nonfarm in open country and in small communities. A rising level of off-farm employment further blurs the distinction between farm and nonfarm (Rudkin, Elder, Rosenfeld, & Conger, 1992).

As might be expected, comparisons of farm and rural nonfarm families generally rank the former much higher on proximity to parents and on frequency of contact with them (Lee, 1988, 1989). However, Lee's study in the state of Washington is based on the perspective of the older generation. The issue is whether the elderly parents live near and see a child frequently, not whether a particular child reports interacting frequently with his or her parents, the focal point of this study. The Iowa study focuses on the perspectives of adult children toward their parents.

Lee's review (1989) of intergenerational studies in rural America acknowledges the diversity of family ecologies but generally ignores this fact in drawing conclusions. He notes that studies have not adequately addressed the caregiving dynamics of rural families and then proceeds to disregard the substantial variety in this category. He concludes that the burden of care should be greater among rural families, owing to their economic limitations, but fails to note that full-time farm families are relatively well-off when compared with the typical rural nonfarm family. Clearly, the existing literature presents a confused and confusing portrait of intergenerational continuity and change among rural families.

No study to date has investigated the effects of farm and nonfarm career choices among middle-aged adults on relations with elderly parents who made their livelihood in farming. And little is known about the intergenerational effects of farm loss during the "Great Farm Crisis of the 1980s" among the adult sons and daughters of farmers. Rosenblatt (1990, p. 147) observed very different responses among fathers to the farm loss of their sons.

One man noted that his father "tried to be kind of supportive, but it was his farm and we lost it. . . . To this day he hasn't said much." Another father received an assurance from his son that he still has all of his financial investment and then concluded: "Well Grandpa doesn't give a rip. Great-grandpa doesn't really give a rip. So it seems to me it's you, and you've got to put food on the table. You've got to take care of your family. Do it however you have to."

Rosenblatt did not consider the life history of father-son relations and its implications for the father's response to the son's loss of the farm, but studies (Elder & Caspi, 1990) suggest that farm loss most likely amplified the initial state of the relationship. Crises frequently accentuate the initial disposition or quality of relationship. Negative, explosive fathers may well have become more negative in relation to sons after the farm loss.

In our study of intergenerational continuity and change across rural Iowa families, we focus on the adult sons and daughters of Iowa farmers. All of these offspring have children of adolescent age in 1990 and thus are in the middle years (about age 40). Their parents range in age from the mid-50s to the early 90s. Some of the sons embarked on a farming career, whereas other sons and daughters sought their fortunes in the nonfarm world.

We explore the opportunities and motivations that led them into farming or nonfarm situations, examine the G2 generation's perception of the supportiveness, negativity, and demandingness of the parent and in-law generation (Mangen, Bengtson, & Landry, 1988; Roberts, Richards, & Bengtson, 1991), investigate the provision of care for needy parents, and explore some relational implications of farm loss among adult sons and their parents.

This design provides an explicit historical timeline and focus on the transition into and out of farming, with a clear distinction between farm and rural nonfarm families. However, by comparing these groups within a regional sample of north central Iowa, we employ a very conservative test of the kinship implications of farm and nonfarm choices among farm-reared Iowans.

Nevertheless, compared with the nonfarm group, we expect the following on kin relations:

1. Entry into farming through marriage or employment will be linked to greater proximity and contact with both parents and in-laws among Iowa men and women.
2. Entry into farming will be associated with more intensive emotional relations, both negative and positive.
3   Farm-based Iowans will be more involved in providing care for elderly parents, regardless of proximity.
4   Men who lost their farm will report more strained relations with father and mother, when compared with men who are still farming.

The distinctive contrast for men on the farm and in nonfarm settings involves relations with parents, not in-laws. Men who are working on the home farm remain under the supervisory eye of their parents. Hence they are most likely to experience an unusual degree of negativity and demandingness. For women the contrast is reversed because farm life for them entails close relations with the husband's mother and father.

We turn now to a more detailed account of the Iowa sample, generations, and study measurements.

SAMPLE, GENERATIONS, AND MEASUREMENTS

Data for this study come from the G2 generation of the Iowa Youth and Family Project, a study of rural families who were recruited from eight agriculturally

TABLE 2.1   Intergenerational Comparisons of Men and Women from Farm Backgrounds

	Parent - Son Life Histories, N = 272		Parent - Daughter Life Histories, N = 200	
	Father / Mother	Son	Father / Mother	Daughter
Birth Year				
median	1918 / 1922	1949	1921 / 1924	1950
Education				
% H.S. grad.	53.6 / 81.9	98.2	57.5 / 73.5	98.5
% college grad.	3.3 / 2.9	24.3	2.0 / 1.5	21.0
Relative Education				
% wife more	46.7	30.1	42.5	29.0
% husband more	13.6	29.8	18.0	31.0
Family Size				
median	6	5	6	5
range	3-16	4-13	3-16	4-9
Farm Activity				
median years farmed	31	-	34	-
% currently farming	53.9	45.2	59.5	37.5
Women's Employment				
% employed	19.5 (ever)*	86.0 (current)	27.0 (ever)*	87.5 (current)

*Percentage of G1 mothers ever employed during G2's childhood (ages 5-16).

dependent counties in the north central region of the state. The first wave of data collection started in January 1989 and produced a total of 451 two-parent households with a seventh grader and a near sibling. This figure is approximately 78% of the eligible families in the region. The second wave of data collection occurred in the winter and spring of 1990 and included 94% of the original families. We shall draw on these two waves of data in the analysis. In each year, the four members of each household completed survey forms and interviews. Family interaction on specific observational tasks were videotaped and then coded.

G1 and G2 Generations

In the G2 generation, we include only men and women who grew up on farms. A farm background is defined as having: (a) a G1 father whose primary occupation was farming or (b) G1 parents who were involved in farming for at least 9 years, starting while the G2 son or daughter was still at home. Table 2.1 compares key aspects of the life histories of the G1 parents and their offspring, members of the G2 generation.

In the far left column we find the parents of the G2 men. The fathers of these men typically launched their farming careers in the 1940s and 1950s, a time when land prices were low and farm commodity prices were stable and high (Friedberger, 1989). The farm crisis of the 1980s had little effect on the careers of these men because their land was paid for, their debts were low, and their capital resources were high. Shaped by the hard times of the 1920s and 1930s, these men typically pursued a cautious management style that avoided heavy indebtedness and relied on family labor.

The younger generation, however, faced a very different world, one initially seductive for the expansionary instincts of the ambitious and then devastating as the economy lowered land values by two thirds. A good many of these young men had college degrees in agriculture and training in agribusiness techniques, but they were not immune to the widespread decline. A number plunged heavily into debt and eventually lost their farms. Indeed, one out of three men in the Iowa sample who had entered farming had to leave the field by the end of the 1980s. Most of the men who entered farming began their careers in the late 1960s and early 1970s, approximately 10 or 12 years before the crash.

Educational upgrading distinguishes the generations, as one would expect, but the change also shows variation by gender. In the G1 generation, women were most likely to have an educational advantage over their husbands, a difference that fades sharply in the G2 generation. The declining educational advantage of women partly reflects shifting priorities on the education of farm sons, as well as the importance of advanced education for nonfarm employment.

Equally noteworthy is the increasing prominence of gainful employment among women with children still at home, from less than 30% to more than 80% in the G2 generation. This apparent change needs to be qualified, however, by the difficulty in obtaining accurate estimates of farm women's employment. Recollections of mother's work status also leave much to be desired on accuracy.

Most of the G1 parents are still living and, in fact, are in relatively good health. Three quarters of the fathers and 85% of the mothers are living and roughly two thirds of these parents are described as having good or excellent health. The mothers' median age is 66 and the fathers' is 68, so most of the parents have not yet reached the ages when health declines become marked. Nearly all (95%) of the mothers and fathers maintain independent residences, but gender differences in the rate of widowhood have led to differences in living arrangements. About 20% of the mothers are living alone compared with less than 10% of the fathers. Eighty percent of the fathers and just two thirds of the mothers are living only with a spouse. Approximately one quarter of the mothers and 40% of the fathers are reported as still working. Interestingly, the labor force participation rate reported for the mothers is as high in the later years as it was for the years when the G2 child was living at home.

Forty-five percent of the farm sons are currently engaged in farming as are 37% of the farm daughters through marriage. We shall first investigate opportunity and motivational determinants of this life career, and then compare the lives of farm and nonfarm men and women on key life events, accomplishments, and relations with kin. Before turning to this comparison, we review a series of measurements that are used in the analysis.

Measurements

Different dimensions of relations between the G2 parents and their own parents and parents-in-law are considered—interaction, relationship quality, caregiving behavior, attitudes about caregiving, and early relationship experiences.

Interaction with Kin

Proximity to kin is measured in seven categories ranging from coresidence to living more than 250 miles from each other. Frequency of contact with kin (in person, by phone, or by mail) during the past 6 months is reported in six categories ranging from daily contact to no contact.

Relationship Quality

Demandingness of relatives is assessed with a single item regarding how often the person "makes too many demands on (you) for help and support." Responses included never, rarely, sometimes, and often. The measure of negativity in the G1-G2 relationship includes responses to two items, one regarding "conflict, tension, or disagreement" in the relationship and the other asking "how critical" the G1 relative is of the G2 respondent. The measure of supportiveness combines responses to three items, regarding how much the G2 respondent can "depend" on the parent or in-law, how much "concern and understanding" the G1 relative displays, and how much the G2 respondent feels "appreciated, loved, or cared for" by the G1 relative. Responses to the five items used in the measures of negative and positive affect range from 1 (not at all) to 4 (a lot).

Caregiving

Attitudes toward helping older parents are measured with two indices. The concern for self-index (α, .86 for women; .85 for men) combines responses to seven items regarding worries that caregiving will interfere with one's own life. The concern for parents index (α, .82 for women; .76 for men) includes six items that address fears for the aging parent's health and well-being. Respondents were asked to how strongly they agreed or disagreed (1 to 5) with a series of statements. The indices are the average item response. Actual helping behavior is measured with yes-no responses to questions regarding the provision of sick care or assistance with transportation or shopping.

Early Family Experiences

We also relate current G1-G2 relationship characteristics to the G2 sons' and daughters' reports of childhood family experiences. Information on these relationships was collected in the first wave of the study, whereas current relationship quality was assessed using data from the second wave. This separation in data collection reduces the problem of recollected relationship reports being influenced by current relationship quality. G1 parents' marital conflict is measured with a single item regarding whether the marriage had a lot, some, or hardly any conflict. Recalled parental rejection is an index of five items (α is approximately .85 for the four G1-G2 pairs) concerning the degrees of trust, care, faultfinding, dissatisfaction, and blame the G2 sons and daughters felt in their childhood relationships with their parents. Parental hostility is assessed with four items from the NEO Personality Inventory (Costa & McRae, 1985), which concern the degree to which the parent was violent and the frequency with which the parent was angry at the way people treated him or her, argued with others, and lost his or her temper (approximate α, .86).

RESULTS

Pathways to Farming

In the Cornbelt, with its grain and livestock agriculture, the typical transition to farming involves the sons of men in farming. Intergenerational succession usually evolved over a lifetime of arrangements (e.g., partnerships, etc.) that culminates in retirement during the father's mid-60s. The traditional emphasis on intergenerational continuity in family farming among Midwest farmers of German extraction (Salamon, 1992) appears in a sample of nearly 1,000 Iowa farmers. Friedberger (1988, p. 83) found that "an intervivos transfer by a German farmer was a reasonable predictor that a farm would stay in the family more than one generation." However, the age at transfer was quite late. "Many sons had to wait until they were middle-aged before they had a chance to assume ownership." In our sample of Iowans, mainly of German ancestry, some of the sons of farmers on the home farm were still waiting to assume full ownership in 1991, and one third had left farming completely.

We lack full details on intergenerational succession in family farming, extending from the son's first working relationship with his father to a career in later life. Also, sibling responses to inheritance decisions in the estate plan are unknown. The Iowa study was never designed to investigate such matters. Nevertheless, intergenerational strains in this succession should be expressed in affective sentiments, a domain well charted by the data at hand. Before moving to this topic, however, we turn to the family influences that led some farmers' sons and daughters into farming and others into nonfarm pursuits.

Choosing a Job and Mate

Occupation and marriage define the principal pathways to farming for sons and daughters of Iowa farmers, respectively. In both cases, we are referring to decisions and actions that typically occurred during the 1950s and 1960s, a relatively prosperous time for family-based agriculture. We asked the adult sons and daughters about their early family situation and the socioeconomic standing of the family and farm operation. Using 13 different measures, we compared men and women who entered family farming with adults who did not by using a test of the difference between means (t-test) and a discriminant function analysis. The complete details of this research, reported elsewhere (Elder, Robertson, & Conger, forthcoming), show that both the early family environment and socioeconomic origins had something to do with transitions into farming among these Iowans.

Men who entered farming were not more likely to be a firstborn or lastborn, but they were apt to have fewer brothers. The number of brothers differs significantly between farm and nonfarm men, but there are clearly many exceptions where even a large number of brothers did not close the option of farming. Friedberger (1988, p. 133) tells the story of an Iowa farmer who managed to launch nine of eleven sons in farming between 1938 and the 1960s. In most cases, the father worked out a low-interest loan for run-down property with the Farmer's Home Administration or Land Bank, and then proceeded to sell the land well under market value to one of his sons on contract.

Iowa men who have farmed tend to come from families with greater financial resources, a higher recalled standard of living. Their fathers ranked higher on education, had fewer episodes of unemployment, were more involved in the management of the farm, and spent more years in farming when compared to the fathers of nonfarm sons—men who never entered farming. By farm management, we refer to men who owned and operated farms as opposed to leasing or laboring on them. Each of these differences is statistically significant.

The recall of early family characteristics is likely to express errors of memory and the distortion of contemporary experiences. This is the case for socioeconomic aspects of the family and it is even more applicable to the field of remembered emotions. The remembered quality of early family experiences may express present day feelings as well as childhood realities. For our purposes, we focused on memories of parental unhappiness and quarreling, depression, hostility, rejection and harsh parenting. The recall of parental unhappiness and conflict is most characteristic of the social origins of men who entered the world of farming, when compared to the nonfarm men. No other relational factor made a difference.

Overall we find that opportunity for farming, as indexed by socioeconomic factors, played a greater role than early family relations in distinguishing between farm and nonfarm trajectories. In a discriminant function analysis, both socioeconomic and family characteristics emerge as statistically significant. One discriminant function arranged the predictors in order of magnitude—farm involvement, years farmed, standard of living, unemployment, marital conflict, number of brothers and education. The model accounts for 22 percent of the variance in the farm-nonfarm choice, and correctly classifies 74 percent of the men.

We carried out similar comparisons on the daughters of farm parents in the G1 generation, keeping in mind that the target here is marriage. What factors differentiate farm daughters who married into farming from those who married men in the nonfarm world? Socioeconomic conditions that played such an important role in shaping the life trajectory of men were not important for the women, though early family relations do stand out as influential. The only statistically significant factors are the educational level of the father, and, again, the recalled quality of his marriage. That is, women with college-educated fathers who had a good marriage were most likely to marry into farming: they were roughly 4 times more likely to make this life choice.

What is the marital significance of a college-educated father on the family farm? For daughters, this factor has less to do with socioeconomic achievement than it does for sons, but it may well tap personal qualities and a way of life that are attractive in the opposite sex. College-educated fathers would be more likely than the less educated to favor gender equality and mutuality in family life, and to link farm and the larger community through an extended breadth of perspective. An affectionate, conflict-free home is part of this family pattern as a desirable way of life.

It is noteworthy that a quality parental marriage is linked to a farm trajectory among men and women. In both cases, the more discordant and unhappy the parental marriage, the more appealing the options beyond farmstead and farming community for sons and daughters. As among *Children of the Great Depression* (Elder, 1974), the desire to leave home seems to have been reinforced and even accelerated by family conflicts and deprivation among members of this Iowa generation.

Life Course of Farm and Nonfarm Adults

Did entry into farming and nonfarm employment lead to major differences in the timing of family events, in educational level and the relative education of spouse, in women's employment and family economic level, and in contact with relatives? As shown in Table 2.2, life-course differences are remarkably small.

Farm and nonfarm men followed similar timetables on family events, and they occupy similar economic positions. The only difference involves the educational advantage of wives. Farm men are more likely to be married to better-educated wives than are nonfarm men, a difference that partly reflects the better education of the latter. The same conclusions apply to women who entered into farming and nonfarm settings through marriage. They married and had their first child at the same age and enjoy similar economic standing today. Farm women enjoy an educational advantage over their husbands, but nonfarm husbands tend to be better educated than their wives.

This social similarity ends, however, when we turn to the nearness of kin (parents and in-laws) and the extent of frequent contact, whether face to face or by phone and letter. Farm and nonfarm offspring may be living in the same general region, eight north central counties, but their involvement in farming has much to do with proximity and contact with parents and in-laws. Men involved in farming are more likely to live close to parents than are the nonfarm men, as one might expect; however it has no bearing on closeness to in-laws. Frequency of contact is likewise linked to farming and parents. Among women, marriage into farming entails close proximity to in-laws and frequent contact with them, for the most part. However, mother remains the sociometric star. Four out of five farm women report contact with mother at least once a week.

How would the contrast between farm and nonfarm adults turn out if we compared the parental contacts of siblings? Little if anything is known about the siblings and their relationships, though one can imagine differences arising between the sibling on the farm, and nonfarm brothers and sisters. Some of the brothers may have partnerships in a farm and thus share the task of caring for elderly parents. Other brothers may have turned most of the responsibility over to a sister. In any case, a more complete picture of the social embeddedness of el-

TABLE 2.2   Characteristics of Middle-Aged Men and Women by Current Farming Status

	MEN			WOMEN		
	Farm (n = 123)	Nonfarm (n = 149)	Probability Level	Farm (n = 75)	Nonfarm (n = 125)	Probability Level
Age at Marriage (X)	23.3	22.8		21.4	20.7	
Age at First Birth (X)	25.6	24.7		23.9	23.3	
Education						
% H.S. grad.	99.2	97.3		98.7	99.2	
% college grad.	21.9	26.2		26.7	17.6	
Relative Education						
% wife more	36.6	24.8	*	36.0	24.8	
% husband more	24.6	34.2		22.7	36.0	*
Economic Status						
women's employment	85.4	86.6		82.7	90.4	
median income, 1989	40,100	37,450		39,750	37,050	
Proximity to Kin (% < 25 miles from:)						
Mother	84.0	59.2	***	76.2	51.3	***
Father	86.2	63.5	***	72.2	52.0	**
Mother-in-law	62.0	54.9		89.5	50.5	***
Father-in-law	60.5	53.4		92.6	50.7	***
Contact with Kin (% weekly contact with:)						
Mother	82.3	57.8	***	80.0	65.1	*
Father	84.5	61.8	***	70.4	56.7	
Mother-in-law	37.0	40.6		64.9	37.6	***
Father-in-law	39.5	38.1		68.5	37.8	***

*p < .05
**p < .01
***p < . 001

derly parents and aging is needed for an understanding of the role of siblings in contact with parents.

The transition of farm boys and girls to farming involves much greater continuity than the experience of leaving home for nonfarm choices. Does this continuity and the changes accompanying the nonfarm career ensure large differences on traditional, family values? We do not have the option of tracing these values from family life and childhood to the adult years. But are farm and nonfarm men and women different on family values or preferences?

During the second wave of data collection, we asked members of the G2 generation a series of questions on parent care. One set dealt only with the believed impact on the individual, such as "I want to help my parents, but I worry about what will happen to my own life," and "I worry that helping my parents will take all of my resources." Seven of these interrelated questions were averaged to form an index of "concern about self." Farm life and culture seems to have little to do with this individualistic orientation, though we find no evidence of any difference by residence among men and women.

Does concern for parents distinguish between farm and nonfarm men and women? Six interrelated items capture feelings of concern about the welfare of parents, such as "I feel I should keep in close touch with my parents to be sure nothing is wrong" and "I have a nagging sense of concern about my parents." We averaged the scores on these questions to produce a single index. Parent concern is slightly more intense among farm than among nonfarm women, but the difference is not reliable for men or women. Overall we find no conclusive evidence of any difference between Iowans who grew up on a farm and then either entered farming or launched a nonfarm career. The common background in farming may have ensured a common ethos of values and attitudes.

Relations with Parents and In-Laws

At the time of our second wave of data collection (1990), the typical member of the G2 generation was entering the 40s, and their parents were in the seventh and eighth decades of life. Among men and women engaged in farming, half of the surviving fathers and fathers-in-law were still farming. What are the consequences of this situation for relations with aging parents and in-laws?

If men who currently farm report close proximity and more interaction with fathers than do nonfarm sons, as the data suggest, their relations with father may combine the positive sentiments of support and appreciation with both critical judgments and parental demandingness. Even if they live independently, as all but two of the Iowa men do, these young farmers remain under the watchful eye of their parents. The problematic pair for women who married into farming is the husband's parents, and perhaps especially the husband's mother. Women who married a farmer are likely to experience the pleasures and irritations of close relations with an elder relative. Their independence and self-worth may be jeopardized by a mother-in-law's frequent challenges in household management and childrearing.

Table 2.3 compares farm and nonfarm members of the G2 generation on four dimensions of relationship quality concerning parents and in-laws: frequency of contact, the demandingness of the relationship, the negativity of the relationship, and the supportiveness of each parent and in-law. To determine

TABLE 2.3   Relations to Parents and In-Laws among Rural Married Men and Women in Iowa, in Means

Dimensions	Work Patterns of Men			Marriage Patterns of Women		
	Farm $\bar{X}$	Nonfarm $\bar{X}$	Prob. Level[a]	Farm $\bar{X}$	Nonfarm $\bar{X}$	Prob. Level[a]
Contact (hi = 6, lo = 1)						
Mother	4.60	3.82	.001(.06)	4.46	4.02	.05(.60)
Father	4.86	4.01	.001(.01)	4.12	3.73	.07(.30)
Mother-in-law	3.31	3.18	.45(.69)	3.95	3.34	.01(.54)
Father-in-law	3.35	3.10	.22(.52)	4.22	3.23	.001(.04)
Demandingness (hi = 4, lo = 1)						
Mother	1.97	1.67	.02(.06)	1.93	1.88	.78(.92)
Father	2.02	1.64	.007(.02)	1.77	1.51	.09(.08)
Mother-in-law	1.78	1.72	.62(.83)	1.95	1.69	.08(.09)
Father-in-law	1.73	1.61	.32(.41)	2.03	1.52	.002(.01)
Negativity (hi = 4, lo = 1)						
Mother	1.69	1.74	.68(.57)	1.67	1.87	.22(.13)
Father	1.81	1.65	.19(.30)	1.69	1.63	.69(.75)
Mother-in-law	1.67	1.80	.24(.31)	2.00	2.00	1.00(.99)
Father-in-law	1.57	1.80	.09(.09)	2.05	1.71	.04(.05)
Supportiveness (hi = 4, lo = 1)						
Mother	3.61	3.65	.63(.41)	3.84	3.55	.008(.03)
Father	3.59	3.63	.72(.44)	3.76	3.48	.01(.06)
Mother-in-law	3.31	3.28	.77(.84)	3.25	3.22	.85(.87)
Father-in-law	3.37	3.21	.19(.23)	3.16	3.11	.77(.94)

[a]P values for means adjusted for proximity are enclosed by parentheses.
[b]Maximum Ns for farm to farm (Men[Women]): Mo = 67 (43); Fa = 59 (40); Mo-in-law = 73 (40); Fa-in-law = 60 (37). Maximum Ns for farm to nonfarm (Men[Women]): Mo = 89 (92); Fa = 70 (83); Fa-in-law = 97 (82); Mo-in-law = 87 (61).

whether the observed differences between farm and nonfarm are a function of proximity, we show the probability level for the unadjusted means and the *p* level (within parentheses) for an analysis of the means adjusted for the influence of geographical closeness.

Demanding Parents and In-Laws

Proximity and intergenerational contacts point to the farm family as the primary locus of emotionally intense relationships, especially of a negative sort, and we find this most vividly expressed in the perceived demandingness of parents for men and of in-laws for women. It is important to note, however, that overly demanding parents and in-laws are in the minority in the Iowa sample. For example, only a fourth of the farm women and men describe the husband's parents as sometimes or often demanding. The figures for other G1-G2 pairs are even lower.

Farmers claim they interact most frequently with the father (among both parents and in-laws), and the wives of farmers rank interaction with the mother slightly higher than contact with their father-in-law. Perceived demandingness tends to be attributed to parents and in-laws who are most frequently contacted, with one exception—the mothers of women who married farmers. These women are plausible marital examples for their daughters. Father-in-law also ranks especially high on demandingness among the wives of farmers.

The feeling that parents or in-laws are overly demanding stems in part from structured family situations that place these older kin in proximate roles of observation, evaluation, and authority. For example, farmers whose fathers still play an active role in the farming operation are two times more likely to report a demanding father than are men with retired fathers. Different views on farming may lie at the heart of a son's perception of an overly demanding and critical father.

In Howard Kohn's (1989, pp. 38–39) evocative story of his aging father, as "the last farmer," he recalls a trip to "inspect" one of his brother's cornfields. Pointing to some of the rows, his father said, "see how thick he's planted, way too thick. Defeats his purpose. Guarantee you he'll get a lot of stalk and few cobs. And the air won't get through to dry the cobs that he does get." At no point in this lengthy narration did the father acknowledge that his son had been getting more bushels per acre than he.

Kohn notes that "through all my father's differences with my generation of farmers—and with my generation, period, ran a single, simple objection: 'you guys are in too much of a hurry to get ahead.'" As Kohn saw it, these differences were the differences between the "generation that came out of the Great Depression and the generation of the FFA (Future Farmers of America) that came into prominence after World War II. The FFA had educated (his brothers) in the holy writs of modern farming—the 'Commandments' as my father refers to them: Thou shalt plant rows close together (my father thought this was greedy and counterproductive)."

Consumer and childrearing decisions may well be a major source of divisiveness for the wives of farmers and their in-laws. The historical time of the in-law generation favored what Barlett (1993, p. 4) calls a cautious management style in which farm families "avoided debt, preferred direct control over farm tasks, accepted a more modest standard of living, and expected hard manual labor and personal attention to detail to be the keystones to success." The spread of consumerism through all levels and sectors of society after World War II takes the contemporary form of demanding material aspirations in farm families, especially among children and mothers. The farm crisis of the 1980s raised serious questions about the wisdom of anchoring rural family life around material gain, and the older generation is likely to have been a prominent source of such critical doubt. The belief that "the good things in life" came too fast and easily to the postwar generations is commonly expressed by elderly survivors of the rural depression, 1920s through the 1930s.

The felt negativity of parents and in-laws shows the same pattern of association with farm families that we observe with the perception of demandingness, but the overall picture is more complex. The similarity is restricted to farm men who are most likely to report conflict and criticism from their own fathers and from farm wives who are most apt to point to their in-laws and especially the father-in-law. Mothers-in-law may be a problem for a number of farm and nonfarm women, but fathers-in-law remain even more of a problem on the farm. For the most part, however, felt negativity does not vary significantly between farm and nonfarm status, and it is not at a high level within the sample as a whole.

Before turning to feelings of parental supportiveness, it is worth asking whether parental demandingness and negativity reflect a self-other orientation of the middle generation toward the care of parents. We have found that life-course variations by farm and nonfarm status are not linked to attitudes of self- or parent concern. Farm-reared offspring in farm and nonfarm situations do not differ on such attitudes. However, adults who score high on self-concern are more likely to report that their parents are overly demanding and negative (see Table 2.4).

This applies to men and women, their elderly mothers and fathers, and both farm and nonfarm settings. Especially on farms, self-oriented sons and daughters are most likely to complain about the demandingness of father. By comparison, self-orientation has less to do with perceptions of parental supportiveness. This is also the case for attitudes of concern for parents. The index of such attitudes is generally unrelated to perceptions of parents as overly demanding, negative, or supportive.

Supportive Kin and Early Family Experience

Problems of kin tend to fade in significance when they are compared with the acknowledged supportiveness of parents and in-laws. Mean levels of supportiveness are high among members of the G2 generation, regardless of farm or nonfarm status.

This is especially true for the daughters of farm parents who married into

TABLE 2.4   Reported Relations to Parents by Self Orientation of Middle-aged Men and Women in Farm and Nonfarm Settings, Correlation Coefficients

| | Self-Orientation, Men | | Self-Orientation, Women | |
| | Farm | Nonfarm | Farm | Nonfarm |
Relations to Parents	r	r	r	r
Relations to Mother	(n = 66)	(n = 89)	(n = 43)	(n = 91)
Demandingness	.34**	.37***	.27	.29**
Negativity	.14	.25*	.24	.21*
Supportiveness	− .06	− .03	− .27	− .22*
Relations to Father	(n = 59)	(n = 70)	(n = 40)	(n = 83)
Demandingness	.35**	.17	.42**	.28**
Negativity	.19	.07	.37*	.11
Supportiveness	.19	− .07	− .28	− .19

*p < .05
**p < .01
***p < .001

farming. Perhaps through marriage to a local boy, these women ended up on a farm that was near to the parental homestead. Such proximity could make frequent contact with parents possible, though proximity alone cannot account for the strength of the intergenerational bond between farm wives and their farm parents. Women who married out of farming perceive less support from their parents.

For the most part, we gain little understanding of affectional solidarity between the generations by comparing the divergent life courses of farm-reared men who stayed in farming and those who left for nonfarm employment. At least from the vantage point of the middle generation, the G2 farmers and those who pursued nonfarm options feel equally appreciated by their parents. However, these different life courses have implications for how past family experience affects current relations.

Men who decided not to farm reported more early family conflicts and harsh parenting than the men who entered farming. Likewise, women who married out of farming were more likely to describe their family background in terms of less affection and happiness. Accounts of early family experience from the first wave of data collection do not alter the picture on perceived supportiveness in Table 2.3, but they do indicate that troubled relations with parents during childhood may persist into the later years of life.

The imperatives of intergenerational contacts on a farm may ensure the con-

TABLE 2.5 Reported Supportiveness of Parents by Recalled Early Family Experiences, Correlation Coefficients

Recollections of Parents & Childhood	MEN		WOMEN	
	Farm	Nonfarm	Farm	Nonfarm
Mother	(n = 67)	(n = 89)	(n = 43)	(n = 92)
Marital conflict	− .03 p < .05	− .34***	− .22	− .46***
Felt rejection	− .34**	− .56***	− .49***	− .59***
Recalled hostility	− .28* p < .01	− .63***	− .42**	− .49***
R²	.14	.42	.31	.40
Father	(n = 59)	(n = 70)	(n = 40)	(n = 82)
Marital conflict	.06	− .18	− .31	− .43***
Felt rejection	− .24	− .16	− .28	− .57
Recalled hostility	− .07	− .28*	− .20	− .35
R²	.07	.08	.14	.37

*p < .05
**p < .01
***p < .001

tinuity of problematic relations and also positive change. The need to get along in a farming operation would strengthen the hand of conflict resolution and accommodation. By contrast, early animosities could live on in the lives of parents and children who do not have to do business with each other. The empirical evidence for continuity is substantial (Rossi & Rossi, 1990; Whitbeck, Hoyt, & Huck, 1994), but the degree of continuity depends on gender and context.

Table 2.5 shows correlations by farm and nonfarm between parental supportiveness and recollections of conflict between parents, felt rejection from each parent, and parent hostility. This recollection is based on the first wave of data collection, and thus it was not obtained when we asked questions about intergenerational contact and affection in the second wave. The life-span continuity of intergenerational sentiments is stronger among nonfarm men and women than among the farm-based adults, and it is stronger among women than among men.

Women show the greatest stability in relation to their mothers, as do men. By contrast, the father-son relationship shows little if any continuity, unlike the father-daughter relationship. Family continuities among women have been attributed by some to the general life-span stability of their family roles. Men experience this continuity through their mothers, whereas women experience the family theme in their own lives *and* in the lives of their mothers. From this vantage point, there is reason to expect very little continuity in the relation of fathers and sons, and this is what we find. However, recollections of early family experience are not the same as prospective measures, and we cannot be sure of their meaning until prospective data on family relations are linked across the life course.

Caring for Elderly Parents

To conclude our examination of relations with parents and in-laws, we turn to the provision of care in two areas: transportation and illness. In the second wave of data collection (1990), the G2s were asked whether they provide transportation for their parents and care during illnesses. The question did not ask for frequency or specify the time frame. Women were more likely than men to claim that they provided help during sickness of either parent (37% vs. 30%), whereas men were slightly more likely to help out parents in the arena of transportation (21% vs. 19%). Assistance for in-laws comes from both men and women. They were roughly equally as likely to assist on transportation (12% for both) and to help out during illnesses (18% vs. 17%).

Farmers and farmer's wives were closer geographically to parents and in-laws, respectively, than were nonfarm men and women, but this mattered very little in the tendency to help out (see Table 2.6). For the most part, farm-based men and women were more likely to claim they helped their parents on transportation and sick care, when compared with the nonfarm men and women, but the differences are not statistically reliable. Farm women also show a greater tendency to help in-laws than their nonfarm counterparts. These differences, such as they are, do not vary with adjustments for proximity, age, and health of parent and in-law, and the number of sisters.

The most noteworthy finding is the prominence of rural farm women in the caregiving role for parents and in-laws during illnesses. These differences are consistent and substantial, given the small sample size. Medical care and maintenance in rural Iowa is heavily dependent on family care, and this is particularly the case for isolated farmsteads. The burden of such care has fallen most heavily on women, a pattern that may be changing with the dramatic upswing in women's off-farm employment.

Provision of financial assistance is another way adult children may help aging parents, but the transfer of money from the G2 to the G1 generation was not prevalent among our families. Less than 5% reported giving money to their parents. The receipt of financial assistance, in the form of loans or gifts from parents, was much more common. Roughly 5% of the farm-reared men and women reported loans from parents, and one third received gift money. Farm

TABLE 2.6   Provision of Care for Parents and In-Laws by Middle-Aged Men and Women

| | MEN | | WOMEN | |
| | Farm | Nonfarm | Farm | Nonfarm |
	%	%	%	%
Transportation				
Mother	23.9	15.8	18.6	17.4
Father	20.3	14.3	7.5	12.0
Mother-in-law	10.9	12.4	20.0	11.0
Father-in-law	6.7	10.3	18.9	4.9
Sick Care				
Mother	32.8	27.0	46.5	32.6
Father	35.6	27.1	35.0	24.1
Mother-in-law	15.1	16.5	30.0	17.1
Father-in-law	15.0	16.1	21.6	13.1
Number of Cases				
Mother	67	89	43	92
Father	59	70	40	83
Mother-in-law	73	97	40	82
Father-in-law	60	87	37	61

and nonfarm men and women were equally as likely to both provide and receive financial assistance.

These comparisons and others up to this point involve the intergenerational relations of couples from different social worlds, in and out of farming. However, couples also have a common social origin, on a family farm. No doubt, larger intergenerational differences would have been observed if our sample had been drawn from the Midwest or entire country, and if we had compared farm couples with nonfarm families that had no background in farming.

The comparisons also ignore the potential intergenerational consequences of farm loss during the "great farm crisis" of the 1980s. Nearly 30% of the Iowa men who entered farming had lost a farm by the end of the 1980s, with slightly less than half going through the experience during the decade. Loss of the farm often meant loss of a family heritage and tradition. Because Iowa farms are typically passed down across the generations, any farm failure and loss had, in potential at least, serious repercussions for relations between the generations. In simplest terms, a farm loss meant the loss of other people's money, status, and tradition, and not merely a personal loss.

Financial Crisis, Farm Loss, and Relations with Parents

The Iowa farm crisis began with an inflationary cycle at the beginning of the decade, passed through a stage of rapid deflation (collapse of land values) and collective denial in 1982 to 1983, and then entered a confrontation and mobilization phase as people sought ways of achieving relief (1984 to February 1985) (Friedberger, 1988, p. 191). In our Iowa sample, most of the farm losses were concentrated around 1983 to 1985. Such events were at least several years removed from our initial survey in 1989, but the painful loss remained just that. In another study, the wife described the loss as something like a "death in the family" (Rosenblatt, 1990, p. 106).

> *I was sad. We cried a lot. In fact we compared it to when I lost my mom two years ago. I mean the feelings are still there. I still cry. It still hurts. You've lost something that's really important.*

The loss also resembled a family death in relation to its consequences for others, for parents and siblings. One of the Iowa farmers noted that continuing contacts with debtors and the prospect of losing the family farm perpetuated a deep sense of personal guilt for letting his father down. "I feel as if I let him down, even though he has been dead many years." When asked how he is handling the problem in 1990 (occurred in 1983), he replied, "not very well. It definitely influences us today. I think about it every day. One minute I think I should quit farming. . . . And the next minute I think I can't give up yet."

Financial obligations to parents discouraged some couples from getting out; these were obligations to protect the loans and collateral posed by relatives that helped them get started. In an era of diminished land values, the sale of a farm had little chance of recovering the money invested in the place during more prosperous times. One farm couple was haunted by the prospect of saving their own situation while losing nearly all of the $100,000 that their parents had invested in the farm.

To capture fully the family dynamics associated with the loss of the home place, we would need to have records that document the son's entry into farming with help from parents, the arrangements between father and son over the years, and the details on how the farm was lost—the intergenerational negotiations, the alternatives explored with lenders, and so forth. Unfortunately, the Iowa study was not designed to collect such information with adequate detail. Relations between middle-aged parents and their elderly parents were necessarily secondary in the project to an understanding of families under economic pressure.

Nevertheless, we can at least explore the relation between farmers and their own parents who have farmed and consider the quality of this relationship even before the farm crisis, as recalled today. To do this, we compared the full-time farmers in 1990 with men who had lost their farm on five dimensions – proximity, contact, demandingness, negativity, and supportiveness. Both groups of men had grown up on a farm.

The results of this comparison showed surprisingly little impact from the farm loss. As expected, the displaced men are living farther away from parents than farm parents and they see their parents less often ($p < .02$). However, both groups of elderly fathers appear equally supportive, and neither ranks high on negativity or shows any difference on this behavior. Displaced men see their fathers as less demanding ($p < .01$), but this situational result is clearly expected given the transition out of farming and close supervision. For the most part, then, we find no evidence of even a minor rupture in relationship between displaced farmers and their fathers, but, of course, we have only the account of the younger generation. The elderly fathers might well have a different story to tell. We also lack specific details about the business relationship between father and son before the farm loss, and about the loss itself. The term "displaced farmer" may well combine different agricultural histories that have contrasting implications for father-son relations.

What about relations with mother? Historically, the dissatisfaction of women with farm life – commonly known as the "woman problem on the farm" – has played a major role in directing farm sons out of agriculture (Fink, 1992). How did farm loss register on sons' perceived relation to mothers? We find no evidence that the mothers of displaced farmers are seen as less supportive than the mothers of farmers, but they do rank significantly higher on negative attitudes ($p < .04$). This level of negativity is modest at best, however, and is well below the perceived degree of parental support. Nevertheless, the attitude difference raises questions about the traditional attachments and preferences of farm parents. Fathers may be more accepting of the loss than their wives.

In actuality, we are not able to provide an adequate test of the assumption that loss of a farm strains intergenerational relations without knowing something about the precrisis state of these relations. Unfortunately we do not have such information. Our best option is to assume that the precrisis relationship resembles contemporary reports on the quality of parent-child relations during childhood. Two such reports are described in the section on measurement; remembrances of feeling rejected by parents and memories of the hostility of parents.

Overall we find modest evidence that negative accounts of parenting during childhood are correlated with felt demandingness, negativity, and the lack of supportiveness in current relationships (see Table 2.7). These correlations tend

TABLE 2.7   Contemporary Relations with Father and Mother by
Recalled Parent Behavior in Childhood among Farming and Displaced
Men, in r Correlations

Recollections of Parent Behavior in Childhood	Father			Mother		
	Farm n = 59	Displaced n = 24	Difference (p value)	Farm n = 67	Displaced n = 36	Difference (p value)
	r	r	r	r		
Felt Rejection by Parent in Childhood						
Demandingness	− .03	.44*	p < .05	.10	.50**	p < .05
Negativity	.25*	.18		.35**	.36*	
Supportiveness	− .24	− .14		− .34*	− .24	
Parental Hostility						
Demandingness	.10	.34		.16	.22	
Negativity	.11	.21		.30**	.38*	
Supportiveness	− .08	− .41*		− .28*	− .16	

*p < .05
**p < .01

to apply to both farm and displaced men but the remembered hostility of father is only predictive of nonsupportive relations with him today among men who lost their farm. Memories of paternal rejection are linked to the felt demandingness of parents, mother as well as father, among the displaced men, but not among the farm men. These findings are consistent with the notion that the farm crisis accentuated negative relations with father and mother, but they are little more than suggestive of the social and emotional legacy of this deprivational time in family experience. The personal legacy for displaced families may be more vivid in memory and contemporary reality.

DISCUSSION

This portrait of elderly Iowans in relation to their middle-aged sons and daughters is drawn at the end of the greatest rural economic decline since the Great Depression. Seen only from the perspective of middle-aged offspring, these farm-based Iowans have lived a life with beginnings that date well before the New Deal of the 1930s. They have known truly hard times in rural America as well as the unparalleled stretch of prosperity after World War II. Their children grew up in the 1950s and 1960s, and a large number of the boys served in Vietnam. By the early 1970s, most of the children in this study had married and launched a family.

The times were attractive for a career in farming and for leaving the home-place for more distant endeavors. Both sons and daughters followed these different paths. At the end of the 1980s we find them in the Iowa study, describing relations to parents that are both similar and different. They are similar in the degree of supportiveness they attribute to both mother and father, and they are different in proximity of residence, frequency of contact, degree of demandingness, and parental negativity. The difference characterizes sons who are farming most particularly and also, in more specific ways, the in-law and parent relations of daughters who married into farming.

This intergenerational study represents an analogue of a historic family dynamic in which intergenerational continuities and change in work life give shape to different family forms. The family economy responds to altered circumstances with different social adaptations and individual choices, such as outmigration. Industrialization is one of the master transformations of this kind and the decline of agricultural employment is one aspect of this change. The present study has relevance to rural depopulation and outmigration, a process that has been underway in the American heartland since the turn of the century, though no study up to the present has directly investigated its implications for intergenerational relations, exchange, and caregiving.

In the state of Iowa a drastic collapse of land values during the early 1980s accelerated this population decline. Iowa lost more of its population to outmigration than any other state except West Virginia. As a result, the rural population in the study region has aged dramatically, with the median age of half of all communities exceeding 39. This compares to a median age of 34 for the state. A substantial proportion of the G1 generation in this study currently resides in or near declining communities that are losing their ability to provide services for the elderly. The rural elderly are becoming more dependent on family support as even local churches lose the resources to provide outreach services. However, continuing outmigration of the young from agricultural counties would tend to shrink the base of kin support for elderly parents and in-laws, and weaken the flexibility of this support. Caregiving that is dependent on a few relatives implies more of a burden than assistance from a diverse network of kin.

The great farm crisis of the 1980s brought bad times to a good many of the Iowa families, farm and nonfarm, placing additional strains on the relationship between older and younger farmers. A son's farm loss meant a loss of tradition, lifetime investment, and anchorage for the older generation. It also had profound economic repercussions for the local community. Indeed, the rural economy declined by nearly 50% and a good many farmers reached the end of their credit line. All of these considerations suggest that displaced farmers are likely to have ended up with more negative relations with father and mother than full-time farmers. We do not find such an outcome, though men who did not get along well with father during childhood were most likely to feel the same way if they suffered a loss of their farm.

What are the broader implications of farm loss and rural outmigration for the relation between brothers and sisters, parents and children in the displaced farm families, and grandparents and grandchildren? Just as class differences reduce contact between siblings (Adams, 1967), there is reason to expect similar intergenerational effects among siblings who are separated by loss of the family farm, and by pathways in and out of farming. Children who have experienced the loss of a family farm show the imprint of this traumatic event in their tendency to feel more rejected by parents when compared with children in other family situations (Conger & Elder, 1993). This feeling reflects in part the depressed affect of parents during the farm crisis and their preoccupation with the problem of economic survival. Rural grandparents in the Midwest may well establish an important bridge to opportunity for their young grandchildren in a time of great adversity and uncertainty. They survived difficult times during the 1930s and have achieved financial security for the later years.

Our sample of rural families in an eight-county region does not enable us to estimate the full implications of rural depopulation and farm loss. The sons and daughters of farmers who chose different pathways in adulthood, farm and nonfarm, still occupy a similar world. The same is true for men who are still farming and those who had to leave the farm. For the most part they live relatively close to each other and to their aging parents. Even so, it is clear that farming entails both positive and negative features of intergenerational relations. Young men feel the long hand of parents in their demandingness, and young women report the same problem with their in-laws. They tend to carry a slightly heavier burden of caregiving than nonfarm sons and daughters, but perceive no less emotional support from parents. Will the intergenerational implications of farm and nonfarm choices be more pronounced or different within a broader region of the country? This question deserves attention toward understanding the kinship effect of the historic decline of the farm population.

REFERENCES

Adams, B. N. (1967, June). Occupational position, mobility, and the kin of orientation. *Annual Sociological Review*, *32*, 364–377.

Barlett, P. F. (1993). *American dreams, rural realities: family farms in crisis*. Chapel Hill: University of North Carolina Press.

Bogue, D. J. (1985). *The population of the United States*. New York: Free Press.

Conger, R. D., & Elder, G. H., Jr. (1994). *Families in troubled times: Adapting and change in rural America*. Chicago: Aldine.

Costa, P. T., & McCrae, R. R. (1985). *The NEO Personality Inventory manual*. Odessa, FL: Psychological Assessment Resources.

Elder, G. H., Jr. (1974). *Children of the Great Depression: Social change in life experience*. Chicago: University of Chicago Press.

Elder, G. H., Jr. (1981). History of the family: The discovery of complexity. *Journal of Marriage and the Family, 43*, 489–519.

Elder G. H., Jr., & Caspi, A. (1990). Studying the lives in a changing society: Sociological and personological explorations. In A. I. Rabin, R. A. Zucker, & S. Frank (Eds.), *Studying persons and lives* (pp. 201–247). New York: Springer.

Elder, G. H., Jr., Robertson, E. B., & Conger, R. D. (forthcoming). Fathers and sons in rural America: Occupational choice and intergenerational ties across the life course. In T. K. Hareven (Ed.), *Intergenerational relations and aging*. Chicago: Aldine.

Fink, D. (1986). *Open country, Iowa: Rural women, tradition, and change*. Albany: State University of New York Press.

Fink, D. (1992). *Agrarian women: Wives and mothers in rural Nebraska, 1880–1940*. Chapel Hill: University of North Carolina Press.

Friedberger, M. (1988). *Farm families and change in 20th century America*. Lexington: University Press of Kentucky.

Friedberger, M. (1989). *Shake-out: Iowa farm families in the 1980s*. Lexington: University Press of Kentucky.

Goode, W. J. (1963). *World revolution and family patterns*. New York: Free Press of Glencoe.

Haines, M. (1979). *Fertility and occupation: Population patterns in industrialization*. New York: Academic Press.

Hareven, T. K. (1982). *Industrial time and family time*, New York: Cambridge University Press.

Hareven, T. K. (1987). Family history at the crossroads. *Journal of Family History 12*, ix–xxiii.

Kohn, H. (1989). *The last farmer: An American memoir*. New York: Harper & Row.

Lee, G. R. (1988). Kinship ties among older people: The residence factor. In R. Marotz-Baden, C. B. Hennon, & T. H. Brubaker (Eds.), *Families in rural America: Stress, adaptation, and revitalization* (pp. 176–182). St. Paul, MN: National Council on Family Relations.

Lee, G. R. (1989). Rural families: Intergenerational relations. Presented at the annual meeting of the American Sociological Association, San Francisco.

Lipset, S. M., & Bendix, R. (1959). *Social mobility in industrial society*. Berkeley: University of California Press.

Lyson, T. A. (1984). Pathways into production agriculture: The structure of farm recruitment in the United States. In H. K. Schwarzweller (Ed.), *Research in rural sociology and development* (pp. 79–104). Greenwich, CT: JAI Press.

Mangen, D. J., Bengtson, V. L., & Landry, P. H., Jr. (1988). *Measurement of intergenerational relations*. Beverly Hills: Sage.

Mooney, P. H. (1988). *My own boss?: Class, rationality, and the family farm*. Boulder, CO: Westview Press.

Roberts, R. E. L., Richards, L. N., & Bengtson, V. L. (1991). Intergenerational solidarity in families: Untangling the ties that bind. *Marriage and Family Review, 13*, 11–43.

Rosenblatt, P. C. (1990). *Farming is in our blood: Farm families in economic crisis*. Ames, IA: Iowa State University Press.

Rossi, A. S., & Rossi, P. H. (1990). *Of human bonding: Parent–child relations across the life course*. New York: Aldine.

Rudkin, L., Elder, G. H., Jr., Rosenfeld, R. A., & Conger, R. D. (1992). The context and meaning of women's paid employment for rural couples. Presented at the symposium on rural/farm women in historical perspective, Davis, CA.

Salamon, S. (1992). *Prairie patrimony: Family, farming, and community in the Midwest*. Chapel Hill: University of North Carolina Press.

Shribman, D. (1991, April 24). Iowa towns shrivel as the young people head for cities. *Wall Street Journal*, pp. A7–A8.

Whitbeck, L. B., Hoyt, D. R., & Huck, S. M. (1994). Early family relationships, intergenerations solidarity, and support provided to parents by their children. *Journal of Gerontology: Social Sciences, 49*, S85-94.

Commentary:
Disruptive Events and the Life Course

John Myles and Susan Morgan

During the past two decades, Glen Elder's name has become synonymous with the effort to track the effects of major historical events on the way individuals, families, and households live out their lives. His major message to the discipline, or at least one of them, is that history matters, or perhaps even that history matters the most. Processes of individual change are inextricably linked to processes of historical change, and especially to those events both large and small that provide the markers separating past and present, before and after. How individuals age is not something that can ever be read off from a set of developmental sequences embedded in the human psyche or canonized in abstract theoretical generalizations. How men or women experience and cope with identical life transitions and states varies dramatically as a result of the way in which their biographies have been touched by larger social processes and the events that provide the markers of historical time.

As a research strategy, Elder has urged us to pay special attention to "disruptive events" such as wars and depressions since such events draw attention to process. His strategy is like that of organizational sociologists such as Selznick (1957) who insist that only in periods when routine breaks down do the commitments and power relations that maintain organizations become truly transparent to the observer and, frequently, to the participants as well.

Elder's concern with the historical event, and the "disruptive" historical event in particular, has led him to adopt, quite self-consciously, a model of research design rather different from what the typical social science undergraduate is taught

61

in the textbooks. In the standard approach, we are taught to begin with the outcome, the dependent variable that we then attempt to trace back to antecedent causes. Such an approach is "standard" not only in contemporary multivariate modeling, but also in both classical and contemporary exemplars of historical sociology. One can think of the efforts of Marx and Weber to explain the origins of modern capitalism or Barrington Moore's efforts to explain the origins of revolution.

From the very outset of *Children of the Great Depression* (1974, p. 6) to his more recent reflections (Elder, 1987), Elder has eschewed the standard approach in favor of one that begins with the "big event" and then moves on to trace out its multiple consequences. The upshot is that rather than a narrowly focused study where a single consequence is linked through a causal chain to past events, Elder's strategy begins with the event and follows that event through "multiple lines of consequences, each branching off in a different direction" (Elder, 1987, p. 195). In more familiar language, the motivator of the analysis is the independent rather than the dependent variable.

Elder's is an ambitious strategy, and like all ambitious strategies it carries with it considerable risk. Rather than modeling a single outcome, the investigator must model many. Demonstrating a causal link between a historical event and some outcome still requires (a) an adequate theory of the outcome in question, (b) specification of the process that generates the outcome, and (c) identification of the way in which the historical event alters the process. In the language of multivariate analysis, Elder's strategy does not absolve him from developing a correctly specified model of the process generating the outcome. Rather, it requires him to construct many such models, a demanding task indeed.

A second feature of Elder's strategy is that it requires great patience, at least if the event in question is relatively recent. As Elder demonstrated in *Children of the Great Depression*, it takes time for the effects of the event to be realized. The event that motivates the present study by Elder and Rudkin is comparatively recent, the collapse of the agricultural economy of Iowa in the 1980s. Some of the outcomes of this collapse will be virtually instantaneous; others may take many years to unfold. To complete their study, Elder and Rudkin have little choice but to wait.

The outcomes explored in this chapter, as we would expect, are multiple: the movement in and out of farming between generations, the quality of interaction and social relations between generations, and the effect of farm loss on social relations between generations. In all of these cases, efforts to develop well-specified models of the processes in question are in an early stage of development and, as a result, not always convincing. Consider Elder and

Rudkin's conclusion that there is no evidence of even minor ruptures in social relationships between displaced farmers and their fathers. They may well be correct. But it may also be the case that the effects of farm loss have been suppressed by an empirical model that is poorly specified. To illustrate, consider Elder's (1974) demonstration in *Children of the Great Depression* that the effect of the "event" depended on the subject's age and stage in the life course at the time when the event occurred. There is no way of knowing from the present analysis whether there is a similar life-course dependency for the effect of farm loss. More worrisome, perhaps, is the fact that the sample design, which truncates variation in several independent variables, may well preclude estimation of such effects because members of the G2 generation are all approximately of the same age.[1]

But by its very nature, however, Elder's research strategy is an ambitious one with a long time horizon, and it behooves us to be patient as the authors work through the problems of model construction and wait for the effects of the event in question to unfold. Indeed, the main function of the present chapter would seem to be to establish benchmarks for further work. Although the downturn in Iowa's agricultural economy motivates the analysis, determining its effects, if any, is not central to this chapter. Only a small part of the analysis (one of four hypotheses) deals with the effects of the downturn, and instead the analysis appears to be working toward a more general understanding of intergenerational relations among Iowa farm families. This is precisely the sort of exploratory work required to develop models that will allow them to turn their attention to estimating the effects for the recession. What might we expect to learn after this preliminary work is done?

To study families under "economic pressure" in this context could mean two things. At the macrolevel, it would mean comparing intergenerational relations during a period of recession with intergenerational relations during a period of prosperity. To do this, Elder and Rudkin will have to wait for conditions to improve for Iowa Farmers (if they ever do) and then collect new data to determine differences in family relations during periods of prosperity and decline. But at the microlevel, there is much to be done.

The fact that there is little difference between those who lost their farms and those who did not indicates that the first task is to account for variations *within* these two groups rather than between them. Some farm families are presumably able to weather the effects of recession better than others, and the recession will be a more stressful life event for some families than others. One might reasonably expect variations in intergenerational relations to be both cause and effect of such differences in individual responses to economic pressure irrespective of actual success or failure in hanging on to the family farm. For organizational sociologists, periods of crisis are times when organizations reveal their true value commitments. What is this organization for? So too with families. Living through a crisis together may reinforce or weaken family bonds irrespective of outcome. Elder and Rudkin might consider the possibility that, *post facto*, the quality of intergenerational relations will not hinge on whether the farm was retained or not but on how well each side of the generational divide lived up to expectations of appropriate behavior during the crisis. We might expect G2 farmers who lost their farms to hold different views of their G1 fathers depending on whether the G1 fathers had risen to the occasion and done everything expected to prevent this outcome. We would guess that some G1 fathers were more able or willing than others to provide economic support to their middle-aged farm sons and daughters in difficulty. Intergenerational transfers of capital may even have made the recession a source of economic opportunity for some farmers, allowing them to buy up farm land from the less fortunate. The types of intergenerational family strategies for coping with economic pressure, their success or failure, and the extent to which they conform to normative expectations for dealing with such situations presumably has much to do with how the generations get along and perceive their relations with one another after the fact.

Elder and Rudkin's study of intergenerational relations among these Iowa farmers has implications that extend beyond the declining agricultural communities of the American Midwest. Because they involve transmission of capital, intergenerational relations among farm families are different. For wage and salary earners, the intergenerational transmission of status and wealth depends largely on the ability to provide their children with human capital (education) rather than physical capital. The former occurs early in the life course, whereas transmission of the family business typically occurs later in the life course. During periods of economic downturn, wage and salary earners can provide accommodation to their adult children, and, indeed, multigeneration households have risen sharply in the 1980s. Family capital provides other kinds of opportunities for intergenerational support but also for intergenerational conflict as Arensberg's classic study of Irish farmers demonstrated.

Throughout most of the 20th century, farmers, merchants, and other small business owners have been a class in decline. As a result, small property owners have been at the periphery of concern among social analysts interested in emergent trends and the long-term future of Western industrial societies. Were this trend to continue, Elder and Rudkin's examination of intergenerational relations among Iowa farmers would be of interest only as a historical footnote on the way things were in the past. Since the 1970s, however, all this has begun to change. What we once called the "old middle class," the self-employed and small employers in small family-owned businesses, has enjoyed a remarkable resurgence. We are not about to see the return of the family farm. But if rising trends in self-employment in services and manufacturing continue, we shall find ourselves doing more studies of the sort Arensburg conducted among Irish farmers but now in American cities. As a result, Elder and Rudkin's study of Iowa farmers—a family-based industry in distress—offers us not a glance to the past but rather a glimpse into the future.

NOTE

[1]A more technical quibble concerns Elder and Rudkin's comparison of Zero-order correlations to reach this conclusion. As Duncan (1975) and others have pointed out, comparison of standardized regression coefficients or zero-order correlations across populations may be potentially misleading by confounding differences in the effect parameter (the slope) with differences in the variances of the variables.

REFERENCES

Duncan, O. D. (1975). *Introduction to structural equation models*. New York: Academic Press.

Elder, G. H., Jr., (1974). *Children of the Great Depression*. Chicago: University of Chicago Press.

Elder, G. H., Jr. (1987). Families and lives: Some developments in life course studies. *Journal of Family History. 12*, 179–199.

Selznick, P. (1957). *Leadership in administration*. New York: Harper & Row.

Commentary:
Rural Families as a Model for
Intergenerational Transmission

Martin Kohli

OVERVIEW

Some of sociology's most basic concerns now center on the macro-microlink, or vice versa (cf. Alexander, Giesen, Münch, & Smelser, 1987). But it is still an area where programmatic statements abound and successful empirical strategies are few. Among the latter, the work of Glen Elder and his coauthors has been a prominent example. The project that Elder has pursued over the last decades consists of articulating the changes in the societal and economic macrostructure with processes on the mesolevel of the family and on the microlevel of individual personalities as they unfold over the life course. As he has shown repeatedly, the family is a key link between the macro- and the microworlds. For those who study intergenerational relations, it is most welcome to have this type of analysis now extended to the later stages of the life course.

In their present study (Elder, Rudkin, & Conger, this volume), the authors have taken agriculture as one more window on the consequences of economic decline: on how economic hardships affect the family, and through it, the life course of its members. The agricultural crisis of the 1980s makes it possible to repeat this feature of the path-breaking *Children of the Great Depression* (Elder, 1974).

But agriculture is more than that. It is also a window on the family effects of modernization, both economically and culturally. In economic terms, farm families are still marked by tradition in the sense that they are not only units of con-

66

sumption but also of production. For analyzing intergenerational relations in the context of the family, this gives an especially rich material. In cultural terms as well, farming represents a special blend of modernity and (at times very obstinate) tradition.

Farm families being so special, one might conclude that they stand for an increasingly defunct stage of the modernization process and are not well suited for studying the mainstream of intergenerational relations today. In my view, the opposite is true. Farm families are an explicit model for aspects of intergenerational relations that, although hidden, remain important for a wide range of family settings. Thus, they offer a privileged access to some of the contemporary contradictions of modernity.

The contradictions focus on how behavior is regulated in the different domains of society. The conventional view of modernization until recently was one of increasing functional differentiation between subsystems, with the economy as the domain of instrumental or profit orientation, and the family as the domain of affective or expressive orientation. Intergenerational relations are one of the fields where this neat separation proves to be wholly inadequate. It is obvious today that these relations cannot be assessed without considering all four modes of interpersonal orientation: personal utility maximization, affective solidarity (or conflict), normative constraints, and moral commitments. How these orientations are mixed is visible (e.g., in caregiving, monetary transfers, or inheritance). In farm families, this mix is particularly manifest.

This speaks to a basic controversy in contemporary sociology: the controversy between utilitarian and normative theories of action. If Talcott Parsons were still alive and theorizing today, he would have chosen intergenerational relations in the family as a testing ground on which to take on proponents of utility maximization and rational choice theories. He could have demonstrated the importance of normative and moral obligations in a field that is increasingly usurped by utilitarian models. Conversely, he would have had to concede the relevance of utility orientations even in relations between direct kin. The controversy is also about the place of social relations and nonutilitarian orientations in the economy itself, in other words, about the social embeddedness of economic activity (cf. Granovetter, 1985; Kohli, 1987). Family businesses—and farms in the Western world are still largely family businesses—are an excellent case for examining how economic considerations take precedence over, or are constrained by, interpersonal solidarity and moral obligations.

The focus of this chapter is on Western Europe, where on the whole the persistence of tradition may still be stronger than in the U.S. Farming is the sector that has longest resisted what Habermas (1984) has termed the "colonization of the life world" by modern market structures and market identities. On the other hand, it has been confronted with massively changing constraints and op-portunities including those of the highly regulated agricultural "market" regime of the European Union (EU). And today, it has become the field of a new con-flict between market identities and ecological identities, giving the "interweave of work, family, and nature" (Elder et al., this volume) a new moral turn.

The following sections proceed from the macro- to the meso- and micro-level. First, I focus on some structural features of agriculture that are relevant for intergenerational issues; second, I address the place of farming and the farm in the family lineage; and third, I go into some impacts of the family economy on personal relations.

STRUCTURAL FEATURES OF AGRICULTURE

In some basic structural respects, agriculture today is homogenous across most of the developed world. In North America and Western Europe (excluding the Mediterranean rim and Ireland), the share of the labor force in agriculture[1] no-where exceeds 10%. In many countries, it is substantially lower, with Great Britain (at 2.2% in 1990) closely followed by countries such as Belgium, the United States, Sweden, and Germany, all below 4% (cf. Eurostat, 1992, p. 129). Thus, farming has become the business of a small minority. As will be seen, however, the present extent of farming is not an adequate reflection of its importance in the social fabric; attention has to be given also to the extent of farm origins in today's older generations.

The special character of farming is highlighted by another common struc-tural feature: it has become highly age concentrated. Throughout the Western world, agriculture is the industry with by far the highest proportion of older workers. Among the six EU countries for which we have the relevant data on the industry-age mix (for 1985), the share of workers older than age 55 in agri-culture is typically twice as high as that of the next highest industry. A fifth of those employed in agriculture in the Netherlands are older than age 55, and more than 30% in France and Denmark, with England, Belgium, and Germany falling in between (Jacobs, Kohli, & Rein, 1991, p. 70). This striking feature of the demography of agriculture can be explained by two factors: the rapid shrink-age of the agricultural work force, with correspondingly low rates of new en-trants, and the tendency for older farmers to retire later than is the case in other fields, or not at all.

In other respects, agriculture seems less homogeneous, especially between Europe and North America. Continental Western European agriculture is more traditional than the United States, with large parts still marked by traditional ownership structures, traditional production lines, and traditional locally based identities. However, the structural change away from agriculture has been more sweeping. As Elder et al. (this volume) note for the United States, about 15% of the total labor force were still employed in agriculture in 1950 compared with less than 3% (2.8% to be exact) in 1990. In the same period, German agriculture declined from 23.8% to 3.4%, and French agriculture from 36.5% (in 1946) to 6.1%. The most extensive evolution has occurred in the European peripheries such as Italy, Spain, and Greece, but also Scandinavia. Finland had 70.6% of its labor force engaged in agriculture in 1920, still 46.0% in 1950, and only 8.4% in 1990. For Italy, the corresponding figures are 55.7%, 40.0%, and 9.0% (cf. Eurostat, 1992; Flora, 1987). Although the rate of decline from 1950 to 1990 in Finland is similar to that of the U.S., the social significance of the decline is much larger. In 1950, Finland was a country where agriculture and forestry still dominated the work force, while in 1990 they have shrunk to a small minority. These figures give an idea of how different the typical experience of growing up has been for today's grandparents, parents, and children. More than two thirds of the present Finnish retirees were born in farm families. This is what they refer to today when in interaction with their grandchildren they recollect their own childhood. It is an intriguing question to what extent the current social idealizations and images of old age take their distinctiveness from this basic rural origin, and how they will change with the succession of generations with different biographical roots.

Thus, economic modernization in continental Europe has come in a more abrupt way than in the United States. The same is true for the consequences of historical-political discontinuities and ruptures, as, for example, in Germany. During the immediate postwar years, German society was shaken by massive forced migration from the lost territories in the East and later by migration from East to West Germany. For these migrants, the attachment to their place of origin was reduced to individual memory, or to collective memory organized through the "homeland"-based movements that were both political pressure groups and folkloristic associations. Only now, after more than 40 years, are these territorial origins revisited and, in some instances, reclaimed.

As another consequence of these discontinuities, agriculture in East Germany—and to varying degrees, in the other Eastern countries as well—has been industrialized and collectivized, creating a new class of agricultural laborers. For the social history of the German Democratic Republic (GDR), this is one of the most interesting and original phenomena. If the core topic of social history is the formation of classes, the shifting of their boundaries, and their eventual dissolution, this new agricultural class is highly significant, as significant perhaps as the better-known "new class" of bureaucrats.

In the GDR, the agricultural wage laborers received rather high salaries (higher than in many service occupations and in some industries), normal social security benefits (including vacations and maternity leaves), and often new collective housing (apartment buildings) constructed for them at the edge of the traditional villages where their large factory-like agricultural enterprises also were located. Thus, there has been a proletarization of agriculture but on a comparatively high benefit level. It was more easily achieved in the northeastern regions of the GDR with their structure of large-scale estates with dependent laborers still partly in place in 1945 but met with more resistance in the southwestern regions with their tradition of independent family farming. It will be most salient to see how much of the traditional agricultural identities have persisted under these circumstances and how they will now fare in the brutal transition to a market economy. Given their former benefits, many of these agricultural proletarians are reluctant to reconvert themselves into (or become) private farmers.

Of course, to speak of a "market" economy in Western European agriculture today is only partly appropriate. To a large extent, farmers depend on publicly regulated prices, or are directly subsidized by the state. Despite their decreasing size, the agricultural populations are still an important factor in the politics of European nation-states, and especially of European integration. This is partly due to the share of agricultural expenses in the public budgets. In the EU, expenses for agriculture still comprise more than half of the total budget (1991: 58%) (Läufer, 1992, p. 229). But for the usual type of structural analysis, the high political weight of agriculture remains puzzling. Pointing to the budget shares is not a sufficient explanation; it is itself in need of being explained. Why are farmers' protests in countries like France so effective, even to the point where they jeopardize a new world trade agreement? One may try a historical explanation: Politicians remember that in former times regimes have been toppled by fights over bread prices. A more recent historical aspect seems to be more significant, however: The farmers still enjoy a strong backing by parts of the industrial and service populations that remember their agricultural roots.

THE ROLE OF THE FARM IN THE FAMILY LINEAGE

Studying family farms requires sensitivity for the importance of place. This is an underrated variable in contemporary sociology that has taken its inspiration from the breakdown of local life worlds and the mobilization of social relations. In many cases a farm might be a piece of land that allows a family to operate a family business and thus to reproduce itself economically—a piece of land that may be acquired and sold like any other capital good. But such a complete commodification of land is restricted by the high attachment to place that is characteristic for many farm families. By holding on to their land, they also conserve the place of origin for those kins who have moved to the industrial or service sector. For France, it has been pointed out (Segalen & Zonabend, 1986, p. 509f) that rural origins in the sense of localization in a precise "terroir" (territorial unit) are conditions for the continuing strength of kinship relations. This is not only a question of intergenerational memory but also of its objectivation in space. The farm is the house and land to which the continuity of the family is linked materially as well as symbolically.

In the history of the rural European family, this attachment to place is perhaps the most prominent feature. The obligation toward the family farm ("estate thinking") has typically taken precedence over all other considerations, including those for one's individual well-being and that of other persons. An impressive example is given by Imhof (1984, p. 142) in his study of the demography of preindustrial Germany. He reconstructed the history of one of the farms in his study area (Northern Hesse) from 1552 to the present and found an uninterrupted line of 16 owners all from the Hooss family. During this period, the farm was always transferred without partition. In three instances, the owner was a woman – the widow of the previous owner. Eleven of the owners, however, were direct descendants in a generational lineage, and 10 of them (including the present owner) had the same name: Johannes Hooss. This represents a strategy of stability that may have been particularly successful in this case, but is indicative of wider processes. Families traditionally have been about continuity – continuity of persons, of social and cultural capital, but also of material capital. There was a strong normative obligation for family heads to transmit at least as much capital as they had inherited themselves (Bourdieu, 1963; cf. Schultheis, 1993, p. 421). Today, this obligation can still be felt; under the modern conditions of schooling as the major system of status distribution, it increasingly takes the form of securing for the descendants a "good education." In a traditional farm family linked to an economic enterprise and a place, the major family capital was the land holding; losing it represented the worst damage to family continuity.

As indicated by the data on the rapid decrease of the agricultural population cited earlier, leaving the farm has become a very common experience in this century. One would therefore expect its moral significance to have weakened. Modern farm families may increasingly replace material continuity embodied in the farm holding by status continuity (or status improvement) through education. Moreover, concern for one's past family lineage, including the lineage aspects of farming, may be increasingly out of step with a society oriented more toward the achievements of the future than the ascriptions of the past. But tradition still has its weight, albeit in differing degrees and forms. This is strikingly shown by Bohler and Hildenbrand's (1989) qualitative study of how successors are recruited in West German family farms. The authors point out that to secure the continued operation of its farm, the family has to mobilize the traditional motives of "estate thinking." The problem is that they are increasingly at odds with the requirement of being an enterpreneur in a modern market environment, as well as with the cultural trend toward individualization. In this contradictory situation, some of the families react defensively, by modernizing only to the extent that is necessary to keep the family farm business viable. Others are more innovative and ready to sacrifice traditional elements of farming for new business concepts such as agroindustrial farming or modern ecological farming. Which variant is played out depends not only on the present economic opportunities and the present personal orientations, including the orientations of spouses, but also on the family tradition. The latter is marked by the status of the family farm in the local community and also by the local pattern of inheritance.

For all variants, the family tradition remains a conscious (if not always positive) point of reference. One of the cases analyzed by Bohler/Hildenbrand is that of a sixth-generation family farm in a mountain village with a traditional pattern of impartibility. Even though the farm has always been one of the largest in the village, and among those with the highest prestige, its economic viability is increasingly problematic. But for the son, it is clear that he will continue to operate the farm and, thus, in his words, "make" the seventh generation. The commitment to the family farm takes precedence over other possible—and possibly more profitable—economic careers. But today, this commitment is not simply a case of stubbornly following an ascriptive mode of life. Continuing a family farm against increasing economic odds represents to some extent a personal achievement. Tradition thus becomes the resource for a new individualized identity.

In another case, the family had lost its male heirs during the war, and one of the daughters finally married a refugee from the East who as a farm worker in the village was not an adequate match in terms of status but had proven his ability for farming. As a consequence, the family moved to a somewhat marginal position in the local community but also opened itself for enterpreneurial innovations. This tradition—a structural compromise between a modern achievement orientation and the old principle of perennial continuity of the farm—prepared it to accept another fundamental change proposed by the present successor, namely, toward an ecological ("biodynamic") production. In a third case, the innovation takes the form of a highly rationalized agroindustrial business. The young farmer who has succeeded his father continues the latter's enthusiasm for modern technology; before taking over the farm, he had completed his occupational education by going to work on a U.S. farm for 18 months.

In the Iowa sample analyzed by Elder et al. (this volume), there are links in the opposite direction: It is mainly of German ancestry. Whether these origins still influence the behavior of present-day farmers may be impossible to ascertain. But as the authors note, (this volume, p. 53) farms are typically passed down across the generations in Iowa as well, and the loss of a farm means "the loss of other people's money, status, and tradition, and not merely a personal loss." It is the failure toward one's ascendants and toward the family heritage that is at stake here, highlighted by moving interview citations that capture the traumatic impact of the event. Interestingly, there is no reference to the loss for one's descendants—to having failed in one's obligation toward future generations. This would be the strongest indication for the continuing vitality of the concept of family farm.

A major issue in the intergenerational transfer of control over a farm, as evoked both by Bohler and Hildenbrand (1989) and by Elder et al. is the possible conflict between fathers and sons over how to farm properly. The Iowa farmers of the older generation have learned their lesson in the Great Depression and have always been critical of their sons wanting to make it too fast. They may have seen this as taking risks that would jeopardize the family farm. The sons now learn their lesson in the crisis of the 1980s. The lesson is a familiar one in farming. Traditionally, farmers have always and everywhere learned to be cautious—to build up reserves for hard times and to distrust the institutions of the modern world (such as banks offering them loans). Farmers have tended to be conservative not only in their preoccupation with continuity of the family lineage but also in their stubborn view of how to do business. This may be linked to the larger kinship dimension of the family. If the larger family is mobilized financially to contribute to keeping up the farm, it can, in turn, count on the farm as a safety net in times of crisis in the industrial and service economy. Under conditions of economic insecurity, as has been demonstrated by anthropological studies, such as Scott's (1976) study of the "moral economy" of southeast Asian peasants, it is more rational for peasants to pursue a strategy of security than of maximization of returns by taking risks. The experience of the farm as a family safety net applies not only to the developing world, but also to economic breakdowns such as in Germany after 1945, or in Eastern Europe (to the extent that families still have control over farms) after 1989. Thus, the conflict over the proper way of farming between fathers and sons is relevant much beyond the intergenerational pair that is empirically concerned. They are players in a drama that involves more than their own selves.

IMPACT OF THE FAMILY ECONOMY ON INTERGENERATIONAL RELATIONS

Given this background, it is surprising and significant that the loss of the farm by the sons in the study by Elder et al. has had little impact on intergenerational relations (this volume, p. 55). Not being able to honor this commitment to the family lineage does not lead to more conflict between fathers and sons. As the authors note, they lack full details on this point; grouping together all farm losses "may well combine different agricultural histories that have contrasting implications for father–son relations" (this volume, p. 55). But to the extent that this result is valid for involuntary displacements from the farm, it seems to indicate that family relations even here have become highly individualized. Sons are allowed to have a life of their own; their personal well-being and that of their own family of procreation takes precedence over any criteria of lineage and of the farm as a material embodiment of lineage.

Intergenerational succession in a family business such as a farm is linked to issues of control over the property. For the older generation, transferring the property is not so much "retirement" in the sense of leaving work as what Plakans (1989) in his overview of traditional Europe has aptly called "stepping down" in the sense of surrendering control. The results from the Iowa sample (Elder et al., this volume, p. 41) correspond to the traditional pattern for Northern and Western Europe: Intergenerational succession evolves over a lifetime, and the final transfer occurs rather late in the life of sons.

Succession also poses the issue of inheritance. Sørensen (1989) has systematically discussed retirement as a consequence of how "individuals and their families and households are matched to positions in social structure" (1989, p. 198), and shown how in traditional Europe this match was shaped by inheritance patterns. These patterns seem to have been largely a function of the opportunity structure in terms of the availability of land, with regions (and periods) with high population pressure on land tending toward impartibility of the estate (unigeniture), tempered in various degrees by payments and dowries to the noninheriting descendants. Impartibility was a solution for preserving the match between a family and a property, but a problem for the "politics of the family" by creating inequality between descendants. The problem has become more acute with the spread of the modern normative idea of equality. In fact, as documented by the classic studies by Wilhelm Riehl and Frédéric Le Play, much of the 19th-century agrarian world was torn by the conflict between older patterns of impartibility and the new democratic rules of equal partition (as introduced, e.g., by the Code Napoléon). Tocqueville saw the imposition of equal partition as breaking the intimate link between the family and the farm holding, which would destroy both of them. Conservative authors such as Riehl and Le Play argued similarly that equal partition would undermine the family lineage tradition as well as the authority of the family head. The latter argument is reminiscent of the way microeconomists today pose the problem of inheritance: Bequests are rational only insofar as parents, by selective bequeathing, try to maximize their own lifetime utility by manipulating the behavior of children toward them (Bernheim, Schleifer, & Summers, 1985; cf. Wolfe, 1989, p. 223f).

Inheritance today is gaining increasing attention in sociology and economics both because after the historically unprecedented accumulation of wealth since the 1950s its empirical importance has grown and because it poses the basic theoretical problem set out in the introduction: that of the dynamic interplay between personal utility, affective solidarity and conflict, normative constraints, and moral obligations. In future studies, we will need a more complete picture including information on what there is to inherit in a family, what the inheritance expectations of the adult children are, and who finally gets what in what parts. We will also need details on coresidence patterns and how they are dealt with, reminding ourselves that in many European farm regions, the traditional pattern has been one of separate households but with very close proximity (*Altenteil; or special living unity for the retired farm couple*). Such information will allow us to examine whether and how the distribution and the timing of inheritance is being used as a control instrument in intergenerational relations—as a handle that the aging parents retain on their adult children including their obligation for caretaking.[2]

Within the family economy, inheritance is only one form of intergenerational transfers. It is usually preceded by regular patterns of other forms, such as donations and services. In the Iowa sample, transfers of money from adult children to their aging parents were not prevalent; transfers in the opposite direction were much more common (Elder et al., this volume). This corresponds to the general picture from studies of intergenerational wealth flow. As shown, for example, for France (cf. Attias-Donfut, 1993), there is a substantial flow from parents to their adult children and grandchildren—a flow of money but also of services, such as child care (which may be essential for mothers to be able to participate in gainful employment). There is thus "a private exchange cycle . . . operating in the opposite sense than that of national redistribution which deducts money from those active to benefit those retired" (Attias-Donfut, 1993, p. 3). The welfare state transfers may themselves be an important resource for this private exchange. In some countries, the elderly have become an asset for the rural family economy because they are pension recipients, and thus a steady source of cash income independent of the vagaries of agricultural production and agricultural markets.

I have so far stressed inheritance and other intergenerational transfers as part of the transmission of the family farm. However, transfers from parents to children come in other forms as well. Those descendants who do not inherit the family farm may receive assistance to set up a new farm on their own (as in the cases cited by Elder et al., this volume). Farming can become a family style much beyond the family farm ("occupational inheritance"). In farm families, there are characteristic patterns of socialization for collective concerns instead of purely individual goals. Elder et al. (this volume) provide vivid examples of the career choices of farm children, contrasting women and men, and on the life course of those who leave the farm, as opposed to those who remain. In a qualitative study, Bertaux and Bertaux-Wiame (1988) have tried to extend this line of analysis to family mobility across several generations. Taking the example of a French rural artisanal family, they show not only the commitment to the family business but also the persistence of the family style with those members of successive generations who leave the family business. Even those who choose (or are launched by their parents into) other occupational fields retain a similar habitus and pursue similar strategies. In this sense, intergenerational transmission can again be seen to include not only material but also cultural and social capital.

CONCLUSIONS

I have argued that farm families, with their special mix of tradition and modernity, highlight some aspects of intergenerational relations that are relevant for other families as well where they are less readily observable. Farming has become the life form of a small minority; migration out of farming has been one of the most massive of the structural changes that Western societies have experienced over this century. But in Western Europe, the tradition of farming is still prominent in societal memory, not least because today's elderly have to a large part still grown up on farms. For a farm family, the farm is not simply a means of production like any other commodity; continuing the operation of the farm may be an important dimension of family continuity. However, the reference to tradition is colored by the cultural trend toward individualization. Even in cases of loss of the family farm, the criteria of personal development seem to take precendence in intergenerational relations over those of commitment to the lineage tradition; in cases of successful intergenerational transmission of the farm, the reference to tradition may be the basis for a new individualized life form.

ACKNOWLEDGMENTS

Despite my own lineage tradition, my professional interest in the rural world is new. It has taken me more than two decades of sociological writing to remember the fact that all four of my grandparents were born on farms, with the men being forced to move away to some other career because they did not inherit and the women being attracted to these nonfarming farm boys. I am grateful to Glen Elder and his coauthors for having challenged me into this memory work and to Dale Dannefer—whose farm background is more recent—for his comments. Of course, the preceding will not be able to do justice to the whole range of the problems involved, nor to the variations in patterns of intergenerational transmission.

NOTES

[1]Here and in the following discussion, "agriculture" includes other primary-sector employment (forestry and fishing).

[2]In the study by Elder et al. (this volume), the parents are still too young, so the test of care is yet to come. There is also an issue of sample design: The sample picks up only those who have remained in the region and thus constitutes "a very conservative test" of the consequences of moving to nonfarm employment for intergenerational ties. Even though in the study the spatial proximity to parents is lower for nonfarming children, it is likely to be considerably higher for those in the study sample than for all nonfarming children of these parents.

REFERENCES

Alexander, J., Giesen, B., Münch R., and Smelser, N. J. (Eds.). (1987). *The micro-macro link*. Berkeley: University of California Press.

Attias-Donfut, C. (1993, July). *Economic crisis and the redefinition of intergenerational solidarity*. Paper presented at the XVth International Congress of Gerontology, Budapest.

Bernheim, B. D., Schleifer, A., & Summers, L.H. (1985). The strategic bequest motive. *Journal of Political Economy, 93*, 1045–1076.

Bertaux, D., & Bertaux-Wiame, I. (1988). Le patrimoine et sa lignée: Transmission et mobilité sociale sur cinq générations. *Life Stories/Récits de vie, 4*, 8–26.

Bohler, K. F., and Hildenbrand, B. (1989). Normalbiographie oder Individualisierung? Zum Strukturwandel in der Rekrutierung von Nachfolgern bäuerlicher Familienbetriebe. *Bios, 2*, 221–238.

Bourdieu, P. (1963). La société traditionelle: Attitude à l'égard du temps et conduite économique. *Sociologie du travail, 1*, 24–44.

Elder, G. H., Jr. (1974). *Children of the Great Depression*. Chicago: University of Chicago Press.

Eurostat. (1992). *Statistische Grundzahlen der Gemeinschaft*. Luxemburg: Amt für amtliche Veröffentlichungen der Europäischen Gemeinschaften.

Flora, P. (1987). *State, economy, and society in Western Europe 1815–1975* (Vol. 2). Frankfurt: Campus.

Granovetter, M. (1985). Economic action and social structure: The problem of embeddedness. *American Journal of Sociology. 91*, 481–510.

Habermas, J. (1984). *Theory of communicative action*. Cambridge: Polity Press.

Imhof, A. E. (1984). *Die verlorenen Welten*. München: Beck.

Jacobs, K., Kohli, M., & Rein, M. (1991). Testing the industry-mix hypothesis of early exit. In M. Kohli, M. Rein, A.-M. Guillemard, & H. van Gunsteren (Eds.), *Time for retirement: Comparative studies of early exit from the labor force* (pp. 67–96). Cambridge: Cambridge University Press.

Kohli, M. (1987). Retirement and the moral economy: An historical interpretation of the German case. *Journal of Aging Studies, 1,* 125–144.

Läufer, T. (1992). Haushaltspolitik. In W. Weidenfeld & W. Wessels (Eds.), *Europa von A-Z* (pp. 225–234). Bonn: Europa Union Verlag.

Plakans, A. (1989). Stepping down in former times: A comparative assessment of "retirement" in traditional Europe. In D. I. Kertzer & K. W. Schaie (Eds.), *Age structuring in comparative perspective* (pp. 175–195). Hillsdale, NJ: Erlbaum.

Schultheis, F. (1993). Genealogie und Moral: Familie und Staat als Faktoren der Generationenbeziehungen. In K. Lüscher & F. Schultheis (Eds.), *Generationenbeziehungen in "postmodernen" Gesellschaften* (pp. 415–433). Konstanz: Universitätsverlag.

Scott, J. (1976). *The moral economy of the peasant.* New Haven: Yale University Press.

Segalen, M., & Zonabend, F. (1986). Familles en France. In A. Burguière (Ed.), *Histoire de la famille* (Vol. 2., pp. 497–527). Paris: Armand Colin.

Sørensen, A. B. (1989). Old age, retirement, and inheritance. In D. I. Kertzer & K. W. Schaie (Eds.), *Age structuring in comparative perspective* (pp. 197–213). Hillsdale, NJ: Erlbaum.

Wolfe, A. (1989). Market, state, and society as codes of moral obligation. *Acta Sociologica, 32,* 221–236.

CHAPTER 3

Intergenerational Patterns of Providing Care in African-American Families With Teenage Childbearers: Emergent Patterns in an Ethnographic Study

Linda M. Burton

D uring the past three decades, dramatic increases in the number of African-American unwed adolescent mothers have spawned a plethora of social science research on the quality of care families provide for the children of teen parents (Alan Guttmacher Institute, 1981; Furstenberg, 1991; Hayes, 1987; McCluskey, Killarney, & Papini, 1983; Vinovskis, 1988). This research has almost exclusively focused on the care that the maternal grandmother and young teenage parent provide for the child (Apfel & Seitz, 1991; Furstenberg, Brooks-Gunn, & Morgan, 1987; Pearson, Hunter, Ensminger, & Kellam, 1990; Tinsley & Parke, 1982). The caregiving responsibilities and practices the young father, grandfather, great-grandparents, siblings, and other extended kin are rarely examined in existing studies (Burton, Dilworth-Anderson, & deVries, in press). Moreover, the caregiving needs of other family members, such as a frail elder, are not systematically considered as factors that influence the provision of care for the teenage parent's offspring (Burton, 1990; Burton & Dilworth-Anderson, 1991).

The provision of care in families with teenage childbearers is intuitively more complex and diverse than current research suggests. The diversity and complexity are inherent functions of the variable family networks teenage parents are embedded within. Existing ethnographic studies suggest that the family networks of teenage parents are quite heterogeneous (Burton & Jarrett, 1994; Ladner, 1971; Stack, 1974). For example, some of the familial networks of teen parents include only a maternal grandmother and the child, whereas others may comprise three, four, and even five generations of extended blood and non-blood-related kin (Burton & Bengtson, 1985; Kellam, Ensminger, & Turner, 1977; Wilson, 1986). The variable composition of family networks suggests that there may be diverse sets of care providers and recipients across teenage childbearing families. Consequently, research that focuses only on the patterns of care the teenage parent and her mother provide for the child may miss the range of constellations of caregiving responsibilities and practices families with teenage parents engaged in.

This chapter examines the diversity and complexity of caregiving in families with teenage childbearers. Descriptions of 14 intergenerational patterns of providing care identified in a 5-year ethnographic study of adolescent childbearing and among low-income African-American families living in a northeastern urban community are presented. The families studied involve four and five generations of parents, children, extended, and fictive kin. The provision of care, in this study, is broadly defined to include the following family-based activities: (a) socializing and parenting of children; (b) providing *extensive* instrumental (e.g., baby-sitting, financial assistance, and housing) and emotional support to adolescent, young-adult, midlife, and elderly family members; and (3) meeting the daily needs (e.g., bathing, feeding) of family members who cannot provide care for themselves (e.g., frail elderly parent, handicapped child, a severely disabled mid-life adult, or a drug-addicted young adult).

In describing the 14 patterns of providing care identified in this ethnographic study, this chapter addresses three questions: (a) What types of family networks are teen parents and their children embedded within? (b) Who are the primary providers of care within these family networks? (c) What are the patterns of providing and receiving care across generations in families with adolescent childbearers?

DESCRIPTION OF THE ETHNOGRAPHIC STUDY

Case history data from an ongoing 5-year ethnographic study of teenage childbearing in African-American families are used to provide illustrations of (a) the variable family networks within which teenage parents and their children are embedded; (b) the range of care providers and recipients in these networks; and (c) patterns of providing and receiving care across generations in families. The ethnographic study began in June 1989 and is being conducted in a northeastern United States city where over 51% of the residents are African-American. Until 1993, this city had the second highest rate of adolescent childbearing in its state, particularly among African-American teens. It now has the third highest.

Data for this study are being collected using a two-stage, multimethod approach. Stage 1 involved gathering data that provided insights on community patterns concerning family networks and intergenerational caregiving. These data were used to identify the 14 patterns of intergenerational care provision presented here. These patterns will be tested further in Stage 2 of the study. Stage 2 comprises structured interviews with 150 early childbearing African-American families who reside in this community.

The patterns of intergenerational provision of care described in this chapter emerged from the analysis of data collected during stage 1 of the study using five qualitative strategies: (a) in-depth open-ended interviews with 48 African-American families; (b) participant observation in family activities; (c) field observations (community ethnography); (d) focus groups; and (e) interviews with formal and informal community leaders. Patterns of the intergenerational provision of care were first identified in the data collected from the 48 families and then validated by data collected through participant observations, focus groups, field observations, and interviews with formal and informal community leaders.

The in-depth qualitative interviews with the 48 ($N = 232$) African-American families were conducted over a period of 3 years. The families were recruited for participation in this study through contacting teenage mothers in the community. The teen mothers were identified through social service agencies, local churches, and community informants. The young mothers ranged in age from 11 to 18 years and had each given birth to a child within the year they were contacted for participation in the study.

Each teen mother was asked to define her family network and to solicit the participation of family members for the study. The family networks that the young mothers identified were quite diverse. Twenty-one of the teens identified their family network as four-generation female lineages including themselves, their grandmother, mother, and their child; six described three-generation female lineages that included themselves, their mother, and the baby; five identified their families as four-generation female lineages but included siblings, their boy-friends, and friends in their definition of family; four outlined three-generation female lineage but also included siblings, boyfriends, and personal friends; seven described their families as including their mothers, fathers, siblings, the father of the baby, and his family; two indicated that their family comprised four genera-tions of both their maternal and paternal lineages; and three noted that their families included their maternal grandfather, their mother, themselves, and the baby. All family members specified by the teens were interviewed in 26 of the families and only available members in the remaining 22 ($N = 232$). In the 22 families all members were not interviewed because they either refused, were ill, or left the area before the study was completed.

All family members who participated in the study were interviewed sepa-rately. Each interview was tape recorded and was 2 to 3 hours in length. Family members were asked to respond to open-ended questions concerning family composition, the provision and receipt of care across generations in the family, and the effects of teenage childbearing on family structure and function.

As the patterns of intergenerational provision of care emerged in the data collected from the 48 families, other data collection strategies were employed to validate the caregiving processes they described. First, participant observation in the baby showers, weddings, funerals, and holiday celebrations of 23 of the 48 families yielded behavioral observation data on how families actually distributed intergenerational caregiving responsibilities. Second, field observations, which were also conducted over a period of 3 years, involved both observational assess-ments and discussions with community residents about how families with teen-age parents who lived in their neighborhoods provided care for their members. Third, the focus-group strategy, comprising nine groups of four to six African-American community residents, was employed to discuss variability in family structures within neighborhoods, community norms concerning adolescent childbearing, and family roles and responsibilities in providing care for its mem-bers. Two of the groups included midlife and elderly females, three comprised adolescent and young-adult females, two were composed of adolescent and young-adult males, and two involved midlife and elderly males. Fourth, inter-views with informal and formal community leaders and service providers pro-vided additional perspectives on the issues faced by African-American, adoles-cent-childbearing families in the community. The community informants included ministers, school officials, health care providers, school counselors, journalists, welfare case workers, and neighborhood block leaders. They pro-vided feedback on how accurately the patterns of intergenerational caregiving derived from the interviews with the 48 families reflected the realities of family life in their community.

Seven African-American field researchers collected the qualitative data. The data generated from each of the strategies were transcribed and then analyzed using the grounded theory approach (Strauss, 1987). The grounded theory approach is a style of analyzing qualitative data using a specific coding paradigm to generate conceptual patterns. The 14 patterns of intergenerational care provision were identified and validated using this strategy.

THE PATTERNS OF INTERGENERATIONAL PROVISION OF CARE

The patterns of intergenerational provision of care that emerged from the ethnographic study are presented in Figures 3.1 and 3.2. Figure 3.1 displays patterns of care that were observed in multigeneration families in which a single person in the family assumed primary responsibility for the care of other family members. These patterns represent the caregiving dynamics observed principally in female lineages. Figure 3.2 illustrates patterns in which intergenerational care is provided by more than one family member (co-caregivers). These patterns reflect the participation of men in intergenerational caregiving activities. The symbols used in the patterns indicate the following:

G1 = great-grandmother (the grandmother of the adolescent mother)
G2 = grandmother (the mother of the adolescent mother)
G2f = grandfather (the biological or step father of the adolescent mother)
G3 = the adolescent mother
G4 = the adolescent mother's infant/child
G3s = the sibling (brother or sister) of the adolescent mother
G3f = the biological father of the adolescent baby
G3sf = the surrogate father of the adolescent's baby (often the adolescent mother's current boyfriend)
G3p = a friend of the adolescent mother
→ = this individual provides primary care to the recipient; care includes the following activities: parenting, socialization, providing extensive instrumental and emotional support, and taking care of the recipient's daily needs
– · – → = this individual provides backup care (see Figure 3.2: patterns 2 to 4) or marginal (see Figure 3.1: pattern 7; see Figure 3.2: pattern 1) care to the recipient

These symbols will also be used in the description of the various patterns as they are outlined subsequently.

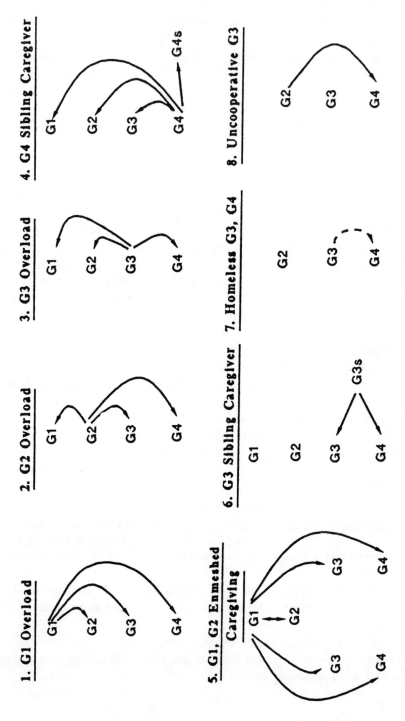

Figure 3.1. Models of care provision: one generation as source of primary care.

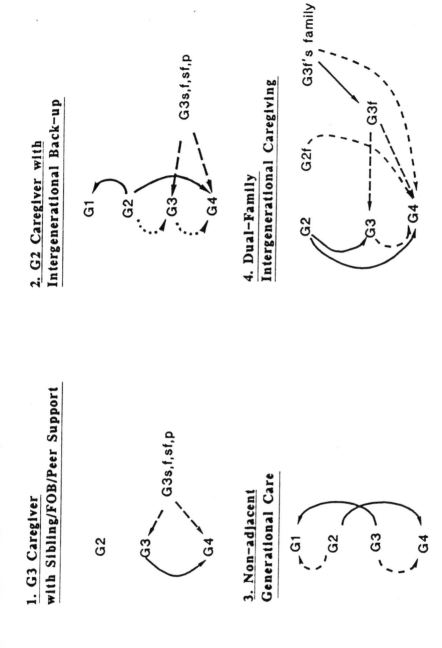

Figure 3.2. Models of care provision: multigenerational co-caregivers as source of primary and "back-up" care.

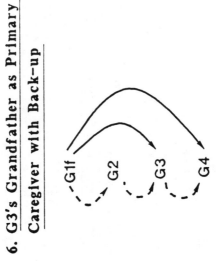

6. G3's Grandfather as Primary
Caregiver with Back-up

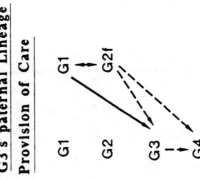

5. G3's paternal Lineage
Provision of Care

Single Caregiver Patterns

Pattern 1: G1 Overload

This pattern (see Figure 3.1) represents a maternal female lineage multigeneration family structure in which the great-grandmother assumes primary responsibility for the care of multiple family members in the extended kin network. Within this family network, there are usually two or more generations of females that have been adolescent childbearers. As such, the great-grandmother (ages 46 to 60), grandmother (ages 27 to 38), and adolescent mother (ages 13 to 18) are often "early occupants" in their respective roles. Given their early transitions to their family roles, G1 (great-grandmother) typically emerges as the most responsible care provider. G1 provides economic support and baby-sitting for G2 (grandmother); continues to parent G3 (adolescent mother); and also assumes the role of surrogate parent to her great-grandchild, G4.

The family situation of Thelma Johnson, a 53-year-old great-grandmother, is illustrative of this pattern of intergenerational provision of care. Thelma has a 38-year-old daughter, Sandy (G2), who is the mother of five and grandmother of six. Thelma has taken primary responsibility for raising one of Sandy's daughter's, LaShawn (G3), who is a 15-year-old mother of two. Thelma offered this description of how she provides care in her family:

> *Oh yeah! I have been taking care of all these kids for a mighty long time. Sandy needs so much help with her children. She needs money and food all the time. I had to take care of her when she had surgery six months ago. Who else would? LaShawn, I raised from a baby. Now she got two kids and I'm doing it again. I bathe, feed them, and everything. Three generations I raised. Lord Almighty! I'm tired, tired, tired. Sick too. . . . Who's gonna take care of me?*

Eight of the 48 families interviewed demonstrated the pattern of caregiving described by Thelma. Data from the focus groups and interviews with community informants indicated that this pattern was possibly prevalent in approximately 25% of the African-American families with teenage mothers who resided in the community.

In addition, participant observation data on the caregiving behaviors of the great-grandmothers in these families suggested that their overloads of responsibility in providing care for others was adversely affecting their health. Because of their extensive intergenerational caregiving responsibilities, these G1s often experienced considerable stress in their roles. The stress typically manifested itself in heightened physical illnesses and psychological problems, such as depression. Eloise Taylor, a 60-year-old great-grandmother explains:

Nobody realizes how much taking care of all these people takes out of you. You get sick all the time but you don't even take time to take care of yourself. I got a friend who is in the same situation as me. She is really sick. She probably won't live too much longer But she doesn't get any help. I'm going down that same trail. This is kind of scary.

Pattern 2: G2 Overload

The family network composition in this model is comparable with that described in the G1 overload pattern of providing care. However, the grandmother (G2) in this family network assumes responsibility for the care of multiple generations of family members. In these families, G3 is usually the first-generation teen mother. Consequently, G2 and G1 are much older than the grandmothers and great-grandmothers in pattern 1. G2's caregiving responsibilities, in this model, include meeting the daily needs of G1 (her frail elderly parent) and parenting G3 and G4. Beverly Richards, a 46-year-old grandmother, whose family represents this pattern described her caregiving responsibilities as follows:

I was really surprised when my daughter got pregnant. It could not have come at a worst time. I have to take care of my mother who is senile. And now I'm taking care of my daughter's baby too. Beside that, I still got to be a parent to my daughter even though she's a mother. She still is a baby in some ways too. This is tough. This is really, really tough.

The pattern of caregiving Beverly describes was observed in 4 of the 48 families studied. The focus group data and interviews with community residents indicate that this pattern was not as common among families in the community as the G1 overload pattern.

Pattern 3: G3 Overload

This pattern is similar to pattern 1 in that G1, G2, and G3 were all teen mothers. G3, however, assumes primary responsibility for the care of her family members.

The adolescent mothers in these families are quite mature and "well connected" to social services. They also, quite often, have had mentors (e.g., high school teacher) outside of the family who have helped them develop responsible caregiving behaviors. The types of care that G3 provides to G1 include meeting G1's daily maintenance needs (frail elderly grandparent) or being G1's primary source of emotional support. With respect to G2, G3 is often responsible for parenting her mother's (G2) children as well as her own (G4). G3 also contributes a significant portion of her own income to the family's support.

The caregiving behaviors of Denise, an 18-year-old mother of two, is representative of the patterns of caregiving observed in comparable family networks.

Denise is a senior in high school and at the time she was interviewed was providing care for her 2-year-old twin daughters, her mother who is an alcoholic, and her grandmother who has cancer. Denise remarked:

> Yes, this is a lot of responsibility. Sometimes I have to miss school because the demands on me are so great. But, I have a counselor at school who has helped me to organize my time. I manage to do all of this because I know how to get help. I think this is preparing me for greater things in life. Some girls my age can't do half the stuff I do.

Three of the families involved in the study demonstrated this pattern of providing care. Community informants indicated that this was not a particularly common pattern of caregiving in families within the community, but they suspected that more teenage mothers were involved in this caregiving pattern than they had formal knowledge of.

Pattern 4: Sibling Caregiving

This pattern emerged in the research as a result of serendipitous findings in the field observations. These findings concern the temporal organization of drug sales in two of the neighborhoods studied (Burton, 1991). While investigating the sale of drugs between the hours of 10:00 p.m. and 6:00 a.m., two of the field researchers independently observed families where G1 to G3, because of their drug addiction, were unable to provide care for their children consistently. The children (G4) (7- to 9-year-old children) in these families assumed the responsibility for the care of their younger siblings (e.g., getting them ready for school and feeding them), and also cooked, cleaned, and ran errands for G1 to G3. Unlike the three preceding patterns, this one represents a female lineage in which the G3 was in fact a teen mother but is now 7 to 9 years older. Observed primarily in persistently poor families, this pattern may reflect what happens in the distribution of caregiving responsibilities in families with young mothers that become addicted to drugs or alcohol several years after the birth of their child.

Two of the 48 families interviewed represented this pattern. Data gathered in the focus groups and through community informants suggested that this pattern of caregiving is one of increasing prevalence in the community. Community service providers argued that this pattern is one that is observed in multiproblem families where teenage pregnancy is the least of the problems that the family is experiencing.

Pattern 5: G1-G2 Enmeshed Caregiving

In three of the families studied, there were two G3 teenage siblings in the female lineage that were concurrently pregnant. What is particularly interesting about these families concerns the relationship between G1 and G2 and how that relationship affected the distribution of caregiving responsibilities across generations. Working with a clinical psychologist and community service providers to analyze data from these families, it was determined that G1 and G2 operate like "one person" in providing care to their offspring. Working together, metaphorically speaking, as "siamese twins" the G1-G2 unit provides economic and emotional support for the adolescent mothers and their children.

Delores, a 54-year-old great grandmother, and Patricia, her 39-year-old daughter, exemplify the enmeshed caregiving pattern. Two of Patricia's teen daughters had recently given birth at the time this family was interviewed. One of Patricia's daughters, Stephanie, described the caregiving activities of her mother and grandmother:

> My mother and grandmother do everything for us and the babies. We don't have to worry about a thing. It's a trip to watch them work because they do everything together. They feed the babies together and everything. They act like they can't do anything without each other. This seems strange to me.

Pattern 6: G3 Sibling Caregiver

Only one of the families who participated in the study demonstrated this pattern. In this pattern, the adult sibling (G3s) of the adolescent mother is the primary caregiver in the family. G3s provides economic stability and a home for both G3 and G4. G1 and G2 were usually independently taking care of their own responsibilities unrelated to the life circumstances of G3s, G3, and G4. Connie, the 24-year-old sister of Rochelle, a 14-year-old mother, offered these comments about her caregiving responsibilities:

> I raised my sister from a baby anyway so I expected that I would also be the one to take care of her now. I wish my mother or my grandmother would help but you know how that is. They don't help at all. I wonder who will take care of them when they need it?

Pattern 7: Homeless G3, G4

As a result of the community-based field observations two homeless teen mothers were interviewed for the study. These teens were members of three-generation families. The teen mothers and their mothers (G2) were rendered homeless either shortly before of after their babies were born. The broken arrow in Figure 3.1 indicates that these two young mothers, often overwhelmed with myriad problems, were able to barely take care of their children (G4). In most instances, their mothers (G2) were not in a position, financially or emotionally, to help their daughters parent G4.

Data from the community service providers indicated that the life situation of the two teens interviewed was becoming increasingly common in the community studied. Several service providers noted that most studies of teenage mothers do not include these teens in the study because they are quite transient and consequently difficult to track. One of the social service providers commented on the implications of this transiency for the caregiving needs of these teens and their children:

> *These girls can barely take care of themselves so how can you expect them to be able to take care of a baby? Everyone is in shock in these families. No one knows what to do. We need intermediate caregivers for the grandmothers, mothers, and their children. But we can't get enough funding to help.*

Pattern 8: Uncooperative G3

This pattern is characterized by G2 providing care for her grandchild (G4) with no assistance from her daughter (G3). G3, in these families, is often a "rebellious" teen who runs away from home, skips school, and whose friends tend to be 10 to 12 years older than she is. In discussions about her daughter, G2 may describe G3 as "the child I disown," "my invisible kid," "they gave me the wrong baby at the hospital; she [G3] can't belong to me," "she's her daddy's child, not mine," or "my dead daughter." G2 also claims her grandchild (G4) as "her own child" and vows to do a better job raising G4 than she did with G3. This pattern was prevalent in four of the families who participated in the study. Data from the focus-group discussions suggested that this pattern is fairly common among families in the community but principally among those who would be considered working class.

Co-Caregiver Patterns

Pattern 9: G3 Caregiver with Peer Support

Five of the 48 families interviewed displayed this pattern of caregiving (see Figure 3.2). This pattern is similar to pattern 6 in Figure 3.1. However, unlike pattern 6, G3 assumes primary responsibility for the care of her child (G4) and receives backup support from a combination of her siblings (G3s), the baby's father (G3f), a man who takes on the role as surrogate parent to her child (G3sf), or other female friends who also have young children (G3p). The G2 in this pattern gives little attention to the needs of other family members.

Data collected using the various qualitative strategies described in stage 1 of the research indicate that the adolescent mothers (G3) in this pattern experience a relatively moderate level of stress in providing care for their children. The support they receive from their siblings, boyfriends, and peers appears to help them cope better with the responsibilities of early parenthood. Janine, a 16-year-old mother commented:

> *Taking care of this baby is not as hard as people might think. I get a lot of help from my boyfriend who is not even the father of the baby. My mother doesn't understand what's going on cause she's doing her own thing. You got to build a group of people who can help you when your mother won't.*

Pattern 10: G2 Caregiver with Intergenerational Back-up

This pattern represents a four-generation family network in which G2 assumes primary responsibility for the care of G1 and G4. In this pattern, G3 is often a "very responsible" adolescent who assists her mother in the care of G4 and requires little intensive parental monitoring by G2. G2 receives backup support in this pattern for providing care for G3 and G4 from the adolescent mother's adult sibling (G3s), the biological father of G4, the surrogate father of G4, or the friend of G3. Unlike pattern 2 in Figure 3.1, the grandmothers (G2) in this caregiving structure experience less stress related to their caregiving responsibilities.

Five of the families participating in the study exemplified this pattern. Social service providers indicated that this pattern could also be observed in 15% of the families with teen mothers that lived in the community.

Pattern 11: Nonadjacent Generational Care

This pattern was observed in only two families that participated in the study. It is a pattern of intergenerational care that was identified in a previous qualitative study of a *unique* low-income African-American community. In this community, adolescent childbearing was considered an alternative life-course strategy that generated a system of nonadjacent generational care in female lineages (Burton, 1990). In this pattern the grandmothers (G2) provide care for their grandchildren (G4), and the adolescent mothers provide care for their maternal grandmother (G1). The qualitative data collected from social service providers, community leaders, families, and in the focus groups indicate that the patterns of caregiving exemplified in this pattern are quite *rare* in the current study population. One social service provider who administered a statewide teenage pregnancy program stated:

> *You don't see many families like this in this community. I've mostly seen this type of family caregiving in very isolated rural communities in the center of the state. You don't see this much in urban areas.*

Pattern 12: Dual-Family Intergenerational Caregiving

In this pattern, G2 again assumes primary responsibility for the care of G3 and G4 but also receives considerable support in caring for G4 from G3, G3's biological or stepfather (G2f), and the biological father (G3f) of G4. In addition, G3f's family of origin provide "backup" support in the care of G4. This pattern reflects the most active involvement of **multiple men** in the provision of care in families. Initial analysis of the data also indicate that while, like the other patterns, tensions do arise in the distribution of caregiving responsibilities across generations in families, the G3f's family's positive involvement in the life of G4 may be just as important to the development of G4 as the involvement of G3's family. Seven of the 48 families interviewed represented this pattern of caregiving. Additional data sources suggest that an estimated 25% of the African-American families in the community reflected this caregiving style.

Pattern 13: G3's Paternal Lineage as Providers of Care

Unlike the preceding 12 patterns that are characterized principally by the caregiving duties and responsibilities observed within maternal female lineages, this pattern illustrates the role of the teen mother's paternal lineage in providing intergenerational care. In three of the families interviewed, the adolescent mother's paternal grandmother, not her mother or maternal grandmother, assumed primary responsibility for her (G3) care and the care of her baby (G4). In all three cases, G3 had been raised by her paternal grandmother since birth, even though G3's mother and maternal grandmother were alive. The paternal grandmother in these families received considerable support from G3's father in taking care of G3 and G4. G3's father often lived in the same household as his mother, G3, and G4. He also provided financial and emotional support for all household members. Roger, a 34-year-old grandfather, offered this representative statement:

> *Well, my daughter got pregnant and there isn't much I can do about it but change diapers when needed. I have to help my mother too because if it wasn't for her I would not have a place to live with my family. That's the way it works around here.*

Pattern 14: G3's Grandfather as Primary Caregiver

This pattern represent a four-generation family network in which the maternal grandfather (G1f) provides care for his granddaughter (G3) and great-grandchild (G4). This pattern of providing care across generations was often observed in families where G1f's spouse had died but where he had been involved in raising G3 since birth. G2, in most cases, did not live in the same household as G1f, G3, and G4, but provided backup caregiving support when needed. G1f was typically retired or partially physically disabled but in all cases was able to provide excellent infant care for G4.

This pattern of caregiving was observed in three families. One of the grandfathers interviewed had this to say about the prevalence of this pattern:

> *Many more black grandfathers take care of babies and everybody than you think. We're just quiet about what we do. These babies love us too. Just look at how this one follows me around all the time.*

CONCLUSIONS

The purpose of this chapter was to illustrate the diversity and complexity of patterns of providing care that exist in families with teenage childbearers. Fourteen patterns of providing care that were observed in a 5-year ethnographic study of teenage pregnancy in African-American families were described. These patterns reflect variability in the composition of families as well as the attempts of single- and co-caregivers to meet the needs of family members across the life span.

The intergenerational patterns of caregiving presented here are preliminary in nature. They are based on data collected from a nonrandom sample of African-American families who live in a northeastern urban community. Consequently, the generalizability of these patterns may be limited. Despite the limitations, however, the patterns of caregiving presented here suggest that social scientists need to move beyond the triad—that is, the teen mother, her child, and her mother—as the context for exploring caregiving in teenage childbearing families. Clearly within families there are a range of providers and recipients of care. Understanding that range may lead to more accurate assessments of the caregiving responsibilities and practices of families with teen parents.

In addition the patterns of caregiving described in this chapter raise several questions for future research. (a) What are the norms concerning the care of older individuals and children in families with adolescent parents? (b) How does having a child at a young age affect family processes of providing multigenerational care? (c) What roles do males, grandparents, and siblings play in the care of young children and the elderly in families? (d) Do patterns of providing care in families with teenage parents vary by race?

ACKNOWLEDGEMENT

This research was funded by the Brookdale Foundation, William T. Grant Foundation, and a FIRST Award from the National Institute of Mental Health (No. R29 MH46057-01).

REFERENCES

Alan Guttmacher Institute. (1981). *Teenage pregnancy: The problem that hasn't gone away.* New York: Author.

Apfel, N. H., & Seitz, V. (1991). Four models of adolescent mother-grandmother relationships in black inter-city families. *Family Relations, 40,* 421–429.

Burton, L. M. (1990). Teenage childbearing as an alternative life-course strategy in multigeneration black families. *Human Nature, 1,* 123–143.

Burton, L. M. (1991). Drug-trafficking schedules and child-care strategies in a high-risk neighborhood. *American Enterprise, 2,* 34–37.

Burton, L. M., & Bengtson, V. L. (1985). Black grandmothers: Issues of timing and meaning in roles. In V. L. Bengtson & J. F. Robertson (Eds.), *Grandparenthood: Research policy and perspectives.* Beverly Hills, CA: Sage.

Burton, L. M., & Dilworth-Anderson, P. (1991). The intergenerational family roles of aged black Americans. *Marriage and Family Review, 16,* 311–330.

Burton, L. M., Dilworth-Anderson, P., & deVries, C. M. (in press). Context and surrogate parenting among contemporary grandparents. *Marriage and Family Review.*

Burton, L. M., & Jarrett, R. L. (1991). Studying African-American family structure and process in underclass neighborhoods. Paper presented at the annual meeting of the American Sociological Association, Cincinnati, OH.

Furstenberg, F. F. (1991). As the pendulum swings: Teenage childbearing and social concern. *Family Relations, 40,* 127–138.

Furstenberg, F. F., Jr., Brooks-Gunn, J., & Morgan, S. P. (1987). Adolescent mothers in later life. Cambridge, MA: Cambridge University Press.

Hayes, C. C. (Ed.). (1987). *Risking the future* (Vol. 1). Washington, DC: National Academy Press.

Kellam, S. G., Ensminger, M. E., & Turner, R. J. (1977). Family structure and the mental health of children: Concurrent and longitudinal community-wide studies. *Archives of General Psychiatry, 34,* 1012–1022.

Ladner, J. (1971). *Tomorrow's tomorrow.* Garden City, NY: Doubleday.

McCluskey, K. A., Killarney, J., & Papini, D. R. (1983). Adolescent pregnancy and parenthood: Implications for development. In E. J. Callahan & K. A. McCluskey (Eds.), *Life span developmental psychology.* New York: Academic Press

Pearson, J. L., Hunter, A. G., Ensminger, M., & Kellam, S. G. (1990). Black grandmothers in multigenerational households: Diversity in family structure and parenting involvement in the Woodlawn community. *Child Development, 61,* 434–442.

Stack, C. B. (1974). *All our kin: Strategies for survival in the black community.* New York: Harper & Row.

Strauss, A. L. (1987). *Qualitative analysis for social scientist.* New York: Cambridge University Press.

Tinsley, B. R., & Parke, R. (1984). Grandparents as support and socialization agents. In M. Lewis (Ed.), *Beyond the dyad.* New York: Plenum.

Vinovskis, M. (1988). *An "epidemic of adolescent pregnancy? Some historical and policy con-siderations*. New York: Oxford University Press.

Wilson, M. N. (1986). The black extended family: An analytical consideration. *Developmental Psychology, 22,* 246–258.

Commentary: Intergenerational Support within African-American Families: Concepts and Methods

Linda M. Chatters and Rukmalie Jayakody

OVERVIEW

Social science research concerning the form and functioning of African-American families has a long scholarly tradition, spanning several disciplines. This diverse literature addresses a wide range of issues and employs a variety of theoretical and conceptual models and research approaches (Dilworth-Anderson, Burton, & Johnson, 1993; Taylor, Chatters, Tucker, & Lewis, 1990). Reviews and critiques of this research repeatedly call attention to the significance of ethnic minority perspectives for understanding family phenomena and generating theories and models of the family (i.e., structure, dynamics, and context) that are culturally relevant (Allen, 1978; Dilworth-Anderson, Burton, & Johnson, 1993). This chapter adopts a selective approach in addressing several key issues related to the concepts and methods employed in extant research on intergenerational support within African-American families. First, we explore the contributions of ethnographic and survey research approaches to understanding diverse conceptions of family and supportive relations among African Americans. Where appropriate, the contributions of Burton's work in understanding intergenerational support among African-Americans is highlighted. Second, we establish ethnographic work on intergenerational support within the context of

97

demographic profiles of African-American families more generally, as well as studies employing survey research approaches. Third, we consider the implications of diversity in family structure and the organization of assistance exchanges for the methodological procedures customarily employed in studies of intergenerational support. Finally, we conclude with an examination of various strategies for the synthesis of qualitative and quantitative approaches and concrete ways that they can be employed to increase our understanding of support exchanges within multigeneration families.

CONCEPTS OF FAMILY AND SUPPORTIVE RELATIONS

A tradition of ethnographic and survey research documents the existence of a plurality of family definitions and forms within African-American communities. Burton's work builds on and extends this tradition and focuses our attention on several fundamental issues pertinent to African-American families. They include (a) an appreciation of differences in conceptualizations of the family itself, (b) recognition of the underlying cultural value dimensions along which families are defined (Dilworth-Anderson, Burton, & Johnson, 1993), and (c) considerations of the impact of demographic change on family structure, function, and individual family roles. The relevance of these issues for research and scholarship on African-American families is explored in relation to four specific substantive areas—extended kin relations, fictive kin, the role of men in families, and the nature of intergenerational family relations.

Extended Kin Relations

Central to conceptions of the family among African Americans is the inclusion of individuals who, together with immediate (i.e., nuclear) family members, form an extended kin group. The notion of the extended kin group has significance for how African Americans conceptualize the family unit, the emergence of distinctive household patterns and arrangements, and the provision of support within families. Overall, African Americans are more likely than whites to reside in extended family households (Angel & Tienda, 1982; Beck & Beck, 1989; Farley & Allen, 1987; Hofferth, 1984; Tienda & Angel, 1982) in which intergenerational family members (Beck & Beck, 1989; Cherlin & Furstenberg, 1986), as well as other relatives live. Older African Americans are more likely than their white counterparts to reside with children and grandchildren (Freedman et al., 1991; Lopata, 1979; Mitchell & Register, 1984; Shanas, 1979), and to accept children and grandchildren into households in which they are the head (Mitchell & Register, 1984). Several scholars suggest that explicit cultural norms and values inform conceptions of family among African Americans (Dilworth-

Anderson, Burton, & Johnson, 1993), specifically in relation to extended family relationships (Sudarkasa, 1981) and functioning (Cherlin & Furstenberg, 1986). Alternative explanations for the prevalence of extended living arrangements suggest that coresidence is motivated by primarily economic considerations (Angel & Tienda, 1982; Tienda & Angel, 1982). However, despite controls for socio-economic status, extended living arrangements are twice as common among African-American as among white households (Farley & Allen, 1987) and have been found to operate within middle class (McAdoo, 1978), as well as poor families (Stack, 1974).

Extended kin groups that reside within a single household (i.e., coreside) may incorporate older parents, adult and minor offspring (i.e., children, grandchildren), and non-nuclear relatives. Noted benefits of extended household arrangements suggest that they (a) are an effective means for the pooling and distribution of limited economic resources (Angel & Tienda, 1982), (b) allow a reallocation of paid employment and domestic responsibilities among non-nuclear adults within the household (Tienda & Glass, 1985), (c) provide for the care of dependent family members, and (d) allow family members the opportunity to pursue education and employment (Furstenberg & Crawford, 1978; Hogan, Hao, & Parish, 1990). Conflicts over childrearing philosophies and practices and parenting styles (Goetting, 1986; Stevens, 1988); difficulties related to crowding and the lack of privacy (Alwin, Converse, & Martin, 1985); and problems related to appropriate role allocation, expectations, and behaviors are recognized drawbacks of coresidence. Coresidence, however, is not an essential requirement for definitions of extended family or the types of supportive relationships that transpire within families. Extended kin groups can also be organized around and operate across separate households (Hogan, Hao, & Parish, 1990; Stack, 1974; Taylor, 1988). Ethnographic studies examining extended relationships across households (noncoresident) suggest that several nuclear families may reside in the same neighborhood and cooperate in a number of daily tasks.

Finally, regarding assistance exchanges, extended kin networks are important sources of informal social support among African Americans (Aschenbrenner, 1973; Dressler, Hoeppner, & Pitts, 1985; Hatchett, Corcoran, & Jackson, 1991; Hill, 1972; Martin & Martin, 1978; McAdoo, 1980; Stack, 1974; Taylor, 1988; Taylor & Chatters, 1991; Taylor, Chatters, Tucker, & Lewis, 1990; Wilson, 1986, 1989). Taylor (1986) found that 75% of African-Americans in a national sample received various forms of support from extended family members; higher levels of income, younger age, kin proximity and interaction, and close affective relationships were all associated with receiving assistance. Research that specifically addresses kin assistance to single mothers has focused on either direct financial aid or the existence of extended family living arrangements (Angel & Tienda, 1982; Hofferth, 1984; Hogan, Hao, & Parish, 1990; Tienda & Angel, 1982), whereas other forms of support (i.e., material, informational, and affective or emotional assistance) have received less attention.

Fictive Kin

Historical (Gutman, 1976) and contemporary evidence (Chatters, Taylor, & Jayakody, in press) suggests that the family and kin networks of African Americans often include individuals who are not related by blood or marriage, but who are accorded the same rights and status of kin. A collection of research indicates that fictive kin relationships are an integral component of family networks (Anderson, 1978; Aschenbrenner, 1975; Kennedy, 1980; Martin & Martin, 1978; Stack, 1974; Tatum, 1987). A recent profile of fictive kin relationships (Chatters, Taylor, & Jayakody, in press) found that two out of three African-American respondents indicated that there was someone in their family who was regarded as a fictive kin. Women, younger persons, those with higher levels of education, and Southern residents (compared with residents of the Northeast region) were more likely than their counterparts to indicate that they had a fictive kin relation. Many of the rights, statuses, and responsibilities usually associated with actual kinship are conferred on these relationships, including participation in the obligations of the extended family. Fictive kin relations can be organized in several different ways and involve age-based peer groups (Anderson, 1978; Liebow, 1967) and churches (Johnson & Barer, 1990; Lincoln & Mamiya, 1990), as well as extended families (Aschenbrenner, 1975; Kennedy, 1980; Stack, 1974).

Fictive kin relationships are found in other cultural groups including Anglos (MacRae, 1992; Rubenstein, Alexander, Goodman, & Luborsky, 1991) and Puerto Ricans (Mizio, 1974; Rogler, 1978; Sanchez-Ayendez, 1988), although the specific cultural meanings of these relationships are often quite different (Chatters, Taylor, & Jayakody, in press). Only a few examples of fictive kin relationships among Anglos are noted (Chatters, Taylor, & Jayakody, in press); overall, research on adult friendships rarely examines fictive kinship ties (Adams & Blieszner, 1989; Allan, 1989; Bell, 1981; Rubin, 1986). Matthew's (1986) and Rubin's (1985) descriptions of various relationships that ostensibly mimic fictive kinship bonds fail to identify them as fictive kinships or employ the terms *fictive*, *pseudo-*, or *quasi-kin* in reference to them. Furthermore, accurate estimates of the prevalence of fictive kin are hampered by differences in the definitions and terms that are used to designate these relationships (MacRae, 1992). For example, the term *quasi-kin* has been used to designate individuals (i.e., stepkin) who are related by ties from a previous marriage (Bohannan, 1970; Cherlin, 1992; Furstenberg & Cherlin, 1991). The prevalence of quasi-kin will likely increase among Anglos, because of higher rates of remarriage among this population group (Cherlin, 1992) relative to others (i.e., African Americans and Latinos).

The actual occurrence of fictive kin and quasi-kin relationships, both within and across different racial and ethnic groups, is likely distorted because of a lack of focused and systematic investigation and the failure to use precise definitions. The development of better approaches to examine these relationships is crucial for understanding how individuals think about and define their families. In particular, pertinent information can promote an understanding of the specific ways that both fictive and quasi-kin coincide with or supplement family-based networks, as well as identify the implications these relationships have for conceptual and operational definitions of family support.

African-American Males and Families

Adequate information on the family roles of African-American men and, specifically, adolescent fathers is clearly lacking (Phares, 1992). Pertinent to this discussion, we recognize that the absence of relevant data on adolescent fathers unquestionably limits our understanding of important family phenomena such as adolescent pregnancy, parenthood, and family formation (Lerman, 1986; Marsiglio, 1989; Parke & Neville, 1987). Although recent work attempts to address these questions (Christmon, 1990; Compas & Phares, 1992; Hawkins & Eggebeen, 1991), conventional perceptions of the position of males in African-American families are that men are marginal to the family and fail to function satisfactorily in family roles (Allen, 1981; J. L. McAdoo, 1981).

A small group of studies examining the concept of the provider role (Ball & Robbins, 1986; Tucker & Taylor, 1989) suggests that being an economic provider for one's family is central to how men define their family roles (Cazenave, 1979, 1984) and that feelings of adequacy in the provider role are related to levels of personal income (Taylor, Leashore, & Toliver, 1988). Poor performance in the provider role appears to adversely affect overall perceptions of the quality of life (Bowman, 1985) among married fathers and is implicated as a deterrent to marriage (Darity & Myers, 1986–87; Tucker & Taylor, 1989; Wilson, 1987; Wilson & Neckerman, 1986). Emergent research on adolescent fathers indicates considerable diversity with respect to the timing of fatherhood (e.g., age and employment and educational roles), patterns of participation in the father role, and level of involvement with the child's mother. Among adolescent fathers, involvement in parenting is associated with younger age of the father and of the child. Adolescent fathers are less likely than adult fathers to live with their child or partner (Lerman, 1986; Marsiglio, 1987). However, among adolescent fathers who are nonresidential, minority fathers (primarily African American) are involved in parenting activities to a greater extent than their white counterparts (Danziger & Nichols-Casebolt, 1988). Finally, similar to the provider role notion, minority adolescent fathers who have been employed in the past year are more likely to be involved in parenting activities than those who are not employed (Danziger & Nichols-Casebolt, 1988).

Burton's current research on intergenerational support among African-American families with adolescent childbearers indicates that adult and adolescent males are involved in several types of assistance patterns and support relationships. In addition to the involvement of the father of the baby (G3f), male age-peers are involved as surrogate fathers (G3sf); biological fathers, stepfathers (G2f), and the adolescent childbearer's maternal grandfather (G1f) participate as primary and supplemental providers. The operation of paternal (as opposed to maternal) lineages as care providers (i.e., the adolescent childbearers' paternal grandmother) is also apparent. Together, this emergent work identifies (a) the family relationships (i.e., kin, nonkin, and fictive kin) and supportive activities that adult and adolescent males are involved in; and (b) the economic (i.e., provider role) and family structure factors that function as either incentives or barriers to the participation of males in caregiving and provider roles.

Intergenerational Relationships

Interest in intergenerational relationships and support arises, in part, from several questions and issues concerning the operation of extended kin support networks and their ability to offset adverse social and economic conditions facing various groups of African Americans (Jayakody, Chatters, & Taylor, 1993). One argument suggests that because of the presence of viable kin ties (Hamilton, 1971; Stack, 1974; Staples & Mirande, 1980; Tolson & Wilson, 1990), vulnerable groups of African Americans (i.e., adolescent and single mothers, older persons) are protected from the adverse social and economic consequences associated with their status positions. In contrast, conditions of severe urban poverty and increased social class segregation within African-American neighborhoods are thought to threaten the continued viability of extended kin networks as sources of assistance (Hogan, Hao, & Parish, 1990; Martin & Martin, 1985; Wilson, 1987). In turn, neighborhood conditions negatively impact on the social and economic circumstances of individuals and successive generations of family (e.g., the development of an urban underclass). Reflecting this notion of vulnerable groups, a considerable amount of research on intergenerational supportive relationships among African Americans has examined specific groups of individuals (i.e., single mothers, adolescent mothers, grandparents, and elderly adults) and their involvement in family-based assistance exchanges (Taylor, Chatters, & Jackson, 1993). The literatures addressing the nature of intergenerational family support generally, and specifically, in relation to these identified groups, reflect distinct research and scholarly traditions. Consequently, it is often difficult to reconcile inherent differences in concepts, methods, and research strategies (Soldo & Hill, 1993).

First, with respect to single mothers, intergenerational kinship ties appear to be important for the distribution and amounts of assistance provided to single-parent families (Allen, 1979; Angel & Tienda, 1982; Gibson, 1972; McAdoo, 1980; Tienda & Glass, 1985). Female-headed families are more likely to coreside with extended kin, a situation conducive to the exchange of assistance (Angel & Tienda, 1982; Hofferth, 1984; Tienda & Angel, 1982). Race comparative studies of the support networks of single mothers suggest that African-American female-headed families are less likely to receive financial and other support from kin networks than are their white counterparts (Hofferth, 1984), although African-American mothers have greater access to kin and are more likely to coreside with kin and to receive child care and financial contributions from relatives (Hogan et al., 1990). In contrast, controls for marital status reveal that white mothers are more likely to receive substantial income support from kin (Parish et al., 1991). The interpretation of these and other race differences will be addressed later with respect to methodological issues in comparative studies of family support.

Jayakody, Chatters, and Taylor's (1993) investigation of kin-based assistance (i.e., financial, emotional, and child care) provided to married and single (i.e., never-married, divorced/separated, and widowed) African-American mothers found that household structure, marital status, poverty status, age, region, proximity to family, and kin affinity all predicted support from extended kin. The emergence of significant contrasts involving never-married versus married mothers (for financial assistance) and never married versus widowed mothers (for emotional assistance) underscored the importance of marital status distinctions for understanding family-based support.

Research involving adolescent mothers suggests that the support that they (and their young children) receive from their own mothers has significant beneficial outcomes for their educational achievements, employment patterns (Furstenberg, Brooks-Gunn & Morgan, 1987; Furstenberg & Crawford, 1978), and parenting abilities (Stevens, 1984, 1988). Similarly, Wilson (1989) argues that single-parent families accrue several benefits from the involvement of various family members of different generations. In particular, intergenerational support facilitates the mother's participation in self-improvement activities, increases the quality of child care, and enhances the parenting skills of single mothers. Much of this research underscores the salience of the grandparent role among African Americans, as well as the potential for cultural differences in normative role expectations and behaviors. Especially important with respect to intergenerational exchanges is the active participation of grandparents and their supportive contributions in the areas of child care for younger generations (i.e., grandchildren), parenting activities, and discipline (Cherlin & Furstenberg, 1986; Hogan, Hao, & Parish, 1990).

Finally, a small body of work examines the support resources of older persons in relation to their adult children (Chatters, Taylor, & Jackson, 1985; Chatters, Taylor, & Neighbors, 1989; Taylor, 1985, 1986; Taylor & Chatters, 1991). The presence of adult children is (a) related to positive appraisals of family life (Taylor & Chatters, 1991); (b) important for facilitating the integration of older adults in extended family networks; (c) critical in determining the characteristics (i.e., size and composition) and functions of the informal support networks of older adults (Chatters, Taylor, & Jackson, 1985, 1986; Chatters, Taylor, & Neighbors, 1989); and (d) associated with a greater likelihood of receiving assistance from extended family (Taylor & Chatters, 1991) and church members (Taylor, 1986; Taylor & Chatters, 1986). Adult daughters, in particular, are most often selected as an informal helper to older African Americans (Chatters, Taylor, & Jackson, 1986). Different age groups display preferred patterns of intergenerational support; young adults tend to rely on their parents, older persons select adult children, and middle-aged persons tend to rely on both their parents and children (Taylor, Chatters, & Mays, 1988).

To summarize, ethnographic and survey research approaches have, to varying degrees and in different ways, focused on the questions of extended family, fictive kin, the family roles of adolescent and adult males, and intergenerational relationships. These substantive areas serve as important background and context for examining African-American families and are central for understanding the specific ways that families are defined and how family-based support is structured and organized. Although not detailed here, investigations based on representative samples of African Americans (e.g., Jayakody, Chatters & Taylor, 1993; Taylor, 1986; Tucker & Taylor, 1989) indicate that sociodemographic factors (i.e., socioeconomic status, marital status, region) are important correlates of family phenomena (e.g., supportive transactions and family structure), suggesting the need to give systematic attention to within-group differences.

Demographic Profiles

Demographic profiles of African-American families demonstrate considerable diversity with respect to the living arrangements of minor (younger than 18 years

TABLE 3.1.   Living Arrangements of Black Children Under 18 by
Marital Status of Parents

Living with both parents	38.45%
Living with mother only	
Divorced	10.63%
Married, spouse absent	11.72%
Widowed	2.18%
Never married	33.28%
Living with father only	3.75%

SOURCE: U.S. Bureau of the Census. Current Population Reports, Series P-20, No. 461, Marital status and living arrangements: March 1991. U.S. Government Printing Office, Washington, D.C., 1992.

of age) children (see Table 3.1). Thirty-eight percent of minor children reside with both parents, roughly 24% live with mothers who are divorced, separated (spouse absent), or widowed, 33% reside with mothers who have never married, and 3% reside with fathers only (U.S. Bureau of the Census, 1992). Twelve percent of African-American children live in households in which a grandparent(s) is the designated head. Of these children residing with grandparents, the majority (62%) live with their mother also, whereas 30% do not reside with either parent. Sixty-two percent of these grandparent households with minor children are maintained by the grandmother only, and 35% are maintained by both grandparents (U.S. Bureau of the Census, 1992). Information on the living arrangements of single mothers indicates that while sizable numbers maintain independent households in which they are head, as many as 25% of African-American single mothers and their children live as subfamily units within the households of relatives where someone else is the designated head (Winkler, 1993). Patterns of household structure vary across married and single mothers (i.e., never married, divorced/separated, or widowed), such that never-married mothers were the most likely to reside with other adults (Jayakody, Chatters, & Taylor, 1993).

Burton's research focuses primarily on adolescent childbearing and its impact on family structure and functioning within distinctive types of family contexts. In particular, this work explores situations characterized by female family lineages, single parenthood, and to a lesser extent, the presence of successive generations of adolescent parenting. Adolescent childbearing, however, occurs within diverse marital, family, and household circumstances. We have relatively little information as to the nature of intergenerational support among families with adolescent childbearers that represents the full range of family contexts within which early childbearing occurs. Studies that employ representative samples of

African-American families would be useful for determining the prevalence of specifically female intergenerational lineages. Continuing research could focus on adolescent childbearing and supportive relationships within the context of current and subsequent (i.e., early marriage, divorce, and remarriage) marital relationships or in families that are not characterized by successive generations of adolescent parenting. In a related vein, adolescent childbearers who marry or cohabit with the father of their child, as well as those who establish independent households, represent important subgroups of this population deserving further study. Finally, the operation of family exchanges that involve transfers across households (i.e., noncoresident) is an important area of inquiry. These brief examples illustrate the variety of demographic and social contexts within which adolescent childbearers and their families can be examined.

Conceptual and Methodological Considerations in Ethnographic and Survey Research Methods

The unique concepts and methods that characterize ethnographic and survey research approaches have, in some instances, hindered an effective synthesis of these literatures. The impact of differences in concepts and methods can be observed in relation to two issues in particular—the framing of questions involving race differences and questions concerning the appropriate unit of analysis for investigations of family support.

Race Differences and Their Interpretation

The investigation and interpretation of race differences has been hampered by various methodological limitations within previous research efforts. Early ethnographic studies of African-American families often document the viability and centrality of kin networks (Aschenbrenner, 1973; Hays & Mindel, 1973; Hill, 1972; Martin & Martin, 1978; Stack, 1974). Interpretations of these findings as pointing to possible cultural differences in supportive networks were made in the absence of appropriate comparative data (i.e., race and socioecomonic status). Recent studies that employ large, national data sets (i.e., Panel Study of Income Dynamics, National Survey of Families and Households, National Longitudinal Survey of Youth) and contain both black and white respondents, reveal that whites receive assistance more often and, on average, receive greater amounts of aid than do blacks. The race disparity is particularly pronounced regarding financial assistance, but has been found for other types of support as well. Among single mothers, whites are more likely than blacks to receive substantial income support (Eggebeen & Hogan, 1990; Hofferth, 1984; Parish, Hogan, & Hao, 1991).

These racial differences could result from disparities in the socioeconomic circumstances of black and white respondents, prompting the employment of controls for income. However, to determine accurately the effects of race on assistance levels, adequate controls for socioeconomic status should be instituted for both support providers *and* recipients. Additionally, wealth rather than income, is increasingly recognized as the critical factor to be controlled for in these analyses. Wealth measures, defined as one's total assets minus all debts, provide a more accurate assessment of a family's economic well-being than does income. Income determinations fail to consider assets such as savings, investments, home ownership, and property. Racial discrepancies in wealth are much larger than racial differences in income; the median net wealth of white households is 10 times greater than the median net worth of black households (Jaynes & Williams, 1989; Oliver & Shapiro, 1989). Comparisons of median wealth for black and white households reveal that whites have nearly 3 times greater wealth than blacks at equivalent levels of annual income. Clearly, a thorough understanding of the financial resources that are available for intrafamily transfers, and the interpretation of race differences in the amounts and types of assistance exchanged must be informed by measures of wealth in addition to those assessing income (Jayakody, 1993).

Studies involving race differences in family support, especially those based on survey research approaches, often employ overly restrictive operational definitions of what constitutes assistance. With respect to financial support, surveys often designate a relatively arbitrary dollar amount as the threshold that defines an event of financial assistance; frequently this amount is either $100 or $200. For example, a survey may assess whether respondents have received $100 or more in the past year from their family. Persons who receive financial assistance in dollar amounts below the threshold level do not qualify as having received assistance. The manner in which the dependent variable has been operationally defined distorts the actual rates of assistance and biases reports of financial assistance in favor of groups with greater financial resources. Even low to moderate levels of financial assistance may constitute meaningful amounts of aid (particularly given racial differences in background wealth) that must be considered in understanding gross race differences in family support. More fundamentally, one could question the exclusive focus on money exchanges as defining financial assistance, to the exclusion of goods and services (e.g., meals and clothing) that have monetary value.

Other survey formats define child care assistance from family as only occurring in situations in which the mother is a participant in the paid labor force. As a consequence, mothers who are not in the labor force but who receive child care assistance from their family are excluded from consideration. Finally, studies frequently restrict definitions of involvement in family support networks to demonstrations of financial aid or child care assistance, or to a particular type of living arrangement (i.e., coresidence). Recent integrative approaches suggest that intergenerational exchanges or transfers can be understood in terms of three systems of currency (Soldo & Hill, 1993). The currencies of time (i.e., provision of services), space (i.e., coresidence), and monetary exchanges (i.e., goods and money) represent the totality of intergenerational exchanges; all three are typically not assessed in studies of support transfers. Alternative survey strategies using open-ended questions or checklist formats provide other means for assessing family support that elicit information on a variety of supportive behaviors (Jayakody, 1993; Jayakody, Chatters, & Taylor, 1993). Restrictive definitions of family transfers are not fully responsive to the task of examining the nature and extent of kin support and underestimate the number of families actively participating in assistance exchanges, as well as the range of pertinent support behaviors.

Unit of Analysis

A basic tenet of ethnographic research is that the family, not the individual, is the focus of research (Rosenblatt & Fischer, 1993). In contrast to this, survey research considers the individual as the appropriate unit of analysis. Survey research approaches adopt the definition of family used by the U.S. Bureau of the Census whereby a family is defined as a group of individuals who live together and who are related by blood, marriage, or adoption. Samples are typically generated based on households (i.e., household units) and the random selection of a respondent from all eligible persons (based on sample and respondent requirements) within the household. Information about the family or household is typically gathered as it pertains to the identified respondent or reference person. Previous discussion related to the prevalence of extended families that exist across households and interhousehold exchanges suggest that a focus on discrete households and single individuals within them is problematic. It is, however, useful to consider why survey research approaches explicitly focus on the individual rather than the family or household unit, and the resulting implications for studying family processes and exchanges.

The identification and use of a reference person is necessary for understanding family relationships for a variety of reasons. First, it is not possible to apriori define a family (or immediate family) except as that designation relates to a specific individual. This is particularly evident with respect to the changes in family configurations that occur following divorce and remarriage. Subsequent to divorce, mother, father, and child(ren) may each form different conceptions of who constitutes their immediate family. Studies of postdivorce families indicate that definitions of the family vary and that no one single definition can be applied or is useful or relevant for all parties (Cherlin, 1992). In postdivorce and blended households, identified family members may reside in different locations yet share enduring relationship bonds (further underscoring the difficulties in defining family membership).

Second, a reference person is essential in studying families longitudinally. Over the life course, families undergo a variety of compositional changes that have implications for family relationships and exchanges. The existence of a stable reference person addresses the fundamental problem of how to link individuals over time when their relationships to one another may change. Further, increasing diversity in family patterns and the timing of role transitions means that relatively few families will conform to the conventional notions of a stable marriage with children leaving home in a predictable manner to begin their own families. Changes in the composition of families could occur because of (a) martial events such as divorce; (b) adult children who leave home to marry or pursue jobs or education; and, in some cases, (c) the return of adult children (and their offspring) to the parental household (Goldscheider & DeVanzo, 1986). Family members may also spend significant periods of time in institutional settings such as the armed forces, universities, nursing homes, hospitals, or jails (Duncan, 1985). Under these circumstances, the individual is logically the appropriate unit of analysis because individuals remain unique and identifiable, whereas family situations may change dramatically. In its early years of operation, the Panel Study of Income Dynamics (PSID) unsuccessfully attempted to classify related individuals in a manner that was independent of time. The PSID solution to the problem of changes in family composition was to establish a fairly comprehensive classification of numerous ways in which a given pair of individuals could be related to one another and code values for that classification in each year that the survey was conducted (Duncan, 1985).

Despite the fact that survey research identifies the individual as the unit of analysis, respondents can and should be examined within the context of their families. A focus on the individual does not preclude the examination of familial and nonfamilial relationships involving this person, nor does it restrict investigations to individuals who reside within the identified household. Numerous examples of families that extend beyond customary household boundaries are found in the research literature. For example, ethnographic studies of poor families document the existence of extensive networks of kin and friends who support one another across several kin-based households (e.g., Aschenbrenner, 1975; Stack, 1974). The consideration of both intrahousehold and interhousehold links are particularly important for studying African-American families and has contributed significantly to our understanding of support exchanges.

Synthesis of Qualitative and Quantitative Approaches

Ethnographic and survey research approaches have both made important and distinctive contributions to our understanding of intergenerational support systems operating within African-American families. This section briefly considers several strategies that involve a synthesis of survey and ethnographic research approaches that would enhance the methodologies that are used to investigate supportive relationships within multigeneration families. Specifically, we present a number of adaptations that can be made to survey research approaches to yield information pertinent to several of the issues that we have addressed here (e.g., family versus household composition, and the role of extended kin, fictive kin, and nonkin in support relationships). Innovative strategies such as kin maps can be used to determine the prevalence of fictive kin relationships within African-American families and the demographic and social correlates of these associations (Chatters, Taylor, & Jayakody, in press). Increases in marital events such as divorce and remarriage are forcing a reconsideration of how families and kinship relations are defined (Cherlin, 1992). Kin maps can be used to investigate the extent to which nonkin peers and quasi-kin (i.e., stepfamily relationships) are incorporated within the family-based support networks of white, as well as ethnic minority families. Further, they may be helpful in determining differential patterns of involvement, and the amounts and types of assistance received from kin, nonkin, and quasi-kin (Bohannan, 1970; Furstenberg & Cherlin, 1991) both within and across distinct racial, cultural, and social class groups.

Research methodologies such as retrospective accounts of family events and life histories are often associated with ethnographic methods. Survey research approaches that have been adapted to gather these types of information can contribute to our understanding of family support over the life course. One survey research technique, the life history calendar (Freedman, Thornton, Camburn, Alwin, & Young-DeMarco, 1988), was developed to improve the quality of retrospective data. Recognizing that discrete events and transitions in the lives of individuals and families can have significant impacts on exchange relationships, the life history calendar can be used to provide accurate information on these past events and assess their impact on family support exchanges. For example, the occurrence of divorce or a nonmarital birth may necessitate increased levels of assistance to a family member. In contrast, obtaining stable employment could lead to a decrease in assistance (particularly financial), while requiring increases in other forms of aid (i.e., child care). The use of techniques such as life history calendars within a survey research format provides the opportunity to examine the impact of various life events and transitions on family exchanges. In a slightly different vein, survey approaches can be used in which more than one member of the same family is interviewed, providing unique data on how individuals within families perceive and are affected by events. Two primary examples of this type of survey include (a) administration of the same questionnaire to two family members in the effort to ascertain potential differences in outlook toward the family environment; and (b) surveys that contain several members from the same family who occupy different generational positions.

Panel studies that investigate individuals and their families over time can track a variety of transitions and their impact on support exchanges. Beginning in 1968, The Panel Study of Income Dynamics (PSID) at the University of Michigan has followed a nationally representative sample of approximately 4,800 households. Individuals comprising this sample have been tracked since that time, whether or not they continued to reside in the original household or with the same individuals. So, for example, adult family members were followed as they grew older, and their children were followed over time as they themselves grew up and formed families of their own. Each year information is collected about the PSID sample members and the individuals with whom they currently live (Hill, 1992). Transitions in marital and employment status, household composition, and poverty are observed, as well as the effects of these transitions on both the individual and the family.

The National Survey of Families and Households (NSFH) (Sweet, Bumpass, & Call, 1988) and the National Panel Study of Black Americans are other surveys that use panel designs and address issues of families and their supportive exchanges. NSFH respondents' original interviews in 1987/1988 (scheduled reinterviews for 1993/1994) provided information on individual and family transitions that occurred during the past 5 years and how these transitions impacted on supportive exchanges (Sweet, Bumpass, & Call, 1988). The National Panel Survey of Black Americans collected data at four time points (beginning in 1979/1980 and most recently in 1992) from a nationally representative sample of African-American adults. Further, at each data collection point, it is possible to inquire about events and changes that have occurred since the last interview rather than focusing only on respondents' status at the time of the current interview. For example, a series of questions regarding family supportive relationships 1 year after the birth of a child would not only inquire about the current pattern of exchanges but also provide an assessment of what had transpired over the course of the year. This strategy, in essence, provides a "moving picture" of the individual and the family rather than a series of static snapshots over time.

CONCLUSIONS

Ethnographic research and scholarship has been at the forefront of efforts that use diverse perspectives to comprehend the nature of intergenerational relations within African-American families. Linda Burton's work has, in particular, considered the impact of personal and social events on the timing, course, and content of intergenerational family roles and supportive relations. These rich and diverse efforts are characterized by the inclusion of a broad range of individual, family, and community factors that affect the structure and functioning of African-American families. Ethnographic research poses critical questions as to the definition and meaning of family (e.g., extended kin and fictive kin), the nature of supportive exchanges (i.e., various types of assistance), and the significance of place in defined geographical locations for the operation and organization of family-based support (i.e., coresidence, and interhousehold exchanges and linkages). Alternatively, survey research approaches that use representative samples of respondents (e.g., socioeconomic status) permit broader generalizations to the underlying populations of interest. Nationally representative samples further allow the investigation of regional variation in relation to these issues, as well as the examination of other factors such as urban/rural differences.

We have provided a selective review of ethnographic and survey research traditions and literatures in the attempt to highlight their commonalities, differences, strengths, and limitations. We believe that by developing meaningful dialogue and exchange between these perspectives, each approach can fruitfully contribute to the other. Several viable research frameworks and strategies for examining family relationships have been suggested that involve the synthesis of concepts and methods from these two traditions. Ultimately, their combined contributions extend beyond the specific context of African-American families to enrich our understanding of intergenerational supportive relationships more generally across diverse groups in our society.

ACKNOWLEDGMENTS

The authors thank Robert Joseph Taylor for comments on earlier drafts of the manuscript. We are indebted to James S. Jackson for his pioneering work in employing survey research methodologies to examine intergenerational relationships among African-American families and in the development of the National Surveys of Black Americans and the Three Generation Family Study data sets, on which portions of this chapter are based.

REFERENCES

Adams, R. G., & Bliezner, R. (Eds.). (1989). *Older adult friendship: Structure and process.* Newbury Park, CA: Sage.

Allan, G. (1989). *Friendship: Developing a sociological perspective*. New York: Harvester Wheatsheaf.

Allen, W. R. (1978). The search for applicable theories of black family life. *Journal of Marriage and the Family, 40*, 117–129.

Allen, W. R. (1979). Class, culture and family organization: The effects of class and race on family structure in urban America. *Journal of Comparative Family Studies, 10*, 301–313.

Allen, W. R. (1981). Moms, dads, and boys: Race and sex differences in the socialization of male children. In L. E. Gary (Ed.), *Black men* (pp. 99–114). Beverly Hills, CA: Sage.

Alwin, D. F., Converse, P. E., & Martin, S. S. (1985). Living arrangements and social integration. *Journal of Marriage and the Family, 47*, 319–334.

Anderson, E. (1978). *A place on the corner*. Chicago: University of Chicago Press.

Angel, R., & Tienda, M. (1982). Determinants of extended household structure: Cultural pattern or economic need. *American Journal of Sociology, 87*, 1360–1383.

Aschenbrenner, J. (1973). Extended families among black Americans. *Journal of Comparative Family Studies, 4*, 257–268.

Aschenbrenner, J. (1975). *Lifelines: Black families in Chicago*. Englewood Cliffs, NJ: Holt, Rineholt, & Winston.

Ball, R. E., & Robbins, L. (1986). Black husbands' satisfaction with their family life. *Journal of Marriage and the Family, 48*, 389–394.

Beck, R. W., & Beck S. H. (1989). The incidence of extended households among middle-aged black and white women. *Journal of Family Issues, 10*, 147–168.

Bell, R. R. (1981). *Worlds of friendship*. Beverly Hills: Sage.

Bohannan, P. (1970). Divorce chains, households of remarriage, and multiple divorces. In P. Bohannan (Ed.), *Divorce and after* (pp. 127–139). New York: Doubleday.

Bowman, P. (1985). Black fathers and the provider role: Role strain, informal coping resources and life happiness. In A. W. Boykin (Ed.), *Empirical research in black psychology* (pp. 9–19). Rockville, MD: NIMH.

Cazenave, N. A. (1979). Middle income black fathers: An analysis of the provider role. *Family Coordinator, 28*, 583–593.

Cazenave, N. A. (1984). Race, socioeconomic status and age: The social context of American masculinity. *Sex Roles, 11*, 639–56.

Chatters, L. M., Taylor, R. J., & Jackson, J. S. (1985). Size and composition of the informal helper networks of elderly blacks. *Journal of Gerontology, 40*, 605–614.

Chatters, L. M., Taylor, R. J., & Jackson, J. S. (1986). Aged blacks' choice of an informal helper network. *Journal of Gerontology: Social Sciences, 41*, S94–100.

Chatters, L. M., Taylor, R. J., & Neighbors, H. W. (1989). Size of the informal network mobilized in response to serious personal problems. *Journal of Marriage and the Family, 51*, 667–676.

Chatters, L. M., Taylor, R. J., & Jayakody, R. (in press). Fictive kin relations in black extended families. *Journal of Comparative Family Studies*.

Cherlin, A. (1992). *Marriage, divorce, and remarriage: Changing patterns in the postwar United States*. Cambridge, MA: Harvard University.

Cherlin, A. J., & Furstenberg, F. F., Jr. (1986). *The new American grandparent: A place in the family, a life apart*. United States: Basic Books.

Christmon, K. (1990). Parental responsibility and the self care image of African American fathers. *Families in Society, 71,* 563–567.

Compas, B. E., & Phares, V. (1992). The role of fathers in child and adolescent psychopathology: Make room for daddy. *Psychological Bulletin, 111,* 387–412.

Danziger, S. K., & Nichols-Casebolt, A. (1988). Teen parents and child support: Eligibility, participation, and payment. *Journal of Social Service Research 11,* 1–20.

Darity, W., & Myers, S. L. (1986–87). Public policy trends and the fate of the black family. *Humboldt Journal of Social Relations, 14,* 134–164.

Dilworth-Anderson, P., Burton, L. M., & Johnson, L. B. (1993). Reframing theories for understanding race, ethnicity, and families. In P. G. Boss, W. J. Doherty, R. LaRossa, W. R. Schumm, & S. K. Steinmetz (Eds.), *Sourcebook of family theories and methods: A conceptual approach* (pp. 627–645). New York: Plenum Press.

Dressler, W., Hoeppner, S. H., & Pitts, B. J. (1985). Household structure in a Southern black community. *American Anthropologist, 87,* 853–862.

Duncan, G. J. (1985). A framework for tracking family relationships over time. *Journal of Economic and Social Measurement, 13,* 237–243.

Eggebeen, D. J., & Hogan, D. P. (1990). Giving between the generations in American families. *Human Nature, 1,* 211-232.

Farley, R., & Allen, W. (1987). *The color line and the quality of life in America*. New York: Russell Sage Foundation.

Freedman, D., Thornton, A., Camburn, D., Alwin, D., & Young-DeMarco, L. (1988). The life history calendar: A technique for collecting retrospective data. *Sociological Methodology, 18,* 37–68.

Freedman, V. A., Wolf, D. A., Soldo, B. J., & Stephen, E. H. (1991). Intergenerational transfers: A question of perspectives. *The Gerontologist, 31,* 640–647.

Furstenberg, F. F., Jr., Brooks-Gunn, J., & Morgan, S. P. (1987). *Adolescent mothers in later life*. Cambridge, MA: Cambridge University Press.

Furstenberg, F. F., & Cherlin, A. J. (1991). *Divided families: What happens to children when parents part*. Cambridge, MA: Harvard University Press.

Furstenberg, F., & Crawford, A. G. (1978). Family support: Helping teenage mothers to cope. *Family Planning Perspectives, 10,* 322–333.

Gibson, R. (1972). Kin family network: Overheralded structure in past conceptualization of family functioning. *Journal of Marriage and the Family, 34,* 13–23.

Goetting, A. (1986). Parental satisfaction: A review of the research. *Journal of Family Issues, 7,* 83–109.

Goldscheider, F., & DeVanzo, J. (1986). Semiautonomy and the leaving home process in early adulthood. *Social Forces, 65,* 187–201.

Gutman, H. G. (1976). *The black family in slavery and freedom, 1750-1925*. New York: Random House.

Hamilton, C. (1971, August 1). Just how unstable is the black family? *New York Times*, p. E3.

Hatchett, S., Cochran, D., & Jackson, J. S. (1991). Black families: Extended family behaviors and support exchanges. In J. S. Jackson (Ed.), *Life in black America*. Newbury Park, CA: Sage.

Hawkins, A. J., & Eggebeen, D. J. (1991). Are fathers fungible? Patterns of coresident adult men in maritally disrupted families and young children's well-being. *Journal of Marriage and the Family, 53, 958–972.*

Hays, W. C., & Mindel, C. (1973). Extended kinship relations in black and white families. *Journal of Marriage and the Family, 25, 51–57.*

Hill, M. S. (1992). *The panel study of income dynamics: A user's guide.* Newbury Park, CA: Sage.

Hill, R. (1972). *The strengths of black families.* Washington, DC: National Urban League.

Hofferth, S. (1984). Kin networks, race and family structure. *Journal of Marriage and the Family, 46, 791–806.*

Hogan, D. P., Hao, L.-X., & Parish, W. L. (1990). Race, kin networks, and assistance to mother only families. *Social Forces, 68, 797–812.*

Jayakody, R. (1993). *Race, family structure and intergenerational exchange* (Working Paper). Ann Arbor: University of Michigan.

Jayakody, R., Chatters, L. M., & Taylor, R. J. (1993). Family support to single and married African-American mothers: The provision of financial, emotional and child care assistance. *Journal of Marriage and the Family, 55, 261–276.*

Jaynes, G. D., & Williams, R. M. (1989). *A common destiny: Blacks and American society.* Washington, DC: National Academy Press.

Johnson, C. L., & Barer, B. (1990). Families and networks among inner city blacks. *The Gerontologist, 30, 726–733.*

Kennedy, T. R. (1980). *You gotta deal with it: Black family relations in a Southern community.* New York: Oxford University Press.

Leibow, E. (1967). *Tally's corner: A study of negro streetcorner men.* Boston: Little, Brown & Company.

Lerman, R. I. (1986). Who are the young absent fathers? *Youth and Society, 18, 3–27.*

Lincoln, C. E., & Mamiya, L. H. (1990). *The black church in the African-American experience.* Durham, NC: Duke University Press.

Lopata, H.Z. (1979). *Women as widows.* New York: Elsevier.

MacRae, H. (1992). Fictive kin as a component of the social networks of older people. *Research on Aging, 14, 226–247.*

Marsiglio, W. (1987). Adolescent fathers in the United States: Their initial living arrangements, marital experience, and educational outcomes. *Family Planning Perspectives, 19, 240–251.*

Marsiglio, W. (1989). Adolescent males' pregnancy resolution preferences and family formation intentions: Does family background make a difference for blacks and whites? *Journal of Adolescent Research, 4, 214–237.*

Martin, E., & Martin, J. (1978). *The black extended family*. Chicago: The University of Chicago Press.

Martin, E., & Martin, J. (1985). *The helping tradition in the black family and the community*. Washington, DC: The National Association of Social Workers.

Matthew, S. H. (1986). *Friendship through the life course: Oral biographies in old age*. Beverly Hills, CA: Sage.

McAdoo, H. P. (1978). Factors related to the stability in upwardly mobile black families. *Journal of Marriage and the Family, 40*, 762–78.

McAdoo, H. P. (1980). Black mothers and the extended family support network. In L. Rodgers-Rose (Ed.), *The black woman*. Beverly Hills, CA: Sage.

McAdoo, J. L. (1981). Black father and child interactions. In L. E. Gary (Ed.), *Black men* (pp. 115–130). Beverly Hills: Sage.

Mitchell, J. S., & Register, J. C. (1984). An exploration of family interaction with the elderly by race, socioeconomic status and residence. *The Gerontologist, 24*, 48–54.

Mizio, E. (1974). Impact of external systems on the Puerto Rican family. *Social Casework, 55*, 76–83.

Oliver, M. L., & Shapiro, T. M. (1989). Race and wealth. *The Review of Black Political Economy, 17*, 5–25.

Parish, W. L., Hao, L.-X., & Hogan, D. P. (1991). Family support networks, welfare, and work among young mothers. *Journal of Marriage and the Family, 53*, 203–215.

Parke, R. D., & Neville, B. (1987). Teenage fatherhood. In S. D. Hofferth & C. D. Hayes (Eds.), *Risking the future: Adolescent sexuality, pregnancy, and childbearing (Vol. 2)*. Washington, DC: National Academy Press.

Phares, V. (1992). Where's poppa? The relative lack of attention to the role of fathers in child and adolescent psychopathology. *American Psychologist, 47*, 656–664.

Rogler, L. H. (1978). Help patterns, the family, and mental health: Puerto Ricans in the United States. *International Migration Review, 12*, 248–259.

Rosenblatt, P. C., & Fischer, L. R. (1993). Qualitative family research. In P. G. Boss, W. J. Doherty, R. LaRossa, W. R. Schumm, & S. K. Steinmetz (Eds.), *Sourcebook of family theories and methods: A contextual approach* (pp. 167–177). New York: Plenum Press.

Rubenstein, R., Alexander, B., Goodman, M., & Luborsky, M. (1991). Key relationships of never married, childless older women: A cultural analysis. *The Journals of Gerontology: Social Sciences, 46*(Suppl.), S270–S277.

Rubin, L. (1985). *Just friends: The role of friendship in our lives*. New York: Harper & Row.

Sanchez-Ayendez, A. M. (1988). The Puerto Rican family. In C. Mindel, R. W. Habenstein, & R. Wright (Eds.), *Ethnic families in America* (pp. 173–195). New York: Elsevier Science.

Shanas, E. (1979). *National Survey of the Elderly. Report to the administration on aging*. Washington, DC: Department of Health and Human Services.

Soldo, B. J., & Hill, M. S. (1993). *Intergenerational transfers: Economic, demographic and social perspectives* (Working Paper). Ann Arbor: The University of Michigan.

Stack, C. (1974). *All our kin: Strategies for survival in a black community.* New York: Harper & Row.

Staples, R., & Mirande, A. (1980). Racial and cultural variations among American families: A decennial review of the literature on minority families. *Journal of Marriage and the Family, 42,* 157–173.

Stevens, J. H., Jr. (1984). Black grandmothers' and black adolescent mothers' knowledge about parenting. *Developmental Psychology, 20,* 1017–1025.

Stevens, J. H., Jr. (1988). Social support, locus of control, and parenting in three low-income groups of mothers: Black teenagers, black adults, and white adults. *Child Development, 59,* 635–642.

Sudarkasa, N. (1981). Interpreting the African heritage in Afro-American family organizations. In H. McAdoo (Ed.), *Black families* (pp. 37–53). Beverly Hills: Sage.

Sweet, J., Bumpass, L., & Call, V. (1988). The design and content of the National Survey of Families and Households (Working Paper NSFH-1). University of Wisconsin-Madison, Center for Demography & Ecology.

Tatum, B. D. (1987). *Assimilation blues: Black families in a white community.* Westport, CT: Greenwood Press.

Taylor, R. J. (1985). The extended family as a source of support to elderly blacks. *Journal of Marriage and the Family, 48,* 67–77.

Taylor, R. J. (1986). Receipt of support from family among black Americans: Demographic and familial differences. *Journal of Marriage and the Family, 48,* 67–77.

Taylor, R. J. (1988). Structural determinants of religious participation among black Americans. *Review of Religious Research, 30,* 114–125.

Taylor, R. J., & Chatters, L. M. (1986). Patterns of informal support to elderly black adults: Family, friends and church members. *Social Work, 31,* 432–438.

Taylor, R. J., & Chatters, L. M. (1991). Extended family networks of older black adults. *Journal of Gerontology: Social Sciences, 46,* S210–217.

Taylor, R. J., Chatters, L. M., & Jackson, J. S. (1993). A profile of familial relations among three–generation Black families. *Family Relations, 42,* 332–341.

Taylor, R. J., Chatters, L. M., & Mays, V. (1988). Parents, children, siblings, in-laws, and non-kin as sources of emergency assistance to black Americans. *Family Relations, 37,* 298–304.

Taylor, R. J., Chatters, L. M., Tucker, M. B., & Lewis, E. (1990). Developments in research on black families: A decade review. *Journal of Marriage and the Family, 52,* 993–1014.

Taylor, R. J., Leashore, B., & Toliver, S. (1988). An assessment of the provider role as perceived by black males. *Family Relations, 37,* 426–431.

Tienda, M., & Angel, R. (1982). Headship and household composition among blacks, Hispanics, and other whites. *Social Forces, 61,* 509–531.

Tienda, M., & Glass, J. (1985). Household structure and labor force participation of black, Hispanic, and white mothers. *Demography, 22,* 381–395.

Tolson, T. F. J., & Wilson, M. N. (1990). The impact of two and three generation black family structure on perceived family climate. *Child Development, 61,* 416–428.

Tucker, M. B., & Taylor, R. J. (1989). Demographic correlates of relationship status among black Americans. *Journal of Marriage and the Family, 51,* 655–665.

U. S. Bureau of the Census. (1992). *Marital status and living arrangements: March 1991* (Series P-20, No. 461).

Wilson, M. N. (1986). The black extended family: An analytical consideration. *Developmental Psychology, 22,* 246–258.

Wilson, M. N. (1989). Child development in the context of the black extended family. *American Psychologist, 44,* 380–385.

Wilson, W. J. (1987). *The truly disadvantaged: The inner city, the underclass, and public policy.* Chicago: The University of Chicago Press.

Wilson, W. J., & Neckerman, K. J. (1986). Poverty and family structure: The widening gap between evidence and public policy issues. In S. H. Danziger & D. H. Weinberg (Eds.), *Fighting poverty: What works and what doesn't.* Cambridge, MA: Harvard University Press.

Winkler, A. E. (1993). The living arrangements of single mothers with dependent children: An added perspective. *The American Journal of Economics and Sociology, 52,* 1–18.

Commentary:
Kindred and Kin: The First and Last Source of Support

Christine L. Fry

More than a hundred years ago Lewis Henry Morgan began the first systematic study of kinship. As true to the evolutionary theory of his time, he was in search of the laws of progress. Since then, we have learned a great deal both about evolution and the diversity of kinship. Evolution and culture are no longer seen as a simple progressive sequence. Instead, intensification of subsistence and risk management are seen as forces involved in the emergence of centralized political institutions or state formation. Likewise kinship failed to match empirically the initial projection of evolution from promiscuity through matriarchy then patriarchy and finally emerging in the families of industrial Europe and America. Quite to the contrary, kinship proved to be challenging in its diversity cross-culturally.

A part of the challenge rests in North American and European concepts of social institutions. As a building block of a culture, institutions have form or structure and make significant contributions in solving human problems. Kinship has almost defied definition as a bounded institution. Elementary definitions of marriage, families, or even a household have proved to be futile in light of the empirically diverse arrangements people have made concerning mating, childrearing, and domestic life. Consequently, comparative approaches to defining kinship have become increasingly multipurpose and multifunctioned.

Despite all the diversity, we know that something identifiable as kinship is basic to all societies. Among our distinctive biological features of our specie are our bipedalism, larger brains, and long maturation rates. This combination proᴜuces difficult child births, a crisis with helpless newborns, and a long-term commitment to childrearing. As a result, long-term bonding between parents and extension of a network of support along genealogical lines is common to our social organization. In other species living in social groups with multiple adult females and males, matri-centered kin groups are also a prevalent theme of social life (Goodall, 1992).

Although families are universal to the experience of being human, they are not all equally important as sources of support. In the simplest of human societies such as the !Kung San (Fry, this volume) kinship gives structure to life and provides a network of security and survival. In more complex societies with centralized state bureaucracies, kinship plays a smaller part in people's lives. First, institutions such as politics, economics, and religion become differentiated from the domestic sphere. Second, security is to be found in these nonkin sources as well as from family. Peasants in many parts of the world decrease their linkages with kin to improve their lot through friendships or dyadic relationships known as patron-clientage. Through these linkages with people of greater wealth and position in the stratification system, access to resources is better assured. State economies are integrated by markets, and security becomes increasingly market based. With an increase of wealth, the family economy diminishes, as individuals are able to purchase the goods and services necessary to survival in market-based mechanisms. Families, for the most part, are no longer economic units except for consumption. They do remain as important units, however, for intimacy and socializing.

Burton's research with African-American families provides insight into the diversity of alternatives people use when dealing with adversity. Her informants have not experienced the increase in wealth that characterizes the history of most Anglo-American families. In these minority families because of discrimination and blocked opportunity, the family economy remains as a primary source of support both socially and economically. An additional challenge faces these families in that a teenage woman has had a child. Both mother who is still a juvenile and her child who is an infant need support. Who among the kindred can be mobilized? What are the creative solutions to the problems of support?

To answer these questions, qualitative methods, such as those employed by Burton, are precisely the most appropriate research strategies. Observational methods are primarily used when the topic under investigation is virtually unexplored. Family life is lived in private. To probe its complexities through questionnaires or formal interviews is to oversimplify or miss some of the complexities of daily life and support. Indeed, the pioneering work of Stack (1974) and Aschenbrenner (1975) has revealed the importance of kin and of female linkages in the social lives of African Americans.

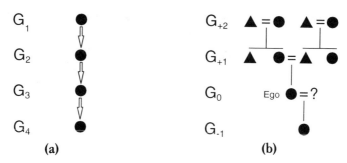

Figure 3.3. Kinship diagram. (a) Mendelian method. (b) The genealogical method.

Participant observation also proves to be a very powerful strategy when the subject matter is highly sensitive and people are not likely to be very responsive to direct questions, and paper and pencils. Teenage pregnancy, birth, and parenting are by and large private matters, but ones that are usually shared with others including researchers. However, because of the need for support from the state, the "culture of welfare" makes these matters highly sensitive. Deviation from the rules of welfare may result in no medical care for the children. Answers to questions may be stereotypic to the reward structure of welfare agencies, unless qualitative techniques are used in an atmosphere of trust between researcher and informants.

DIAGRAMMING ALL OUR KIN: MENDEL OR RIVERS

A necessary first step in mapping the pool of people who can be mobilized to help a teenager who is caring for her infant, is to diagram the social field. Although network analysis may be useful, a focus on kinship is probably more appropriate. Parenting and care for the younger generation is the responsibility of families. From the perspective of anthropology looking into family sociology, it appears as though an alternative way of representation linkages between and across generations has evolved. This is a simplified version of Mendelian genetics with generations appropriately numbered. A "G" is substituted for an "F" (see Figure 3.3a).

An early lesson for anthropologists in trying to map kin terms and relationships is to map kin types anchored in a reference point labeled as "ego." To do so otherwise is to sink into a morass of shifting reference points and confusion between genealogical connections and social relationships. Exotic cultures necessitated the attention to an explicit kinship grammar. This lesson is still important for researchers exploring kindreds among less exotic peoples in industrialized societies.

Some 80 years ago. the genealogical method was invented (Rivers, 1910). As a method it has a grammar. Everything is anchored in an ego (see Figure 3.3b). From this reference point generations are either a 0 or same as ego; a + 1, + 2, or + 3, indicating ascending generations; or a − 1 or − 2, indicating descending generation. Likewise solid lines indicate genealogical linkages. Vertical lines are indicative of descent (parent to child) while horizontal lines are collateral linkages (siblings). Genders of individuals are indicated by circles (females) and triangles (males). The equal sign is reflective of marriage or its equivalent. When people die or when relationships are broken, a simple slash suffices.

What are the advantages of each diagramming tradition? What are the disadvantages? The Mendelian approach has the distinct advantage of being simple and parsimonious. In fact the Mendelian approach works well in diagramming families where one generation is primarily responsible for support (see Figure 3.1). Unfortunately, when a support network is more complicated, the simplicity of Mendel gets in the way as is seen in the tendency to note kin types in the margin of the diagram (see Figure 3.2).

A distinct disadvantage of the Mendelian approach is the problem of the point of reference or the anchoring generation and person. G1 would appear to be a beginning generation. From the perspective of a G4 they are great-grandparents. Does every family have four generations? Do all of the infants have great-grandparents? Although the answer is empirical, it seems a better way to configure the diagram is to anchor it in the focus of the research—the teenage mother. Thus G3 is the anchoring generation. Furthermore, it would be much clearer to use the conventions of genealogical diagramming to use G 0 to note ego's generation, G + 1 for the parents generation, G + 2 for grandparents, and G − 1 for the infant's generation.

If there is a disadvantage to the genealogical method, it is cumbersome in its detail and if there are several families in the sample, we quickly become aware of diversity in kindreds and the people who make them up. Conversely, that may be an advantage. When exploring the comparative unknown, it is important to pay attention to all the detail that is relevant to the research question. In looking at the kindred as a pool of support, this means charting all of the kin, their generations, and their kin types anchored in the individual who is the target of the research—the teenage mother. Only then are we prepared to examine the ways in which the people in the kindred directly or indirectly avoid supporting the teenager with an infant.

CLASSIFICATION: THE TREES OR THE FOREST

A challenge of qualitative research is to display the data in a way that clearly reveals the structure in the data. Qualitative data are rich in detail, and difficult to

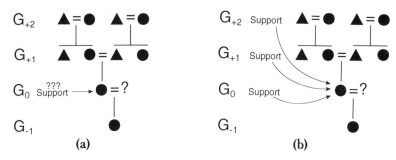

Figure 3.4. (a) Type 1 — Families with problematic sources of support. (b) Type 2 — Families with multiple sources of support.

reduce to a few diagrams or tables. The analysis of qualitative data is a difficult balancing act of being anchored in the detail of people's lives (the trees) as well as the parameters and processes shaping those lives (the forest).

Linda Burton has dealt with this challenge in presenting models of care provision (see Figures 3.1 and 3.2). As a true qualitative researcher Burton is fascinated by the diversity in the structures of support her African-American families have worked out. As a result, we are presented with 14 different support structures. Burton organizes these into two figures that point to a basic difference between the presence of single and multiple providers.

A more parsimonious representation of these two patterns is Figure 3.4. This is an abstraction from Figures 3.1 and 3.2. A generalized kinship diagram is used rather than the Mendelian representation. In type one, the support pattern is seen as problematic through the single arrow. The burden of support falls onto one individual in the web of kin with the concomitant difficulties of caregiver burnout and overburden. Conversely, in type two support is less problematic because there is more redundancy in the support network. More individuals and more generations are involved as is represented in the multiple arrows.

For any kind of research, simplicity in classification is essential. Complexities of ordinary life are indeed interesting, but the purpose of research is to arrive at generalizations about the phenomena we are studying. Linda Burton has taken the first step, but should proceed to a higher level of abstraction that will further clarify research questions and simplify data analysis and the display of the results.

CAUSES AND CONSEQUENCES

Teenage pregnancy, coping with its aftermath and raising the resultant children presents challenges to the families so affected. Burton's research has advanced our knowledge of how some families meet these challenges. her future work will undoubtedly answer further questions dealing with the causes and consequences of the patterns she has discovered. At this point we can offer questions within a simple framework of cause and consequence.

Causes

What are the major differences between families that are able to provide multiple sources of support and those that cannot? Are the families with more problematic sources of support more likely to have fewer kin? . . . more individuals in crisis (drugs, crime)? . . . fewer people employed? . . . or long histories of multiple problems? Also what role does the state play in the configuration of welfare rules? In other words, what are the contributing factors that have shaped these two major types of families?

Consequences

Similarly, what effects do these two types of family support have on their members as well as the teenage mother and infant? Are those families with more problematic sources of support more likely to experience negative consequences? Are these families at risk for child abuse, health problems, depression, or increased reliance on formal supports?

CONCLUSIONS

A frustrating feature of qualitative research is that it usually raises more questions than it answers. Conversely, the generation of questions is a very real strength. Science in its effort to be generalizable and parsimonious also is concerned with validity. A part of our scientific skepticism and concerns with the falsifiability of our research also extends to the way we approach the empirical world. Classification and operationalization are the processes through which theory is linked to the empirical world. Qualitative research permits an immersion in a social world and an opportunity to improve the operationalization of variables and possibly the way we ask our researchable questions.

For African-American families with adolescent childbearers, Linda Burton's research has raised questions beyond those she set out to investigate. African-American families do support members in crisis. Her research looks beyond the stereotype of a strong matri-centric family nurturing all of its members. The fact that Burton found two major types of kin support with 14 subtypes indicates we can no longer talk about *the* African-American family. Instead there are African-American *families*. It is not unusual for qualitative research strategies to reveal a world more complicated than we originally thought. Scientifically, the next step is to incorporate this variance into our classifications and our theories about families as the first and last sources of support.

REFERENCES

Aschenbrenner, J. (1975). *Lifelines: Black families in Chicago.* New York: Holt, Reinhart & Winston.

Goodall, J. (1992). *The chimpanzee: The living link between "man" and "beast"* (Third Edinburgh Medal Lecture). Edinburgh: Edinburgh University Press.

Rivers, W. H. R. (1910). The genealogical method. *American Sociological Review, 3,* 1–11.

Stack, C. B. (1974). *All our kin: Strategies for survival in the black community.* New York: Harper & Row.

CHAPTER 4

Kinship and Individuation
Cross-Cultural Perspectives on Intergenerational Relations

Christine L. Fry

"Around here people are all involved in their families. They can do little else. Kinship occupies all their time. If things are to be done for the community, it is done by outsiders."

Kinship can be either an asset or a liability, or both. Involvement with kin can be all pervasive with clannishness truncating involvement in anything beyond those we call family. Across cultures we expect to find kinship as the dominant institution in simpler, more isolated societies. Somewhat unexpectedly, the introductory quotation was made by an older widow from Momence, Illinois, the community in which I did research for Project AGE. Unlike the people she describes, she herself is an outsider, having married into the community some 40 years ago. Her children, all successful, have moved more than 1,000 miles away. She is college educated and is active as a leader in multiple organizations. Initially, I interpreted her statement as a complaint about leadership in a small town. I recorded it in my field notes and later ruminated about its truth value intertwining themes of kinship, stratification (Momence is working class), and

126

the division between public and domestic spheres of community life. In a very real sense she is right–the work of kinship has its costs. Conversely, it also has its rewards.

In this chapter my intent is to examine major cross-cultural differences in kinship ideologies and resulting expectations about intergenerational relations. On a global basis, families are ubiquitous, but highly variable in form and function. Kinship ideologies are potent features in the lives of individuals either to mobilize a class of people we call "relatives" or to distance ourselves from obligations. To examine the ideology of kin on a comparative basis, this chapter is organized into four sections.

1. *Kinship from whose perspective?* Because kinship is cultural, kin ideologies are in "the eyes of the beholder." In broadening our understanding we must ask the question of whose perspective? Here we combine two viewpoints. The first is an intergenerational perspective that looks at kinship by life stage and changing life courses of individuals connected in the web of kin. The second is the cross-cultural perspective that enables us to understand intergenerational relations as a part of specific cultures and conditions.

2. *Kinship ideologies: collective or individual.* Variability in families is nearly infinite. At the same time variability does not mean chaos. Our window into the ideologies of families is to explore one axis of how domestic units view themselves. Kin can be viewed as a collective unit working and living together across a lifetime. Conversely, kin can be viewed as individuals, differentiating and distinguishing themselves as they mature and grow old, but not necessarily contributing to each others' welfare within a social unit.

3. *Kinship ideologies across cultures and life stages.* In this section of the chapter, the focus is on the communities of Project AGE, and comparisons in social structure and kinship. Here people in seven communities around the world were asked to tell us what is positive and then what is negative about different life stages from the beginning of adulthood to old age. Family life is a major dimension used to describe both good and difficult experiences across adulthood. From these responses, it is clear that involvement with and expectations about kin are linked to specific social and economic conditions.

4. *Implications for models of kinship.* Finally, the implications of this comparative research are brought back home for an understanding of American kinship and a middle-class bias in examining intergenerational relations.

KINSHIP FROM WHOSE PERSPECTIVE?

When we examine intergenerational relations, we see ourselves both coming and going. A look to our seniors gives us ideas about where we are going. A glance toward our juniors reminds us of where we have come from. One moment we are a child, a few years later we become an adult, and then we are old. Because life is a journey through time, we change and obviously those who are linked to us also change. Recognizing that lives move through social structures and historical events, a distinctive framework, the life-course, has emerged primarily within gerontological research. The life-course perspective has become a model of aging. As a model it defines our units of analysis and guides us to interesting questions. For intergenerational relations it reminds us to examine the issue from the viewpoint of life stage. People who are young have a different perspective from those who are old and vice versa. Likewise a middle-aged perspective is distinct from people who are beginning or those who are approaching the end of the life course.

Another viewpoint across cultures reminds us of a plurality of perspectives on the relationships between generations. Why would we ever want to look at intergenerational relations in a cross-cultural perspective? We already have enough perspectives here at home without opening the pandora's box to the 3,000 + cultures of the world. Beyond mere curiosity, there are three important reasons to use the comparative perspective of other cultures.

1. *Science.* Other cultures are the natural laboratory for the social sciences. They have been explored primarily by anthropologists investigating evolutionary and social organizational questions. Each culture is a natural experiment in resolving basic human problems. We expect and find tremendous variation. Scientifically, when the variation does not conform to our predictions, we have encountered an "ethnographic veto." These vetoes can be annoying simply because they tell us our pet theory may be in trouble. Yet they are so important because a troubled theory leads to the search for a better theory that is predictive of more cases.

   Social and cultural phenomena are complex and often messy. This messiness is because we deal with behavior that is conditioned both by circumstance and cultural models about that behavior. These models are learned and are viewed as being perfectly natural by the actors and sometimes by the investigators. Other cultures give us the ability to ask questions of similarity and of differences. In other words we can take something as complex as aging that is both biological and cultural to this laboratory. By discovering what is common to all cultures and what is different, we are on our way to disentangling the cultural specific aspects of the experience of growing old from that which is universal to our specie.

Just as cosmologists are in the process of discovering things about the nature of our universe precisely because they now have the technology to see beyond earth and the solar system, we need to broaden our perspective. We need to look beyond the developed societies to understand fully the nature of aging and the nature of intergenerational relationships. Above all we need to construct theories that are empirically evaluated on data from vastly different kinds of societies.

2. *Iconoclasts.* Often we are pulled to other societies with the hope of supporting myths we have about ourselves. Most often we come away with our myths shattered. There is no Shangri-la. Paradise was not lost. There are no superlongevous populations. A detailed look, however, can reveal some of the uglier facts of life. To solve a crisis of care, an older person can be killed. In technologically less advanced societies, most older people are loved and respected as long as they are intact. However, once the line is crossed into a decrepit category, they are at increased risk for benign neglect, death-hastening behavior, or outright killing (Glascock, 1990).

With myths dispelled, we should ask, why did they appear in the first place? Why is the grass greener elsewhere? These myths are telling us there is something wrong with ourselves. If older people are respected, loved, and cared for in simpler societies, should not we do even better with all of the wealth that passes through our own society? Obviously, the desired answer is yes. Yet sometimes we fall short, causing either remorse or a search for why. Ultimately these myths serve to reinforce norms of what we think we should be doing.

3. *Learning about ourselves.* In the end, we really want to learn something about ourselves. We want to see ourselves as the alien. By putting our own experience and cultural models in comparison with other cultures, we challenge our assumptions. We can see more clearly how institutions work and do not work. It is now that we turn our attention to the institution of kinship and generational relations.

KINSHIP IDEOLOGIES: COLLECTIVE OR INDIVIDUAL

Kinship has been the most studied and the most theoretically dissected of all social institutions. Across cultures kinship is universal, because everyone is bound to others who constitute a special class known as relatives. Kinship is also variable. In fact, it is so diverse that it is nearly impossible to arrive at a minimal definition of family, or even of marriage, to satisfy all cultures. Since the initial comparative work on kinship by Lewis Henry Morgan in 1870, resulting in *Systems of Consanguinity and Affinity of the Human Family*, anthropologists have learned a lot about kinship. Kin have been looked at from the viewpoint of individuals, social actors, groups, and as a system of symbols. Genealogies have been collected. Models of lineages, clans, moieties, and kindred have been drawn along with jural rules and lines of sentiment. Descent and alliance as views of kinship has also dominated our discourse.

One of our major discoveries is that kinship is a versatile institution. It is responsive to economic change and to structural changes in other institutions, which accounts for its variability. Part of the versatility of kinship rests in the distinctness of kinship as a social institution. It bridges nature and culture. Relatives are people to whom one is connected by descent and marriage. Reproduction is natural based on the biology of the parents. Also the main business of kinship takes place within families and households that constitute the domestic or private sphere of a culture. Here behavior is less standardized, and microtraditions are worked out between the people living together. At the same time kinship is cultural. Culture, in contrast to nature, is ordered by rules, understanding, and symbols. Clearly there are rules about mating. There are rules to include and exclude some from membership in a kin unit and terms to identify relationships within the unit. Rules are to be found on power and authority in decision making, and on the transmission of property and resources to the next generation. This is the public side of kinship that is far more standardized than in the private domain. Because of the cultural side of kinship, we find we can make generalizations about a society's family organization. Conversely, we may find even more variety than we bargained for when we investigate the everyday work of kinship. In the domestic domain, where there is privacy, little can be known once the door is closed to the outside world.

MAJOR AXES OF VARIATION: COLLECTIVES OR INDIVIDUALS

Variability across cultures and within cultures may appear to be insurmountable, but anthropologists thrive on describing it. One axis-structuring variation is in the system of descent, or the rules defining membership and the form of kin groups. A major distinction is between unilineal descent, and cognatic or bilateral descent. Concomitant with contrasting rules of descent are disparate answers to the question of what are relatives for?

With unilineal descent the resulting units, usually called lineages, consist of a core of kin of one gender with in-marrying members of the opposite sex. For patrilineal units the image is of a core of males (fathers, brothers, and sons) with wives joining the group through marriage. For matrilineal units the picture is of a core of females (mothers, sisters, and daughters) with husbands marrying in and brothers returning to manage family affairs.

In contrast, cognatic descent is bilateral, using both genders to define the boundaries of being a relative. The image here is one of a circle of kin or a kindred. At the center is a group of siblings united by a core of lineal kin (parents, grandparents, children, and grandchildren). Joining this core are the collateral kin (siblings of the lineals: aunts/uncles and nieces/nephews) and finally their descendants (cousins and great-nieces/nephews). Because each set of siblings has a different kindred (a child's kindred is different than its parents), it is difficult to form a group much beyond the nuclear family or its variants.

What promotes the unilineal or bilateral descent? Undoubtedly, the factors are multiple, but are primarily of political and economic origins. Comparative research has found that denser populations promoting more intensive warfare has contributed to a need for emphasizing exclusive group unity and solidarity (Ember, Ember, & Pasternak, 1974). Under such conditions, unilineal descent groups become the predominant form of kinship. These groups have well-defined memberships and an ideology of exclusive rights over resources and people. Furthermore, there is an association between horticulture (as opposed to foraging) and unilineal descent (Harner, 1970) combined with population pressure and declining resources.

Bilateral descent, in contrast, is known to be associated with conditions that call for flexibility. Where people must be moved to resources or where the key to survival is to be able to activate differentially a less sharply bounded web of kin, we find bilateral descent. We find bilateral descent among hunter and gatherers. We also find bilateral descent in industrialized societies. In fact, with the spread of industry, the kindred and neolocal residence has been the response to this form of economic and political organization (Ember, 1967).

Rules of descent and residence not only reflect the boundedness and rigidity in the kin units formed, but they are also indicative of underlying kin ideologies and expectations about relatives. The contrast is between collective and individual orientations. Collectivist kin ideology sees the lineage as the unit proceeding through time as parents fill the lineage with progeny. Individuals shape themselves into the lineage, being a member and receiving identity, resources, and protection from kin. The image here is of a vessel, filled with kin, who remain or return to the vessel as it journeys through time. Expectations are that relatives work together for the mutual benefit of all across their lifetimes.

Individualist kin ideology also sees families as producing and rearing children. These children, however, do not mold themselves to images of kin. Instead, they proceed to differentiate themselves from kin and become increasingly individuated, seeking significant portions of their identities beyond kinship. It is no accident that flexible kindred composed of individuated individuals and neo-local residence are a part of the industrial order. The labor market provides a new axis of identity and participation on an individual basis, not involving larger kin units. The labor market provides opportunity for individuals who should be prepared to move to where there is labor and opportunity. As individuals of collectivist kin units begin to participate in the industrial order, even they seek refuge in neolocal residence. As is frequently observed in the underdeveloped world, relatives have a tendency to show up and increase their demands on pay day, drawing from the "family fund." Our image here is one of nests with kin nurturing the next generation who some day leave as unique persons. Expectations are that relatives share intimacy, often at considerable distance, but do not necessarily work for each others' benefit across their lifetimes.

We now turn our attention to how people in seven different communities around the world evaluate the relations they have with their kin, how this is shaped by the dynamics of the life course, as well as the social structures in which lives are lived.

KINSHIP IDEOLOGIES ACROSS CULTURES AND LIFE STAGES

Project AGE

Project AGE is a cross-cultural research project that takes a team approach to cross-cultural data collection and analysis. As its major goal, the project sought to investigate how different kinds of communities shape the experience of aging and pathways to well-being for their older members. In shaping aging and old age, the life course is a unit in need of definition within each of the research communities. What are the transitions noting progression through the life course? What are the divisions or age grades? Do we find consensus? Do we find a staged life course or one that is more diffuse in definition? What are people doing in different life stages?

As a team project, the codirectors (Fry and Keith) formulated and coordinated the research design. Principal investigators worked in specific communities around the world adapting that research design in culturally sensitive ways to the local culture. Project members met on a regular basis to discuss research design and problems of analysis, and the project codirectors visited each community while the research was in process. In 1982 the project began in North America and Hong Kong. By 1986, a second phase of data collection was initiated in Ireland and Botswana.

By doing an ethnography of age, we can understand the consequences of other community features for aging and for intergenerational relations.

Communities

Our units of analysis are communities and neighborhoods. Seven research sites were selected on the basis of cultural and structural diversity across these settings. Table 4.1 outlines the differences across the seven communities. They are not representative of the respective nations. They are, however, shaped by national level policies and national social structure. The communities are on four continents (Asia, North America, Western Europe, and Africa). Economies differ ranging from an international port of trade to cattle herding and a combination of foraging and experimentation with farming in a desert habitat. They represent different settlement patterns with urban apartments and public housing at one extreme to cattle posts or small scattered villages around permanent water. Change is ubiquitous, but different in each community. This ranges from near instantaneous response to world markets, suburbanization, outmigration, deindustrialization, and European colonization.

Kinship

Kinship and family organization also varies across our seven communities. For the communities in Ireland and the United States, the pattern is one of a bilateral kindred and neolocal residence (separate households formed on marriage or the beginning of the relationship). In these communities we find the form of kinship organization adapted to the industrial economy. Yet there are differences shaped primarily by level of participation in industry.

Social stratification conditions what people can do and what they think they should be doing. For example, in Swarthmore, Pennsylvania, the upper-middle-class suburb, people control more of their lives and are better able to achieve the ideal. Children receive quality educations and are fully expected to live their adult lives achieving their goals regardless of where that may take them. Consequently most families are not geographically close to adult children. Momence, Illinois, and Blessington, County Wicklon, Ireland, in contrast, are working-class communities with mixed economies. Individuals here are less likely to achieve their ideals. Compromises are made. Children do leave in search of work elsewhere, but some children stay. As a result, kin are more proximate, and extended kin are a part of daily life. Clifden, County Galway, Ireland, in contrast, is marginal to the industrial economy. It is isolated in the beauty of the Conne-

TABLE 4.1   Project Age: Communities and Characteristics (Directors: Christine L. Fry, Ph.D., Loyola University of Chicago, Jennie Keith, Ph.D., Swarthmore College

Community	Researcher	Location	Population	Economy	Family Organization
Research Sites:					
!Kung	Patricia Draper Pennsylvania State Univ.	Southern Africa Botswana North and west Near Namibia in the Kalahari	780	Small-scaled gardening, stock raising & foraging Herding for Herero Crafts No steady wage labor	Bilateral Kindreds Neolocal Residence villages consist of related individuals Kin Proximate
Herero	Henry C. Harpending Pennsylvania State Univ.	Southern Africa Botswana North and west near Namibia in the Kalahari	5000 ± (Seasonal Fluctuation)	Pastoralism Cattle Herding and small animals Some gardening No steady wage	Matrilineal Lineages patrilocal Residence Corporate ownership of cattle Kin Proximate
Clifden	Anthony P. Glascock Drexel Univ.	Western Europe Ireland, County Galway 50 miles West of Galway in the Connemara	805 in Town 851 in Townlands	Farming, Fishing, Shopkeeping Tourism (50% who work, work in tourism-related jobs) 19% Unemployment	Bilateral Kindreds Neolocal Residence Some Kin Proximate Immigration of Kin to Europe and U.S.

Site	Researcher / Institution	Location	Population	Economy	Kinship
Blessington	Jeanette Dickerson-Putman, Indiana Univ. Indianapolis	Western Europe Ireland, County Wicklow 18 miles South Dublin	1322 in town 678 in Townlands	Service, Light Industry, Farming, Commuting to Dublin, 7% Unemployment	Bilateral Kindreds, Neolocal Residence, Kin Geographically Proximate
Momence	Christine L. Fry, Loyola Univ.	North America Midwestern U.S.A. 1 hr. + south of Chicago	3400 in town 4000 in 72 sq. miles around town	Agribusiness, Light Industry, Service, Commuting to Chicago, 19% Unemployment	Bilateral Kindreds, Neolocal Residence, Kin Geographically Proximate
Swarthmore	Jennie Keith, Swarthmore College	North America Northeastern U.S.A. 20 min South of Philadelphia	5950	Service, Commuting to jobs in Philaelphia	Bilateral Kindreds, Neolocal Residence, Kin Geogrpahically Scattered & Usually Distant
Hong Kong	Charlotte Ikels, Case Western Reserve Univ.	Asia Southeastern Coastal City	5 Million +	International Port of Trade, Industrial	Patrilineal Stem Family – Neolocal Residence – Extended households for old

mara where the short tourist season is the major industry. Unemployment is high. The dole is the major source of income. Young people have emigrated, leading to depopulation and fewer kin in Clifden.

Families in Hong Kong have also accommodated to urban industrial life. Family organization is described as a "stem family" and is decidedly patrilineal. These stem families consist of a senior generation (older couple or widow/widower), a son and daughter-in-law, and grandchildren. Once the decision is made as to which son will remain with his parents, other sons on marriage form nuclear families with neolocal residence. Daughters on marriage move to their husband's stem families or form nuclear families. The most prevalent residential pattern is neolocality, but for older people the stem family is the prevalent residential pattern. Household units, stem or neolocal, tend to be economically autonomous from each other with family members participating in the labor market to improve the lot of their household.

In our African sites, we find kindreds and lineages, and virtually no wage labor. Isolated in the Kalahari Desert of northwest Botswana, the !Kung San and the Herero have kinship structures thoroughly entwined in economic production. Unlike their counterparts in the industrialized world, these families are both producing units as well as consuming units. Urban industrial families have emerged as primarily consumption units producing individuals who participate in the labor force for wages. By organizing both what they produce and how they consume, the !Kung and Herero have a domestic mode of production (Sahlins, 1978). This requires a different form of kinship organization or demands different functions from similar forms.

The !Kung San of Dobe have accommodated to this desert environment through foraging and small-scale gardening with bilateral kindred. These families are very similar in form to those in our Irish and American communities. Nuclear families predominate along with neolocal residence. Kindreds, or parts of them, tend to be coresidential in that villages consist of related individuals, and there is extensive visiting of relatives between villages. When foraging was the rule these kindred served as an effective safety net in distributing food from those who had luck in the hunt or in gathering to those who were unsuccessful. Through an ethos of sharing, everyone in camp got some food. The bilateral extension of the kindred increases the pool of kin with whom to visit and share. Generalized reciprocity may sound idyllic, but in reality can be problematic with accusations of being "stingy" and resultant difficulties in mobilizing labor. These strains have become increasingly apparent as mobility has decreased, material wealth increased, and camps have become villages.

Of all the Project AGE communities, only the Herero have unilineal descent with lineages. They have been described as being double unilineal (both matrilineal and patrilineal), but recent evidence is supporting the conclusion that they are matrilineal and patrilocal (Harpending, personal communication, 1992). Pastoralists require a pool of males who can be interdependent with one another for managing cattle herds. Under these circumstances a lineage is the predicted form of kinship. Here villages are headed by a male with a core of his sons and grandsons, and sometimes his brothers. Within this village are multiple households including the males, mother, sisters, and daughters. On marriage, women move to the village of their husband. If a marriage dissolves, she returns to her father's village or if she does not marry, she may remain with her father or brother. Marriage has no correlation with fertility and a significant percentage of women never marry. Thus we have an image of a core of males with women leaving and often returning or never leaving their father's village. However, the cattle define the lineage. Ownership is complex. The head of the village and his male kin are only stewards for many others, mostly their female kin. Thus for the Herero, it is the lineage and the political economy of the lineage that shadows intergenerational relations.

The form, function, and ideology of kinship is clearly different across these seven communities. These differences are related to the socioeconomic and political context in which the seven communities are located. If the work of kinship is work, how does this differ across communities? How is this work evaluated? How does this differ by life stage? To answer these questions we must examine how data were elicited from informants and respondents in each community.

Methods

In each community, our initial questions were: What makes people old? How is social time constructed? How is social time calibrated? What are the cultural markers people need to make judgments about differing degrees of social maturity? To get at these markers we used ethnosemantic or cognitive anthropological strategies. The goal is to use native categories, and native definitions and native boundaries to those categories (emics). What we wanted to avoid was the superimposition of the researcher's categories onto the culture of each community (etics). A variety of techniques can be used to accomplish this that are adaptable to specific settings (Fry, 1986). Age-relevant characteristics were abstracted, and then the line of inquiry turned to how these features were predictive of age or were not indicative of age. Regardless of how the markers of age were derived; they *are anchored in key informant's judgments.*

A longer term goal of this exploration was to arrive at an instrument we call the "Age Game" to be used with a larger sample within each community. These age markers were used as descriptors for "social personae" representing believable men and women (all adults) of differing ages (Fry, 1976, 1986). Thus, more work with key informants resulted in knowing how to combine the markers to describe culturally appropriate personae for each community. These personae formed the basis of the Age Game card sort. Respondents were given a deck of female or male personae (depending on their own gender) and asked to study the descriptions of people on the cards and then to group them by similarity of age or life stage. They were instructed that there was no correct number of groups, and we were interested in seeing how they divided up the life course. Once this was done, the deck with the opposite gender was given to them with the same instructions. The respondents could either use the groups they had sorted for their own gender or could repeat the task separately if they saw major differences in men and women's lives. Before proceeding to the next stage of the Age Game Interview, they were asked to review what they had done and if the sorting remained separate by gender, we asked for them to make the groups as parallel as they could and that they could have a group of one gender. In all subsequent questions we did ask for gender differences.

In no site was this an easy task. The construction of the personae lasted well into the 4th month of fieldwork alone. In some places it was more difficult with instructive lessons. For nearly all of our !Kung respondents, in Southern Africa, and a little under half of the respondents in Clifden, Ireland, the sorting task was baffling. We knew the !Kung field site could be difficult because of illiteracy. Pat Draper with key informants tried to overcome this by devising icons consisting of pictures of activities or social groupings to serve as markers of age. Regardless, the !Kung remained puzzled. Herero respondents, conversely, seemed to have little difficulty, but did not read persona and sort primarily because of poor reading skills. Instead Henry Harpending read the descriptions of personae, and the respondent replied with a linguistically marked age grade differentiated by gender. In the end the analysis of the Herero, the people in Clifden who had difficulty, and the !Kung have led to the conclusion that for individuals who are not participating in or who are marginal to an industrial economy have life courses that are notably different from those more central to urban industrial life (Fry, 1992). Age, per se, is not as salient in organizing their lives nor is the life course perceived as a series of stages. In addition, analysis from other sites has led us to conclude that this kind of sorting task requires some of the analytical skills promoted by formal education, also an institution of industry. For Clifden and !Kung, alternative strategies were used to have respondents divide the adult life course into stages.

The purpose of the age game is twofold. First, we wanted to elicit data that would enable us to analyze variation in the structure of the life course. This involves the markers of age used to create the personae, the ways in which the personae were sorted, and the divisions people saw (ranging from 1 to 11 with an average around 5 for most sites). Second, the divisions created in the sorting task constituted a framework to ask other questions. Some of these are structural, dealing with names, transitions, or thresholds to life stages, and chronological boundaries. Others focus on evaluations and expectations. For each life stage we asked for positive and negative aspects. These were phrased as the good things or best things about that age and conversely the hard things or worse things about being in that age group.

Once our questions were asked, we had respondents do one final age game task. Because all of the age groups were defined by each informant, we needed a more comparable unit for comparison within and across sites. Otherwise, we would be comparing someone who saw a broad 3 or 4 life stages with another who sees a more refined 6, 7, or 11 divisions. For respondents who saw 4 or more divisions, we asked them to regroup the results of their sorting into three groups for the purposes of comparison—a younger group, an older group, and the group in between. On the basis of data from the groups so combined, we have information on the structural properties of these larger groups. For divisions not based on the sorting procedures, the range of differentiation seldom exceeded 3 or 4. Thus regrouping into 3 more standardized categories was based on younger, older, and those in between.

Evaluation of Kinship by Life Stage

In this chapter we employ data from the evaluative responses for positive and negative things about a life stage. The specific questions are "What is good or best about this life stage?" and "What is hard or worst about the same life stage?" Responses to this question were open ended and were recorded for each age group. These were analyzed for content and coded into a limited number of themes for comparison.[1]

Of all the dimensions describing what is hard or good about a life stage across the seven sites of Project AGE, we are interested in kinship. Responses using kin and intergenerational relationships to evaluate a life stage as either good or difficult are our window into the ideology of kinship within each site. Within this dimension are themes about marriage, family, and relationships within and across generations. For each respondent, the standardized grouping of three divisions of the adult life course are used. This means for individuals who created only 3 age groups, there is only 1 group in the youngest standardized age group. Conversely, for those who created 6 age groups there may be 2 age groups in the youngest standardized groups depending on how they regrouped their 6 groups into 3. In examining Figure 4.1, the percentages (bars on the graphs) are reflecting the number of age groups within the young, middle, and oldest part of the life course in which kinship was stated as being a hard or a good thing.

By comparing Figure 4.1a and 4.1b, it is apparent that kinship can be simultaneously positive and negative. In fact, superficially these graphs could be near mirror images. However, a closer examination reveals that across all 7 sites kin are seen as a good thing about an age group more frequently than they are as difficult, especially for the oldest age groups. Clearly for the Herero, kinship is a predominant theme, especially for the middle groups. For all sites, kinship as either a difficult or a good aspect is clearly salient in middle age. If kin can be two faced, what is it that makes them difficult? What is it that can make them a rewarding feature of a life stage? We now turn to the reasons the respondents from each site gave as they evaluated life stages.

Kinship as a Hard Thing

In Figure 4.1a, Herero mentioned kinship in a higher percentage of their age groups. This is especially the middle groups where it is in nearly 80% of the groups. Striking for nearly all of our sites, kinship is mentioned the most frequently for the middle groups and the least frequently as a theme that is hard for the oldest groups. Only for the !Kung does kinship appear as a hard thing in the young groups a little more frequently than in the middle groups. Clifden, as expected, is a little lower in mention of kinship but fits the pattern of most of sites.

What is it about kinship that makes it difficult? Some of the statements are similar across sites, reflecting the dynamics of the domestic cycle and childrearing. Other statements reflect the structural differences in families across sites. We now examine statements made about difficult aspects of kinship for each site organized into young, middle, and older age groups.

Young Groups

Difficulties in establishing relationships and starting families are mentioned as hard things about the youngest groups. The !Kung and Herero express this rather directly as availability of sexual partners.

"If there are no women to sleep with." (!Kung man, young)
"Too many boyfriends." (Herero woman, young)

In the other sites marriage, young children and infidelity are critical issues.

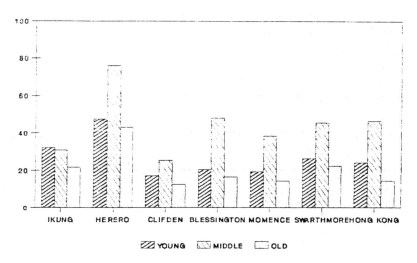

% OF AGE GROUPS IN WHICH MENTIONED
BY STANDARDIZED AGE GROUP
P = .000

(a)

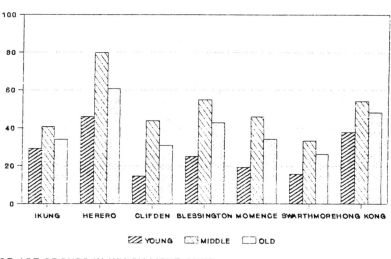

% OF AGE GROUPS IN WHICH MENTIONED
BY STANDARDIZED AGE GROUPS
P = .000

(b)

Figure 4.1.   (a) Kinship as a (a) difficult or (b) good aspect of a life stage.

"Thinking about marriage." (Clifden)

"Losing a girlfriend/boyfriend." (Blessington)

"Realizing marriage requires work." (Blessington woman, age 69)

"Marriage: If it is on the rocks or not; get tired of each other; if do get divorced, how will it affect the kids?" (Momence woman, age 23)

"Being tied down by responsibility for children." (Swarthmore)

"In terms of marriage, when they fall out of love." (Hong Kong)

In the sites with industrial economies differentiating from parents is also a difficult thing.

"Leaving home." (Clifden)

"Living under same roof as parents." (Blessington)

"Relations with family i.e., feelings of rebellion." (Swarthmore woman, age 24)

But there are differences. In Hong Kong leaving parents is hard because one takes on the responsibilities for family (as teenagers they took care of you). Also in the stem family, residentially a young couple lives with the husband's parents.

"One loses the happiness of being a teenager. They lay the path for the future." (Hong Kong)

"Living with the husband's parents, there is difficulty in getting along with them." (Hong Kong)

The !Kung and Herero statements reflect another issue—interdependency of family members in helping each other in providing food.

"When your elders don't give you things and don't take care of you." (!Kung)

"If she does not have a husband to help her and her mother." (!Kung)

"Neglect (not providing for) parents." (Herero man, age 67)

Middle Groups

For the industrialized communities, the respondents in Hong Kong express the major reason kin are difficult the most directly as "having to bear the family burden." Being responsible for children, educating children, and trying to hold marriages together define the burdens of family.

"Bear the burden of family expenses: working and care of family expenses." (Hong Kong)

"Parents are getting older and starting to make demands just as children are."
(Swarthmore)
"Responsibilities of raising family." (Momence)
"You are so wrapped up with the children that you lose contact with the
outside world." (Blessington woman, age 46)
"Tied down with kids." (Clifden)

In Ireland and America, another difficulty is seeing children leave and a concern
for them as they become adults.

"Realizing kids are individuals who will have their own lives." (Swarthmore)
"Losing control of children's lives." (Momence)
"Adjusting to a new life situation when children leave home." (Blessington)
"Family gone away (mature and possibly emigrating)." (Clifden)

!Kung and Herero, conversely, do not see families as burdens nor are they concerned about launching their children. Instead it is interdependency: having a
family, and having children to work and care.

"Having her daughter refuse to work for her." (!Kung)
"No wife to cook for him and his children." (Herero)
"No daughter to work for her." (Herero)

Old Groups

Hard things in the oldest groups, for our industrialized communities, have to do
with relationships with spouses and children who by now are living their own
lives. Most of the concern is with the frequency and quality of relationships
with those children.

"Not seeing your kids and grandchildren often enough." (Clifden man, age
55)
"Getting used to the fact that your children are grown." (Blessington)
"The children not wanting you around." (Momence woman, age 65)
"Children not being as attentive as you would like." (Swarthmore)
"Afraid the children do not love them." (Hong Kong)

Only in Hong Kong do we find concern about abandonment of older people.

"If children are bad to one, they drive you away from home. Then one has
to be a beggar. Those who are the most out of line leave them in the
hospital and do not attend to them." (Hong Kong man, age 21)

In the Kalahari it is interdependency and mobilizing kin for food and care.

> "If you don't have a child you are in pain." (!Kung woman, late middle age)
> "No children to give you care." (Herero man, age 74)

Kinship as a Good Thing

As a good thing about a life stage, kinship is also a major theme (see Figure 4.1b). As with hard things, the Herero mention it more often in their age groups of all life stages. Respondents in most of our communities mentioned kinship as a good thing in 20% to 55% of their age groups. However, in Swarthmore and Clifden in the youngest groups it is a theme for only 15% of the age groups. Across all sites, a common pattern is found. Kinship as a good thing is highest in the middle groups and lowest in the young groups. For the oldest age groups it is somewhere in between, mentioned in 60% of the Herero old groups and a low in Swarthmore at 26%. We now examine statements made about the positive aspects of kinship for each site organized into young, middle, and older age groups.

Young Groups

Sexual partners are good things for the !Kung and the Herero as is the interdependency of working together and looking after parents.

> "Thinking about women and sleeping with them." !Kung
> "Sleeping with men." (Herero)
> "If have husband, glad and can work together." (!Kung)
> "Take care of relatives." (!Kung)
> "Looking after parents." (Herero)

For the Irish and American communities, it is being single, establishing relationships, getting married, the joys of small children, and the togetherness of family that make kinship a good thing.

> "Being single and not tied down with family and mortgage." (Blessington)
> "Single and free to do what you want to." (Momence)
> "Starting your own family." (Clifden)
> "Small children, small problems." (Blessington)
> "Family home life." (Momence)
> "Becoming a parent. Feel you belong to a unit." (Swarthmore woman, age 79.)

Our Hong Kong Chinese also see marriage and children as positive, but a young family represents a turning point. Once the family is formed, responsibility for it becomes a reality.

> "Marriage is a turning point. You have a family and change from having no worries to having a sense of responsibility." Hong Kong woman, age 35

Middle Groups

In the Kalahari, the good things about the middle-aged groups is marriage and interdependence. It is the contributions that spouses and children make in the work effort. Also references are made to feeding elders and obeying them.

> "Marry so they can help each other out." (!Kung man, age 30)
> "You can feed yourself and feed your elders who birth you. You can get things for yourself and give yourself a life." (!Kung man, over age 60.)
> "Many children to do the work, keep the sacred fire, kill mice in our house, daughters work for you." (Herero woman, age 26)

Children and their maturation are the major issues for respondents in Ireland, America, and Hong Kong. They bring joy in and of themselves and the feeling of family.

> "Rearing of family, kids are great fun." (Clifden man, age 40)
> "Family is together growing up." (Blessington woman, age 41)
> "Children are unfolding. The differences in their talents makes it thrilling to watch them grow up." (Swarthmore woman, age 78)
> "Have the second generation; more people to talk; it is fellowship." (Hong Kong woman, age 70)
> "Formed the family: do not have to be perplexed by love." (Hong Kong)

Old Groups

Interdependency with spouses and children again is what makes kinship a good thing in old age for the !Kung and Herero. Only in these groups is being helped or looked after a positive feature. Just as obeying parents was good in the Herero middle groups, commanding children is good in the older groups.

> "What is good is if they have someone to help such as a wife or a husband or a child to bring them things and help them out." (!Kung)
> "Commanding children to milk cattle, bring food, tobacco and tea." (Herero man, age 54)

In Ireland and the United States, clearly it is having a family and enjoying them that makes kinship a good thing.

> "Having family around you." (Clifden man, age 88)
> "Have family, get most enjoyment from family getting together." (Momence man age 28)
> "Seeing both sides of each family: enjoy grandchildren more than your own." (Swarthmore man, age 45)

Only in Swarthmore do we see some concern about abilities to continue visiting the younger generation who is most often geographically distant.

> "Being able to enjoy your family and being mobile enough to visit family." (Swarthmore)

In Hong Kong the hope is that children will be wealthy, listen to what they say, and to have a good family environment. For people in these older groups it is the family that supports them.

> "Hope that the children will get wealthy." (Hong Kong)
> "Hope that the children and grandchildren will listen to what one says." (Hong Kong)
> "If the family environment is good, there are people who support them." (Hong Kong man, age 62)

FAMILY BURDEN

The family burden again emerges as an important component of themes that make kin a positive feature. Only this time it is reversed and can be referred to as the joys of the "empty nest." Being burdened with family, as discussed earlier, can be difficult. Conversely, with the maturation of children the burden is completed. With the empty nest comes the release from the responsibility that is very positive. We find the "empty nest" as a theme most prevalent in Blessington, Momence, Swarthmore, and Hong Kong (see Figure 4.2). For Swarthmore the launching of children and the maturation of children accounts for most of the reasons why kinship is a good thing for the middle and older groups. In Hong Kong it also is a predominant theme in the younger groups as well, primarily because people in these age groups are too young to have experienced the burden. For the most part, individuals in the youngest age groups are unmarried, still dependent on parents and have not formed their families. Inter-

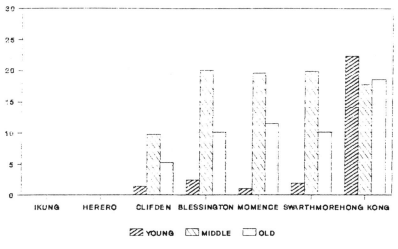

% OF AGE GROUPS IN WHICH MENTIONED
BY STANDARDIZED AGE GROUPS
P = .000

(a)

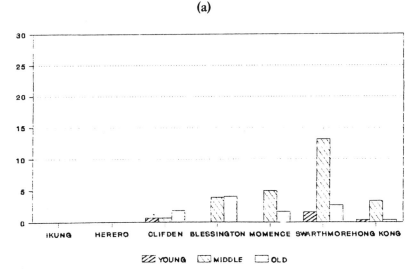

% OF AGE GROUPS IN WHICH MENTIONED
BY STANDARDIZED AGE GROUPS
P = .208

(b)

Figure 4.2. The "empty nest" as a (a) hard or (b) good thing about life
stage.

estingly, the empty nest is not a major issue as a hard thing with the exception of Swarthmore where in nearly 15% of the middle groups it is referenced. In our African communities, the family burden and its decline or the empty nest is never mentioned.

Excerpts from responses for the middle groups reveal that the launching of these children brings the relief of a job done; a sense of relaxation and redirection of family life with a spouse; and especially in Swarthmore, the joys of seeing children find their own ways in successful careers and marriages.

> "Kids are gone. You can go back to do your own thing and enjoy them [adult children]." (Clifden woman, age 32)
> "Children are grown up and parents are a bit relieved of their responsibility." (Blessington woman, age 66)
> "Like a honeymoon with the children gone—enjoy children—go off and enjoy each other." (Momence woman, age 70)
> "Kids coming into bloom; look forward to kids being more responsible for themselves." (Swarthmore woman, age 37)

Hong Kong Chinese see this decline of the family burden a little differently. As children mature, they start working and that money is contributed to their natal family. A male child and a daughter-in-law is expected to remain with parents in the stem family. Thus, for them, once the family burden begins to diminish, it will soon vanish altogether.

> "Children are growing up, working and earning money." (Hong Kong)
> "Have their children to support them; they need not support their kids anymore." (Hong Kong woman, age 27)

DISCUSSION

Everywhere families are important. Every culture has a social institution we recognize as kinship that resolves basic issues of reproduction, enculturation, domestic arrangements, and sometimes production and politics along with other things. Because the underlying basis of kinship is generations and the succession of generations, it is an important dimension of social life across the entire life course both positive and negative. Kinship is versatile in accommodating to variable social and economic conditions. On the basis of the variation we see from the Project AGE communities we ask two questions. First, what is it that these communities can tell us about ourselves? Second, what are the implications of our comparisons for the models and theories we have about intergenerational relations?

When respondents in each community talked about the positive and negative features of different stages of the life course, they told us about an ideal. The ideal that makes for a good life and the problems that could make it difficult. For kinship, these normative statements reveal a lot about the ideology of kin and models of family life. Norms do not necessarily tell us what people are actually doing in their lives and with their kin. Yet norms do tell us what people think they should be doing and can do with their families. Norms also indicate what people are worried about. Finally, differences in social structure are reflected in norms.

Clearly, the !Kung and Herero emphasize the collective nature of their families. Interdependency is a theme of cooperation between kin. On the positive side, one benefits from the work of others as one contributes to their welfare. The down side is mobilizing others to work and the difficulties that emerge when they do not work. Kindred for the !Kung are their safety nets in assuring the quest for food and distribution of food. Likewise, the Herero lineages are another variety of safety net. As cattle herders with wealth on the hoof, Herero lineages are corporate entities. Village owners manage the cattle and labor needed to get them water, pasturage, milked, butchered, or get them to market. When we look at themes in addition to kinship that make things good or hard, for both these communities we find material security and interdependency (dependence in old age) dominant themes. The !Kung also emphasize physical abilities because of the strength required in a foraging and gardening economy.

Unlike the !Kung and Herero, the Chinese in Hong Kong have adapted their stem families to industrial urban life. An ideology of patrilineages links fathers and sons across multiple generations and even to the ancestors who are to be worshiped. Collectivity is expressed in yet a another way. Families as coresidential units are economic units. Work and wages promote the welfare of this unit. Parents invest in children and their studies in the hope they will be successful. Once children begin to work, their wages come back to the family. When the family burden shifts to the younger generation, a parent will live with a son and his family. Successful children contribute to a higher quality life in old age. Families must be responsible for the welfare of their older members. Although highly industrial and dominated by the market, the government of Hong Kong assumes families will meet many of the basic needs of their older members. State-funded welfare programs are directed toward health but not independent living (Ikels, 1993).

Clifden, Blessington, Momence, and Swarthmore are communities anchored in economies that are industrialized and nations that have welfare benefits for older people (the dole, social security, and medical benefits). Although the position in and involvement with the industrial order is different for people in these communities, comparisons with Africa and Hong Kong enable us to explore the question of: "What has this culture of enterprise done to our families?" Kindreds are the expected form of kinship because resources (jobs) are not geographically stable. The market, however, has penetrated more than the form of family organization. It permeates the ideology as well. Responses from these four communities do not reveal the collective interdependency between relatives. Instead, we find individuation and individualized kin.

Individualism certainly predates capitalism, but it has been reinvented in new forms. In kinship this individualism is seen in the way children are seen as both a burden and a delight in the United States and Ireland. Quite some time ago, David Schneider (1968) in his celebrated cultural account of American kinship pinpointed sexual intercourse as the central axis of kin solidarity. Sex is emotionally charged and symbolically a solidarity is produced that transcends reciprocity. A very necessary precondition for children is sex, the recombination of parental genes. With lower fertility, the uniqueness of each child can be cherished. This is exactly what our respondents are telling us as they talk about the joys of seeing children grow and eventually to have lives of their own. Children are also a responsibility both economically and socially. Again, this is what our respondents tell us. Reductions in this responsibility are clearly good things. But it is not just getting rid of the kids and having the nest all to yourself again. Instead there is the anticipation of children continuing to grow, becoming even more of an individual, and making it on their own. There is also the expectation of different qualities in the relationship with adult children.

A man in his 70s from Momence, in the last days of a terminal illness, summarized his life succinctly in one sentence, "The children are raised and the house is paid for." In a very simple way, that is exactly what families do in this culture of enterprise. They create children and raise them as individuals. Educations are paid for through parents' taxes and contributions in tuition. Fledgling individuals are prepared to explore and make their way through the adult world of careers, marriages, and consumerism. Fears are over a failed launch when children come home again, and over becoming a burden to the children once health or financial difficulties are encountered.

A very practical concern of intergenerational relations in urban America is the willingness and ability of generations to respond in supporting each other. What are the consequences of this individuation and solidarity based on sentiment in mobilizing familial support? If solidarity transcends reciprocity, what obligates family members to respond to the needs of kin in need? As Nydegger (1980) points out, emotions are not the best things on which to predicate solidarity. Yet, it seems as though that is exactly what Americans have done. Feelings are very powerful in motivating people to do things. Conversely, primarily because of their volatility they can be switched off or realigned quickly. An argument or a new romance can dissolve a relationship.

Are the kindred of individuated members as fragile as we might believe? Are the older members of these kindreds not receiving a desirable level of support? One is quickly reminded of the iconoclastic work of Ethel Shanas and her colleagues (1968) in the late 1960s. Families were not abandoning their old in industrialized societies. Our research on intergenerational relations reveals considerable support in both directions. Older generations support their children primarily in transfers of wealth. Younger generations help the old primarily in services. Do we have a crisis in care across generations? Or is the care crisis yet another myth?

To answer this question we must consider the effects of social stratification and wealth. Although modernization theory highlights increased vulnerability for older people, industrialization has brought very clear benefits (Gratton & Haber, 1993). Wealth has increased. In early industry, family members worked together contributing to a "family fund" to help the entire family through rough times. With more opportunity and prosperity, families rely less on the family fund for their material security. The ideals of independent households, once attainable by only the wealthy few, are now within the reach of the majority. Intimacy at a distance is further made possible for the majority through state-funded pensions and social security. Wealth accumulated over a working lifetime is augmented, and the need of older people to require the financial help of younger relatives is decreased.

Project AGE communities exemplify the pattern of less reliance on the family fund. Of our four communities whose economy is industrialized, only Clifden is marginal in terms of the penetration of the market. Here we find tourism as the main industry along with a sizable subsistence economy, supplemented by the dole. Blessington and Momence are working class with their citizens working in agriculture or in blue-collar jobs. Swarthmore is an upper-middle-class community where many people are professionals with relatively high-paying jobs. Here the American ideal of achievement is closer to being a reality. Children are launched, and with quality educations, they leave to pursue interesting careers elsewhere in the world. There is little attachment to Swarthmore. Likewise, the parents of most Swarthmorians are elsewhere because they (the children) have moved here to pursue their careers in Philadelphia.

Ironically, those who can achieve this American ideal see the support of parents as a hard thing. Only in Swarthmore do we find the "women in the middle" seeing the simultaneous demands of children and career on the one hand and parents on the other. Children pursuing their own life trajectories, encouraged by their parents, find it painful when crisis strikes the parental nest. Compounding this is the physical distance. Solving problems at a distance is difficult, and moving a parent to Swarthmore can be traumatic with considerable ambivalencies. Even more ironic, many older Swarthmorians see aging in the community as risky and have decided to leave the community long before frailty impairs their functioning (Draper & Keith, 1992).

In comparison, the ideals of achievement are often compromised in Blessington and Momence. Professional jobs are rare. Available jobs involve 9 to 5 pink-collar, blue-collar work, or being a part of a small business or agricultural work. Above all, kin are in the community. Children are launched, but some of them are not launched too far. Caring for a frail mother is not the strategic problem it is when she is living in Idaho. Visiting on the way home from work, picking up groceries when doing your own shopping, sending a grandchild to mow the lawn or wash the windows are accomplished with minor disruptions to daily routines. Such small tasks of daily support are less onerous than transplanting the person in need of help into your home or into a nearby apartment. If there is any movement in Momence, it is from the older person's home to a hospital and then to nursing home, not into a child's home. The work of kin is done in Momence, in Blessington as it is in Swarthmore, only it is a little less intrusive on their lives.

To what extent does a middle-class image of kinship, especially the individuation of children, penetrate working-class families? Schneider's original (1968) study was done with middle-class Chicagoans. Subsequently, this study was extended to lower income families (Schneider & Smith, 1973). One of their findings was that the emphasis put on the growing autonomy of children, in fact, is encompassed by lower class family values. The lower class values are not a separate subculture but deferred middle-class values in the face of real-life choices with limited resources. In Blessington and Momence aspirations for children's lives and careers reflect the compromises of educational costs and opportunities in the labor market. Although the ideology of kinship is individualized and stresses the growing autonomy of children, it is not as extreme as in Swarthmore.

Before we end, we should consider intracultural variations within communities engulfed within the industrial order. Some people are without kin. Some decided not to marry. Couples can be infertile or decide not to have children. Relationships are broken very frequently as is evident in escalating divorce rates. Women have children and raise them without the help of a partner. Matri-focality has become an important variant in American kinship, especially for poor and minority families. We have no solid answers other than communities shape outcomes. Kin substitutes can be cultivated. It remains somewhat unclear what happens to people who have had bad experiences with their primary kin, namely, the children of divorced parents. At this point it appears as though they are less willing to do the work of kinship.

IMPLICATIONS FOR MODELS OF KINSHIP

Everyone has a model of kinship. From our models we answer such basic questions as: Who are our kin? What can we expect from them? What can they expect from me? Cross-cultural research into diverse models of the world reminds us to ask an additional question: Whose model is it? Researchers in gerontology and intergenerational relations have codified representations of family life largely based on folk understandings of the people they study as well as their own cultural backgrounds. Unless we try to see ourselves as the alien through comparative research, cultural models will seem perfectly natural even to researchers. Gerontology by and large is an invention of middle-aged researchers who have developed our understanding of old age over the past four or five decades. These researchers are also academics who are predominately middle-class or upper middle-class in their social origins. Our understandings of how families should work cannot help but be shaped by a middle-aged, middle-class view of kinship. Across the seven communities of Project AGE, kinship themes are usually most prevalent in the middle groups. Intergenerational relations are a concern of the middle aged. Likewise, we know that the image of kin differs by context and class. Thus our view of kin is more likely to be similar to those individuals who shared their experiences in Swarthmore.

Individualism and the market economy are prevalent features of Western industrialized democracies. Families have responded with a distinctive ideology about kin. Families are fairly small autonomous units linked with similar units through genealogical ties. People work for their families and recreate with their members. Families are the locus of intimacy (Bellah, Madsen, Sullivan, Swidler, & Tipton, 1985; Gans, 1988). Families are home, the place where you can be yourself and not worry about bureaucratic matters and the competition that pervades other dimensions of social life. This ideology is true of English families (Strathern, 1992), and as we have seen Irish and American families. In contrast, Hong Kong Chinese, Herero, and !Kung families do not share this image of kinship.

A bone of contention is in how children are viewed. For the !Kung and Herero, children are welcome additions to the domestic labor force, especially as they mature. Relatives are people who work together, making a living across their entire life courses. Children are definitely not expected to leave home on adulthood. Hong Kong families support children in providing as much education as possible to improve their prospects as adults. One son is not expected to depart the nest but remain to support his parents in old age. If the earlier investment in their son is successful, he will be wealthy and their old age secure.

In American and Irish families, children are cherished but for different reasons. Kids are companions, they are fun, and they are even a challenge. As they mature, unlike !Kung and Herero children, they are expected to become autonomous. When they leave, an empty nest is left at home as they set up independent households and ultimately family units of their own. As we have seen earlier (see Figure 4.2), the empty nest is a far more positive than it is negative aspect of middle-aged groups. In fact, a real tragedy for middle-class parents is the failed launch when a child does not leave home or returns home.

With our predominately middle-class, middle-aged view of kinship made clearer with comparative data, we have one more caution. States also make assumptions about families based on their model of what kin can and will do for each other. The Hong Kong government assumes the stem family will assume responsibility in housing and caring for their older members. Welfare benefits are directed toward health and a small allowance, but not toward autonomous living. In an ethnically homogenous but class-stratified society, there probably is considerable agreement on images of families. In an ethnically diverse and pluralistic society such as the United States, common assumptions about kinship may not be warranted. As researchers we should remind policy makers of this pluralism. Policy can change reward structures, which, in turn, can alter the functioning and quality of life within families.

The work of kinship takes time. The observations of the older widow with whom we began this chapter are correct and actually reveal more than I initially thought. Superficially, she is telling me about the difficulties of mobilizing Momence residents for community organizations. At a deeper level, she is telling me about kinship in Momence. She is of the middle to upper middle class, with a middle-class model of family life. The people she is trying to organize and coordinate are working class, with somewhat different expectations about the involvement with kin. As I now look back at her statement, I realize behind her frustrations are slightly different models of family and kinship and their role in community life. Also to middle-aged, middle-class researchers, her statement is a reminder that although families may appear similar to those of the middle class, their expectations and involvement with relatives are not always the same.

NOTE

[1]The texts of the responses were entered into an electronic data base. Researchers from each site coded the data set using site-specific codes. These codes were reviewed by the

project coordinator and translated into 15 themes such as physical issues, concerns of material security, and kinship. Reliability and comparability of the coding and the conceptual boundaries of the themes were then checked by two raters. One rater was a theoretically naive sociology graduate student who checked all theme codes by reading responses across all sites after ordering the data set by themes. The second rater was a project coordinator who read responses for each site again by reading responses after ordering the data set by themes. Any potential disagreements were electronically recorded. The data was returned to the researcher for that site, and questions that are disputes about the coding and translation into themes were negotiated. In this way mistakes in the site-specific coding are minimized, as are problems in translating these codes into themes for comparison. Above all, our goal is to assure comparability in the meaning of the themes and to make explicit the cultural differences across sites. From this point, the themes are then translated into nine dimensions that are broader in meaning.

REFERENCES

Bellah, R, Madsen, R. Sullivan, W., Swidler, A., & Tipton, S. (1985). *Habits of the heart: Individualism and commitment in American life*. Berkeley: University of California Press.

Draper, P., & Keith J. (1992). Cultural contexts of care: Family caregiving for elderly in America and Africa. *Journal of Aging Studies, 6,* 113–134.

Ember, M. (1967). The emergence of neolocal residence. *Transactions of the New York Academy of Sciences, 30,* 291–302.

Ember, C., Ember M., & Pasternak B. (1974). On the development of unilineal descent. *Journal of Anthropological Research, 30,* 69–94.

Fry, C. L. (1986). Cognitive anthropology and age differentiation. In C. L. Fry & J. Keith (Eds.), *New methods for old age research*. Brooklyn: J. F. Bergin.

Fry, C. L. (1992). Changing age structures and the mediating effects of culture. In W. van den Heuvel, R. Illsley, A. Jamieson, & C. Knipscheer (Eds.), *Opportunities and challenges in an aging society*. Amsterdam: North-Holland.

Gans, H. (1988). *Middle American individualism: The future of liberal democracy*. New York: Free Press.

Glascock, A. P. (1990). By any other name it is still killing. In J. Sokolovsky (Ed.), *The cultural context of aging*. New York: Bergin & Garvey.

Gratton, B., & Haber, C. (1993). Rethinking industrialization: Old age and the family economy. In T. Cole, W. A. Achenbaum, P. L. Jakobi, & R. Kastenbaum (Eds.), *Voices and visions of aging: Toward a critical gerontology*. New York: Springer.

Harner, M. J. (1970). Population pressure and the social evolution of agriculturalists. *Southwestern Journal of Anthropology, 26,* 67–86.

Ikels, C. (1993). Chinese kinship and the state: The shaping of policy for the elderly. In G. Maddox & M. P. Lawton (Eds.), *Annual review of gerontology and geriatrics: Aging, kinship and social change*. New York: Springer.

Morgan, L. H. (1870). *Systems of consanguinity and affinity of the human family* (Vol. 17, pp.1–590). Washington, DC: Smithsonian Institution.

Nydegger, C. N. (1983). Family ties of the aged in cross-cultural perspective. *The Gerontologist, 23*, 26–32.

Sahlins, M. (1972). *Stone age economics*. Chicago: Aldine–Atherton.

Shanas, E., Townsend, P., Wedderburn, D., Friis, H., Milhøj, P., & Stehouwer, J. (1968). *Old people in three industrial societies*. New York: Atherton Press.

Schneider, D. M. (1968). *American kinship: A cultural account*. Englewood Cliffs, NJ: Prentice Hall.

Schneider, D. M., & Smith, R. T. (1973). *Class differences and sex roles in American kinship and family structure*. Englewood Cliffs, NJ: Prentice Hall.

Strathern, M. (1992). *After nature: English kinship in the late twentieth century*. New York: Cambridge University Press.

Commentary:
Culture, Social-Structure and Intergenerational Role Relationships: General Observations and the Case of Japan

Carmi Schooler

In this chapter I use Fry's chapter (this volume)—Kinship and Individuation—as a sounding board to raise general methodological and substantive questions about how social structure and culture interact to affect intergenerational role relationships. In doing so, I also review the relevant evidence from my own research on how these factors affect such relationships in Japan.

Fry's chapter, and the Project AGE research program that it describes, make a very obvious contribution by using an ethnosemantic research approach to give us a feel for what people in different cultures consider good and bad about their kin relationships at various stages of their lives. For two of these cultures from the remote Kalahari Desert—the !Kung, hunter gatherers, and Herero, pastoralists—the primary theme of kin relationships is interdependency. On the positive side, one benefits materially from the work of others and gains satisfaction from contributing to their welfare. On the negative side, it is sometimes difficult to mobilize others to work; others' demands can stand in the way of the fulfillment of one's own needs; and if others do not do their share, one can be in real trouble.

Kinship in industrial Hong Kong seems best described in terms of an investment model. Parents tend to see children (as children tend to see themselves) as financial contributors to the household, and as insurance for their old age. In fact, as I will argue later, this pattern becomes rare after a generation or two of industrialization, and actually is more representative of peasant-based agricultural societies.

In the other four societies sampled—Clifden (rural Ireland); Blessington (rural Ireland but with light industry and commuting to Dublin); Momence (small-town Midwest United States); and Swarthmore (college town, mainline Philadelphia suburb)—responses "do not reveal the collective interdependency between relatives. Instead we find individuation and individualized kin. With low fertility rates the uniqueness of each child can be cherished. Children are a responsibility and a pleasure" (Fry, this volume, p. 150).

Despite Project AGE's unusual methodology, these results parallel those of other studies (e.g., Macfarlane, 1986; Thadani, 1978; Thornton & Fricke, 1987). Taken together, these studies suggest the existence of three models of the family differing according to whether kin, particularly children, can be characterized as one of the following:

1. Individual members of a production/consumption cooperative
2. Workers for (and possible inheritors of) the family unit's well-being and insurance policies for the parents' old age
3. Expensive pets (and incidentally promulgators of the "selfish gene")

METHODOLOGICAL ISSUES

As I noted, the general findings of this ethnosemantic research project parallel those of researchers from other intellectual disciplines, and the study's conclusions are congruent with my beliefs. Nevertheless, before discussing the general implications of how culture and social structure affect intergenerational role relationships in Japan, I would like to raise a few methodological issues about the ethnosemantic approach in general, and about the Project AGE studies in particular.

Questions About the Ethnosemantic Approach

I have some questions about the basic assumptions of the approach. Although developing emic kin categories for each culture (i.e., categories that arise from a culture's ethos and that are "natural" to participants in that culture and not imposed from outside that culture's perspective) is laudable, I have a strong suspicion that this approach, in common with many other supposedly culture-free approaches, is actually highly culture dependent. My suspicion is supported by the finding that

> *In the end, the analyses of the Herero, the people in Clifden and the !Kung have led to the conclusion that for individuals who are not participating in or who are marginal to an industrial economy, the life course is not waged and staged. Age, per se, is not as salient in organizing their lives. (Fry, this volume, p. 138)*

Such a generalized conclusion about nonindustrial cultures seems a bit lame when one considers all of those nonindustrialized societies both in Africa and elsewhere where age grading and formal age and cohort groups are among the principal cleavages along which society is formally structured. I think that the real clue to the meaning of the findings for the three "preindustrial" cultures comes in the next sentence:

> *Also analyses from other sites led us to believe that this kind of sorting task requires the analytic skills promoted by formal education. (Fry)*

I strongly suspect that such abstract tasks as the "Age Game," in which individuals are asked to judge or logically manipulate categories, concepts, or stimuli, which they have no experience as viewing as meaningful semantically independent entities in their everyday lives, can readily be performed only by those who have had experience with such tasks. Incidentally, similar criticisms can also be made about the semantically sparse stimuli involved in measures of fluid intelligence (e.g., letters, numbers, or nonfigurative shapes). Empirical support for this suspicion can be found in Ceci's (1990) literature review.

Further questions about the meaning and usefulness of the various emic categories arise when we see how they are analyzed. In fact, it is unclear how the "imperfect" data from the !Kung, Herero, and Clifden were actually used. The more general question, however, is whether collapsing the original nine groups into three loses their original meaning. It is also unclear what happens to the emic approach when the categories are translated into "nine dimensions that are broader in meaning" (Fry, this volume, p. 155). Granted that this attempt to develop emic site-specific measures is a noble one, I am not sure what happens in the massaging process necessary to make cross-cultural comparisons. If one truly believes in the importance of the emic approach, it may be that cross-cultural comparisons become logically impossible. As one who believes that, with care, most concepts and categories relevant to people's everyday lives and beliefs can generally be translated in ways that permit cross-cultural comparisons, I would personally be more inclined to put my effort into trying to develop such cross-culturally comparable terminology beforehand rather than trying to equate emically developed terms. But this is clearly a matter of taste. One compromise that combines minimal external imposition of structure with the evaluation of kinship roles, yet permits the development of statistically sophisticated analyses, is the combination of taxonomic approach and semantic differential rating (of evaluation, potency, and activity) presented by David Heise in earlier conferences in this series (Heise, 1987, 1990).

Concerns About the Communities Sampled

I understand how difficult it is to gain access to communities and to conduct the kind of intensive field work necessary for the type of research reported. Nevertheless, I am somewhat concerned about the nature of the communities chosen and not chosen to be in Project AGE. It is a little strange that there is no North American or Western European industrialized city. All of the Western examples, although presumably enmeshed in industrial economies, are in the far margins of such economies (i.e., Clifden), or in the agricultural or at most light industry sectors (Blessington and Momence), or possibly in a postindustrial phase (Swarthmore). Studying Swarthmore is not only convenient but interesting. Nevertheless, studying someplace like Philadelphia is a necessity. As it is, because the only fully industrialized site examined—Hong Kong—is also the only Asian site studied, we can not tell whether what was found is a function of full-scale industrialization or of an Asian cultural system originally developed in a primarily peasant economy.

Neglect of Differences Within Societies

Clearly, my general point is familiar to the Project AGE researchers. Thus, Fry (this volume) notes:

> In these communities we find the form of kinship organization adapted to the industrial economy. Yet there are differences shaped primarily by level of participation in industry. (p. 133)

Such a potential source of difference should not only have shaped the choice of countries to be examined, it should also have affected both the analyses and selection of subjects within countries.

I am well aware that issues of respondent selection represent central differences between the guild practices of sociologists and anthropologists, with empirically oriented sociologists more likely to favor representative sample-based surveys to intensive questioning of informants. Thus, not only am I struck by the relative lack of comparison between a particular site and other sites in the larger political, cultural, or socioeconomic units to which it belongs, but I am bothered even more by the degree that each of the cultural sites is described and discussed holistically, with not much concern for the social-structural and socio-economic differentiations within each site. My concern is even greater because I believe that some of these socioenvironmental differences among individuals are causally related to the development and maintenance of the cultural differences that are often the focus of anthropologists' interest.

CULTURALLY RELEVANT SOCIAL-STRUCTURAL CONDITIONS

My concern about the causal connection of socioenvironmental conditions to psychological level phenomena, on the one hand, and to cultural level phenom-ena, on the other, derives from my research on the psychological effects of occu-pational conditions, particularly my cross-cultural research involving Japan. Much of this research on Japan deals specifically with how social-structural con-ditions can both influence the acceptance of and possibly change the nature of cultural values regarding kin relationships.

A central aim of this research on Japan is to test the replicability of a series of findings in the United States (Kohn & Schooler, 1983), indicating that job conditions that facilitate occupational self-direction increase intellectual flexibil-ity and promote a self-directed orientation to self and society. Japan represents a particularly appropriate place to test the generalizability of these conclusions be-cause self-directedness is not seen as being culturally valued there. Yet despite this, the results of our survey of a representative sample of 629 Japanese men (A. Naoi & Schooler, 1985; Schooler & A. Naoi, 1988) replicate our original U.S. results by finding that in Japan, as in the United States, occupational self-direction leads not only to ideational flexibility but to a self-directed orientation to self and society. Other findings center on the more extensive relationship in Japan between position in the work organization and psychological functioning. The pervasiveness of this relationship provides evidence for those who empha-size the importance of the organization for the Japanese worker. The organiza-tional effects that were found (e.g., the increase in self-esteem and authoritarian conservatism resulting from ownership, high bureaucratic level, and bureaucrati-zation) reflect patterns of Japanese culture and organizational functioning.

Even stronger evidence of the generalizability of the Kohn-Schooler hypothesis about the psychological effects of occupational self-direction was found among Japa-nese women, the wives of the men in our sample, whom we also interviewed (M.

Naoi & Schooler, 1990). This is the same pattern of results as was found among the U.S. women. Surprisingly, in a culture where self-directedness for women is apparently particularly disvalued, among the employed wives of the men in our sample, as with with their husbands, self-directed work increases intellectual flexibility and self-directed orientations while also leading to less traditional attitudes (M. Naoi & Schooler, 1990). Our evidence also shows that Japanese women are substantially less likely than their husbands to do self-directed work on the job. The resultant occupationally induced lessening of self-directed orientation may contribute to women's accepting cultural norms that keep them in subservient positions.

Data from some of my earlier research on Japanese women provides further evidence of how the social-structurally determined environmental conditions of Japanese women clearly affect the likelihood that they will accept their culture's norms that keep them in subservient positions. In collaboration with Karen Smith (Schooler & Smith, 1978; Smith & Schooler, 1978), I designed a study of the cultural and social-structural determinants of Japanese women's conjugal and maternal role values and behavior. We developed a questionnaire that was administered in 1972 to a sample of 145 mothers of first- or fourth-grade children in four elementary schools representative of the Kobe area. Overall, the general tenor of our findings supported the conclusion of William Caudill and many other observers of Japanese culture that the role of mother is a much more central one than that of wife or couple member. Although our respondents' uncomplaining acceptance of household chores and responsibilities appears to make them fit the stereotype of the selfless domestic desirous of filling her husband's every wish, the women seem to have been more disinterested than willing servants, their husbands being nowhere as important a factor in their social and psychological existence as were their children.

Our findings, however, also suggested the possibility that these values and attitudes were not immutable. They supported the hypothesis that social structural variables related to environmental complexity (e.g., being young, well educated, urban, and having fathers and husbands with high status occupations; cf. Schooler, 1972, 1984) result in an increase in individuality and in the importance placed on the couple relationship and a decrease in such signs of complete absorption in the maternal role as the belief that good mothers always place their children's welfare ahead of their own. We concluded that with "further urbanization and higher educational levels, Japanese women may increasingly emphasize individualism even in their most traditional role, that of mother" (Smith & Schooler, 1978, p. 619).

Japanese Culture, Social Structure, and Care of the Elderly

Further evidence, particularly germane to the topic of this meeting, on how social-structurally determined environmental conditions can effect the acceptance of traditional norms and perhaps ultimately change the nature of these norms can be found in that portion of the research that Michiko Naoi and I did (M. Naoi & Schooler, 1990) that examines attitudes toward caring for the elderly.

Our measures are based on a set of 13 items that literally ask what the respondents think about having elderly parents live with them, as well as about living with their own children when they themselves are older. An extensive series of exploratory and confirmatory factor analyses indicated that this complex of attitudes can best be conceptualized in terms of four factors:

1. General belief that living with elderly parents is good
2. Belief that one should not live with one's parents if this leads to problems
3. Willingness to take in parents if they are ill
4. Desire to live with one's own children when older

The first three of these factors can be made into a second-order factor measuring willingness to live with and care for elderly parents that fits the data well.

Because it seems unlikely that once she has entered the work force a woman's attitudes toward responsibilities for the older generation would affect her level of occupational self-direction, we assumed that the causal direction would be from occupational self-direction to values toward the elderly. Therefore, we modified the model we had used to explore the other effects of psychological conditions by eliminating the reciprocal path from the "psychological" variable to occupational self-direction. When we tested such models, the path from occupational self-direction to our second-order factor measuring willingness to care for elderly parents in one's home is significant, and the path from occupational self-direction to wanting to live with one's children when one is older is negative and close to significant. Thus, our hypothesis that the self-directed orientation resulting from doing self-directed work would decrease people's willingness to put up with the constraints involved in living with the older generation is confirmed.

There is also support for the hypothesis that working in a traditional industry (i.e., one that existed in Japan during the Tokugawa era) increases the traditionalism of family attitudes. Although traditionalism of industry is not significantly related to the second-order measure of traditionalism of attitude toward care of elderly parents, it is significantly related to two of the component factors. Working in a traditional industry increases Japanese women's willingness to take elderly parents into their homes, both if the parents were sick and if doing so would cause problems. In addition, women working in traditional industries are significantly more likely than those working in nontraditional ones to want to live with their own children when they themselves are elderly. These findings that Japanese women working in traditional industries retain traditional attitudes toward the elderly are congruent with earlier findings for Japanese men (Schooler & A. Naoi, 1988). Those earlier findings indicate that Japanese men who work in traditional industries tend to be traditional in their orientations and values.

Another occupational variable that affects attitudes toward the elderly is working in a bureaucracy. Working in a bureaucracy leads to less willingness to take elderly parents into one's home and less desire to live with one's own children during one's own old age. One possible explanation is that bureaucracies may be less likely to permit the flexible work arrangements that are sometimes needed to care for the elderly at home. The findings are also explainable by the hypothesis that working in a bureaucratic setting leads to a more general bureaucratic view of life in which problems are solved through bureaucratic rather than personal arrangements. If this is so, working in a bureaucracy should lead individuals to believe that impersonal agencies rather than families should bear the responsibility for care of the aged.

When we look at the effects of the other variables in our model, we see that coming from a high social status background directly decreases the acceptability of having older and younger generations of adults living together. This is reflected both in a decreased willingness to take elderly parents into one's home as measured by the second-order factor and a decreased desire to live with one's own children when older.

Another possible cause of differences in attitudes toward caring for elderly parents in one's home that we examined is birth rank of the husband. According to the traditional Japanese family system, the oldest son not only inherits the major share of his parents' wealth but also the responsibility of caring for them in their old age. Consequently, it might be expected that women who are married to first-born sons would feel an especial obligation to care for their husbands' parents. There is some evidence that, in the past, husband's birth rank may have affected the likelihood of living with the husband's parents, but that the pattern has changed. M. Naoi, Okamura, and Hayashi (1984), examining the actual patterns of which elderly parents lived with their children, found that among those respondents whose parents had lived with them, but then died, there were more women whose husbands were first-born. However, among those living with their elderly parents at the time of the interview (1983), husband's birth rank did not affect the likelihood of such living arrangements. In this group the major demographic predictor of living with one's parents is whether the parents own a home that provides comfortable accommodation for the children.

We have also modified our analyses to check whether the husband's birth rank affects what the wife thinks about caring for elderly parents. We did this by adding a new variable to the model—whether the husband was first-born—and estimating the path from that variable to traditional attitudes toward living with the elderly. Both for attitudes about living with elderly parents or about living with one's children, such a path, which serves as a control for the effects of husband's birth rank, was not significant, and did not affect the other values in the model. Thus, both the findings by M. Naoi et al. (1984) about actual living circumstances and our analyses about attitudes toward living with parents suggest decreasing acceptance of the traditional Japanese norm that the continuity of the stem family should be preserved by having elderly parents live with their eldest son.

If this is true, and it is consistent with many other findings by myself and others about the increasing acceptance in Japan, albeit sometimes in a very Japanese-flavored way, of new individualistic norms. Thus, in Japan we are witnessing a culture in change, one that is changing as a result of changes in the everyday circumstances individuals face as a result of changes in the social and economic structure of their society.

Causal Connections Among Environmental Conditions, Social Structure, and Culture

I have a full discussion of the issue of the causal connection between environmental conditions, social structure, and culture, particularly as it relates to the interrelationships among environmental complexity, technical development, and individualism throughout the life course, in an earlier volume from this conference series (Schooler, 1990). Several aspects of that discussion are relevant here. The first is that the !Kung also played an important part in that chapter. I noted the preponderance of evidence that immediate-return hunter gatherers like the !Kung, as well as sub-arctic hunter gatherers, had cultures marked by a high degree of individualism, which may well be at least in part a function of their modes of production and related family and social structures. I see this as the first family model (noted on page 158)—one in which kin are individual members of a production/consumption cooperative that they are relatively free to leave.

Interestingly, somewhat similar familial structures and levels of individualism are found in modern industrialized societies. In this model (cf. p. 158) children and (elderly parents) can be seen as expensive pets to whom one is tied through feelings of responsibility deriving from positive sentiments and satisfactions received by the individual. In both the hunter gatherer and modern industrial societies adaptation depends on flexibility. In the case of the immediate-return hunter gatherer societies, such flexibility may only involve individual geographical mobility. In the cases of subarctic hunter gatherers and modern (and postmodern) industrial societies this flexibility also involves intellectual flexibility, which together with a self-directed orientation, is both required and fostered by the complex environmental demands that participants in such societies face.

In agricultural-based peasant societies, familial control of the land is a central issue. In such societies individual geographical mobility is problematic, and environmental demands are generally not as complex as they are in modern societies or among sub-arctic hunter gatherers. Individualism in such societies tends to be disvalued; values and orientations tend to be authoritarian and collectivistically centered on the family. It is in such societies that my second model of kinship generally seems to apply—one in which kin are seen as workers for the family units' well-being and insurance policies for the parents' old age.

As Fry (this volume) notes, C. Ember, M. Ember, and Pasternak (1974) have reached somewhat similar conclusions in examining the determinants of kinship structures. Comparing bilateral and unilateral descent, they find unilateral descent in cultures where denser populations promote intensive warfare, leading to an emphasis on exclusive group unity and solidarity. Besides also being linked to horticulture (as opposed to foraging), these groups have well-defined memberships and an ideology of exclusive rights over resources and people. Bilateral descent, conversely, is associated with conditions that call for flexibility. "Where people must be moved to resources or where the key to survival is to be able to differentially activate a less sharply bounded web of kin, we find bilateral descent. We also find bilateral descent in industrialized societies. In fact, with the spread of industry, the kindred and neolocal residence has been the response to this form of economic and political organization" (M. Ember, 1967; Fry, this volume, p. 131). Clearly bilateral descent is linked to individualism.

As I have discussed in my earlier article (Schooler, 1990), what is unclear is whether, as Macfarlane (1978, 1986) has hypothesized, individualistic values and family practices are a necessary precursor to the original development of industrialism. What does seem to be the case, however, is individual psychological functioning may be more readily amenable to change than cultural and social-structural level phenomena. Consequently, the ensuing cultural conservatism often results in ideologies and customs formed under an earlier set of conditions continuing to affect people's behavior in later but different conditions. This seems to be what is happening in terms of provision for the care of the elderly in Hong Kong. The government policy of depending almost entirely on the family unit for providing such care may well be the result of an ideology formed in a more agricultural period. Granted that the shift of some of the burden of the care for the elderly in Japan from the family unit to the government is no where as far along as it is in the West, nevertheless as we can see from M. Naoi's et al. (1984) research on living arrangements, and M. Naoi's and my research (Naoi & Schooler, 1990) on attitudes toward living with the elderly, a shift is occurring. Because of the psychological effects of meeting the requirements of their environments, individuals in certain, probably increasing, sectors of society are more and more likely to prefer taking care of the elderly in some more individualistically oriented way than caring for them in their own homes. If these trends continue, the ensuing psychological changes may well eventually result in a general cultural change. In a similar way, the culture of Hong Kong is also not immutable.

If we are going to have some idea of how a culture may change, we have to pay attention to differences between individuals in different social-structural positions within a culture. We can not assume that all the members of a society have the same values. To answer its own questions, anthropology needs sociology.

REFERENCES

Ceci, S. J. (1990). *On intelligence . . . more or less: A bio-ecological treatise on intellectual development*. Englewood Cliffs, NJ: Prentice-Hall.

Ember, C., Ember M., & Pasternak B. (1974). On the development of unilineal descent. *Journal of Anthropological Research, 30*, 69–94.

Ember, M. (1967). The emergence of neolocal residence. *Transactions of the New York Academy of Sciences, 30*, 291–302.

Heise, D. (1987). Sociocultural determination of mental aging. In C. Schooler & K. Warner Schaie (Eds.), *Cognitive functioning and social structure of the life course* (pp. 247–261). Norwood, NJ: Ablex.

Heise, D. (1990). Careers, career trajectories, and the self. In J. Rodin, C. Schooler, & K. Warner Schaie (Eds.), *Self-directedness: Cause and effects throughout the life course*. Hillsdale, NJ: Earlbaum.

Kohn, M. L., & Schooler, C. (1983). *Work and personality: An inquiry into the impact of social stratification*. Norwood, NJ: Ablex Publishing Co.

Macfarlane, A. (1978). *The origins of English individualism: The family, property, and social transition*. Oxford: Basil Blackwell.

Macfarlane, A. (1986). *Marriage and love in England: Modes of reproduction 1300–1840*. Oxford: Basil Blackwell.

Naoi, A., & Schooler, C. (1985). Occupational conditions and psychological functioning in Japan. *American Journal of Sociology, 90*, 729–752.

Naoi, M., & Schooler, C. (1990). Psychological consequences of occupational conditions among Japanese wives. *Social Psychology Quarterly, 58*, 100–116.

Naoi, M., Okamura, K., & Hayashi, H. (1984). Living arrangements of old people and some comments about future change. *Social Gerontology, 21*, 3–21.

Schooler, C. (1972). Social antecedents of adult psychological functioning. *American Journal of Sociology, 78,* 299–322.

Schooler, C. (1984). Psychological effects of complex environments during the life span: A review and theory. *Intelligence, 8,* 259–281.

Schooler, C. (1990). Individualism and the historical and social-structural determinants of people's concern over self-directedness and efficacy. In J. Rodin, C. Schooler, & K. W. Schaie (Eds.), *Self-directedness and efficacy: Causes and effects throughout the life course.* Hillsdale, NJ: Erlbaum.

Schooler, C., & Naoi, A. (1988). The psychological effects of traditional and of economically peripheral job settings in Japan. *American Journal of Sociology, 94,* 335–355.

Schooler, C., & Smith, K. (1978). " . . . and a Japanese wife." Social antecedents of women's role values in Japan. *Sex Roles, 4,* 23–41.

Smith, K., & Schooler, C. (1978). Women as mothers in Japan: The effects of social structure and culture on values and behavior. *Journal of Marriage and the Family, 40,* 613–620.

Thadani, V. N. (1978). The logic of sentiment: The family and social change. *Population and Development Review, 4,* 547–499.

Thornton, A., & Fricke, T. E. (1987). Social change and the family: Comparative perspectives from the West, China, and South Asia. *Sociological Forum, 2,* 746–779.

Commentary: Cultural Comparison and Intergenerational Relations

David I. Kertzer

For well over a century, anthropologists have sought to devise methods to permit the proper comparison of cultures. The problems have been formidable, and, indeed, lately a major debate has taken shape over whether meaningful comparison is possible at all (cf. Marcus & Fischer, 1986; Rabinow, 1988; Rosaldo, 1989; Sangren, 1988; Strathern, 1987; Tyler, 1986). The irony is that the very drive to understand other cultures has led some anthropologists to the extreme relativistic position that cultures are incomparable. From this perspective, each culture represents a unique way of viewing the world, expressed in unique concepts and embedded in languages that are not fully translatable. In keeping with this perspective, any use of common measures or common terms to compare cultures robs them of just what it is that makes them unique and translates them into terms that are foreign to them.

In the face of such critical perspectives, however, most anthropologists remain committed to cross-cultural comparison. Yet, even among these anthropologists considerable disagreement remains over how best to overcome the pitfalls of cultural comparison and advance our understanding of cultural diversity. Christine Fry has championed one of these approaches, identified with ethnoscientific procedures. This approach holds the promise of permitting cross-cultural comparison while respecting native categories and ways of viewing the world. However, as we can see in her examination of intergenerational relations, the approach cannot avoid the difficulties inherent in trying to accommodate both cultural diversity and the need for a common language for comparison.

169

Fry begins with the premise that if we are to understand the way different peoples conceive of and divide up the life course, we cannot impose our own categories. Thus, for example, we cannot simply set a chronological age (say, age 60) for the beginning of old age and use this to compare people across cultures. This, of course, is just what is done in most cross-cultural research by economists, demographers, sociologists, and others. By contrast, following an ethnosemantic approach, Fry advocates allowing the people themselves to divide up the life course into meaningful categories (employing, that is, an emic approach) and then use those to see how they view age and aging.

Although this approach has its attractions, many of them soon dissolve when attempts are made actually to do more than simple ethnosemantic ethnography. Indeed, earlier critics of the approach have noted that it tends to locate culture at the level of the individual. It is significant that the approach relies on the use of key informants, and difficulties arise even in generalizing for limited numbers of people in the same cultural setting.

In the case of cultural notions of the life course, we might well ask whether men and women divide up the life course in similar ways. While Fry here homogenizes men's and women's life stages, it is unclear why men and women in a society should be presumed to have corresponding life stages if these are defined emically. For example, people in some societies might divide women's lives according to their stage in the reproductive life course while they divide men's lives on the basis of their progression through other kinds of roles (economic, ritual, or whatever). In such a society—which would seem to represent a rather common case—is it culturally justifiable to speak of men and women as ever occupying the same life stage?

While a person's gender remains unchanged over the life course, the same is not true for age, and we can readily imagine that one's view of the life course differs according to where one stands in it. This, again, is not accommodated in Fry's analysis, and, although it theoretically could be, along with gender, the resulting comparison of seven cultures would soon become exceedingly complex. Do young people divide the life course in the same way as older people? This, on the face of it, seems unlikely, just as it seems unlikely that valuations of the "good" and "bad" aspects of the life stages are viewed similarly by people regardless of their own age.

Even employing an ethnosemantic approach, the anthropologist cannot escape the problem that if we want to compare culture we must use concepts that themselves may be foreign to the cultures we are comparing. Indeed, in this study of the life course and kin relations, the whole analysis is based on a structure that comes from the anthropologist and not from the people being studied, namely, the concept of a life course divided into identifiable and comparable stages.

Fry notes the difficulty her research team had in administering the sorting task that lay at the heart of their methodology, observing that hardly any of the !Kung and little over half of the residents of Clifden could make any sense of it. She concludes from this that "Age, per se, is not as salient in organizing their lives." Taken as a statement of the relative placement of people in a bureaucratic society whose benefits and responsibilities are allocated on the basis of chronological age, this statement is unexceptionable. However, the problem seems to be less one of the salience of age, and more one of the cultural concept of distinct and comparable age groupings.

To obtain the comparability needed for comparative analysis, Fry not only needs to require people in all the cultures to come up with a set of distinct life stages, she also needs to reduce these to the same number. One of the more interesting aspects of the ethnosemantic approach to the life course is, in fact, the variable number of life stages different people come up with. Analysts of aging have long emphasized that the life course is culturally defined, and certainly one implication of this is that different cultures divide up the life course in different ways.

Yet the approach taken by Fry appears to require that all cultures studied have the same number of life stages. Where they actually see more, she requires them to collapse these into three, yet it is no longer clear just what these units represent, because they are no longer culturally meaningful divisions. Moreover, Fry treats them as if they refer to the same portion of the life course, yet it is unclear what theoretical justification can be given for this. One can well imagine one culture where the oldest category begins at the stage of decrepitude, while for another it begins when one's first grandchild is born. In what sense can we use the evaluations people of the two cultures give of life in the "third stage" as referring to the same thing?

Attempting to use scientific procedures to code and quantify the norms and attitudes linked to each of these three life stages raises new difficulties. A content analysis is used of people's comments to determine the frequency with which they mention kinship as one of the "good things" or "bad things" associated with a given life stage. The resulting proportions are used to compare societies and to compare life stages within individual societies with respect to whether kinship is viewed positively or negatively.

The problem that first confronts the ethnoscientist is how to determine what constitutes kinship. Should the definition vary by culture, as the emic approach might suggest? It is not entirely clear what Fry's position is on this. There is some indication that she takes a pluralist stance, believing that native notions of kinship should be employed. This is the only way I can interpret including, for example, "Thinking about women and sleeping with them" as evidence of a positive view of kinship among !Kung for the young life stage or the Herero's "sleeping with men" (see Table 4.1). In some societies, "sleeping with men" would be seen as the opposite of following kinship principles. Yet, if we use native definitions of kinship are we comparing the same "thing?" What possible meaning does it have, in this context, to argue that the !Kung and Herero have a more positive view of kinship among the young than do residents of Swarthmore?

The ethnosemantic approach derived from a desire to establish a rigorous methodology for getting at culture, defined primarily in terms of the way people interpret their world. This method was to make the people themselves the judge of the distinctions that were important to them. The method has generated a good deal of criticism (e.g., Burling, 1964; Harris, 1979, pp. 265–279), not least because it has not lent itself to cross-cultural comparison. Comparison rests on an analytic language that is etic, not emic, and this presupposes a set of concepts developed by the academic community, not by the people being studied.

Such concepts are, of course, implicit in Fry's analysis: the notion of the life course, of life stages, of kinship, intergenerational relations, and so on. The challenge is to develop methods that will best enable us to document cultural diversity while providing a tool kit of concepts and methods enabling meaningful comparison. This turns out to be no easy task, and debates over it continue to divide the anthropological community.

REFERENCES

Burling, R. (1964). Cognition and componential analysis: God's truth or hocus pocus? *American Anthropologist, 66,* 20–28.

Harris, M. (1979). *Cultural materialism: The struggle for a science of culture.* New York: Random House.

Marcus, G., & Fischer, M. (1986). *Anthropology as cultural critique.* Chicago: University of Chicago Press.

Rabinow, P. (1988). Beyond ethnography: Anthropology as nominalism. *Cultural Anthropology, 3,* 355–364.

Rosaldo, R. (1989). *Culture and truth.* Boston: Beacon.

Sangren, P. S. (1988). Rhetoric and the authority of ethnography. *Current Anthropology, 29,* 405–435.

Strathern, M. (1987). Out of context: The persuasive fictions of anthropology. *Current Anthropology, 28,* 251–281.

Tyler, S. (1986). Post-modern ethnography: From document of the occult to occult document. In J. Clifford & G. Marcus (Eds.), *Writing culture.* Berkeley: University of California Press.

CHAPTER 5

Perceived Family Environments Across Generations

K. Warner Schaie and Sherry L. Willis

T he Seattle Longitudinal Study (SLS) has followed panels of multiple cohorts of adults over the past three decades to assess age changes in intellectual abilities over the adult life course. Study participants have been followed over as long as 35 years (Schaie, 1958, 1983, 1988, 1989, 1990a; Schaie & Hertzog, 1986; Schaie & Labouvie-Vief, 1974; Schaie & Strother, 1968). This study has recently been expanded by assessing the adult offspring and siblings of many of our original study participants, thus allowing us to consider issues germane to the fields of developmental behavior genetics and family studies. Data with respect to cognitive similarity among adult family members have been reported elsewhere (cf. Schaie, Plomin, Willis, Gruber-Baldini, & Dutta, 1992; Schaie et al., 1993). The purpose of this chapter is to report data on family similarity in the perception of individuals' family environments, as well as to contrast differences in perceptions within parent-offspring pairs (across generations) to differences within sibling pairs (within generations).

Parent-offspring similarity has traditionally been studied in young adult parents and their children, while sibling studies have primarily involved children and adolescents. In this chapter we report some of the first data on the perception of family similarity of perceptions of family environments between parents and their adult offspring and of adult sibling similarity in such perceptions in adulthood. Perceptions of family environments are considered both with respect to the family of origin (i.e., the family setting experienced by our study participants when they lived with their own parents) and with respect to the current family (i.e., the family reference unit at the time these data were collected). The relation of perceived family environments to reported current intensity of contact between parent-offspring and sibling pairs will also be examined.

ROLE OF DEVELOPMENTAL BEHAVIOR GENETICS

The relatively new interdisciplinary field of developmental behavioral genetics merges developmental and behavioral genetic theories and methodologies and offers exciting possibilities for understanding the origins of change and continuity in development (Plomin, 1986). The new focus of developmental behavioral genetics on change, not just continuity, often surprises those developmentalists who tend to associate the adjectives genetic and stable. However, longitudinally stable characteristics do not necessarily have a hereditary base, nor are genetically influenced characteristics necessarily stable.

A second issue receiving attention by developmental behavioral geneticists is that of nonshared environmental influence (Rowe & Plomin, 1981). In general, behavioral genetic research provides the best available evidence for the importance of environmental influences. Moreover, behavioral genetic research converges on the remarkable conclusion that environmental influences operate in such a way as to make individuals in the same family as different from one another as are pairs of individuals selected at random from the population. In other words, psychologically relevant environmental influences are likely to make individuals in a family different from, not similar to, one another (see Plomin & Daniels, 1987).

DEVELOPMENTAL BEHAVIOR GENETICS AND AGING

From a behavioral genetic perspective, very little is known about the origins of individual differences in cognitive abilities, personality, and adjustment during the last half of the life span (Plomin & McClearn, 1990). Most behavioral genetic research in adulthood in the past has involved family members in their late teens, typically toward the end of high school or at the time of military induction (Plomin, 1986). In the handful of studies that include older adults, the average age of the sample is generally in the 20s or 30s; hence cross-sectional analyses of family resemblance as a function of age are limited. Past genetic studies covering middle and old age were twin studies (cf. Jarvik, Blum, & Varma, 1971; Kallman & Sander, 1949; Plomin, Pedersen, Nesselroade, & Bergeman, 1988). Results from these studies, because of the unusual life circumstances of twins, may be difficult to generalize to the more typical case of family similarities among nontwins.

The research reported here capitalizes on the longitudinal-sequential design of the SLS offering the opportunity to compare young adult and middle aged offspring with their middle-aged and old parents, and to compare sibling pairs from young adulthood to old age. Our family design cannot unambiguously disentangle the contributions of heredity and shared environment because parents and offspring, as well as siblings, at least over some extended period of their lives shared the same family environment as well as heredity. The family design used here, however, has some important advantages over twin and adoption designs. Twins share environmental experiences in common to a much greater extent than do first-degree relatives; furthermore, twin studies estimate higher order genetic interactions (i.e., epistasis) unique to identical twins. Thus, the results of twin studies may not generalize to the usual case of first-degree relatives either in terms of environmental or genetic factors. Early-adopted individuals are difficult to find later in life, and they may differ from nonadopted individuals in terms of the family environments that they experience (Plomin, 1983).

Family studies are valuable because first-degree relatives represent the population to which we wish to generalize the results of behavioral genetic investigations. The family design asks the extent to which individual differences are due to familial factors, whether genetic or environmental, and it provides upper-limit estimates of genetic and shared family environmental influences. One way in which individuals experience shared family environments is to inquire as to the shared perceptions of this environment; this is our current task.

SEATTLE LONGITUDINAL STUDY

The data base to be examined here stems from our inquiry into adult cognitive functioning that began some 35 years ago by randomly sampling 500 subjects equally distributed by sex and age across the range from 20 to 70 years from the approximately 18,000 members of a health maintenance organization (HMO) in the Pacific Northwest (Schaie, 1983, 1989; Schaie & Hertzog, 1986). The survivors of the original sample were retested and additional panels were added in 7-year intervals; a total of more than 5,000 different individuals have been studied at least once. The sampling frame of this project, now known as the SLS, represents a broad distribution of educational and occupational levels, cov-

Study Waves

1956	1963	1970	1977	1984	1991
S_1T_1	S_1T_2	S_1T_3	S_1T_4	S_1T_5	S_1T_6
(N = 500)	(N = 303)	(N = 162)	(N = 130)	(N = 92)	(N = 71)
	S_2T_2	S_2T_3	S_2T_4	S_2T_5	S_2T_6
	(N = 997)	(N = 420)	(N = 337)	(N = 204)	(N = 161)
		S_3T_3	S_3T_4	S_3T_5	S_3T_6
		(N = 705)	(N = 340)	(N = 225)	(N = 175)
			S_4T_4	S_4T_5	S_4T_6
			(N = 612)	(N = 294)	(N = 201)
				S_5T_5	S_5T_6
				(N = 628)	(N = 428)
					S_6T_6
					(N =690)

S = Sample;   T = Time of Measurement

Figure 5.1.   Design of the Seattle Longitudinal Study.

ering the upper 75% of the socioeconomic spectrum. The population frame
from which we have been sampling has grown to a membership of more than
400,000 individuals, but the general characteristics of the HMO remain comparable with its structure at the inception of the study. The study design of the
SLS is given in Figure 5.1.

Throughout the course of the SLS our primary focus has been the investigation of psychometric abilities within the Thurstonian (1938) framework. However, we have also collected data on rigidity-flexibility, lifestyles, some personality traits, as well as the health histories of our participants. To examine
perceptions of shared environments, we began to add appropriate scales for this
purpose beginning with our 1989–90 data collections. Details of the measures
included in the study reported here will be given in the methods section.

We have previously reported our findings on cognitive similarity (Schaie,
Plomin, Willis, Gruber-Baldini, & Dutta, 1992; Schaie, Plomin, Willis, Gruber-
Baldini, Dutta, & Bayen, 1993). Briefly, we found that significant family similar-
ities were observed for parent-offspring and sibling pairs for all ability measures,
except perceptual speed, and for cognitive-style measures of rigidity-flexibility.
The magnitude of correlations for the ability measures were comparable for

those found between young adults and their children (DeFries et al., 1976). Our data also strongly supported stability of parent-offspring correlations over as long as 21 years. Evidence supporting the absence of shared environmental effects on family similarity were provided by analyses of the intensity of current parent-offspring contact.

We had suspected that cohort effects in parent-offspring correlations would result in higher correlations for earlier cohorts, because of a decline in shared environmental influence attributed to an increase in extrafamilial influences in more recent cohorts. This proposition could be supported only for the attitudinal trait of social responsibility (systematic cohort differences on this variable have previously been reported, e.g., Schaie & Parham, 1974). For the cognitive abilities, once again counterintuitively, there seems to be stability or even an increase in family similarity for more recent cohorts. Finally, ability level differences within families equaled or approximated differences found for similar cohort ranges within a general population sample (cf. Schaie, 1990b; Willis, 1989). When broken down by cohort groupings, such differences became generally smaller for the more recently born parent-offspring pairs.

In this chapter we focus exclusively on our subjects' perceptions of their family environment, without attending to the influence of such perceptions on intelligence. Our efforts to measure these perceptions were motivated by the fact that it is extremely difficult to measure current environments objectively, and it is virtually impossible to obtain such information directly over the quality of environments that pertained at earlier life stages of our study participants. We therefore decided that it was necessary to infer environmental quality by asking our subjects to rate both their current environments and their retrospection of the family environment they experienced within their biological family of origin. We are concerned first to examine the usefulness of family environment perceptions to measure environmental heterogeneity. That is, we ask the structural question whether the same dimensions can be used by subjects across and within families to describe their current families and their families of origin. We next examine the substantive issues whether we can demonstrate the existence of generational patterns or secular trends in the perception of family characteristics. We do this by testing whether the strength of family similarity in perception is greater with respect to *shared* than to *unshared* environments. We do this for parent-offspring pairs who have shared the same environment but did so at different life stages, and for sibling-pairs who have shared the same environment at the same life stage. To the extent that we can demonstrate differential strength of perceptions within similar environments as opposed to different environments we will also provide indirect evidence supporting the construct validity of measures of the perceived family environment as indicators of actual family environments.

METHODS

Subjects and Procedure

The participants in the family similarity study consist of the adult offspring and siblings (22 years of age or older in 1990) of members of the SLS panels and their target relatives. Those members who participated in the fifth cycle of the SLS had a total of 3,507 adult children. Of these, 1,416 adult children (M = 701; F = 715) resided in the Seattle metropolitan area. They also had a total of 1,999 siblings including 779 brothers and 1,020 sisters.

The recruitment of the adult offspring and siblings began with a letter containing an update report on the SLS sent to all study participants tested in 1983–85. This letter also announced the family resemblance study and requested that panel members provide names and addresses of siblings and offspring. A recruitment letter was then sent to all siblings and offspring thus identified.

Those who agreed to participate in the study were tested in small groups or individually. Approximately 80% of the subjects tested resided in the Seattle metropolitan area. Other subjects were tested preferably when they visited their Seattle relatives, but approximately 150 subjects were tested in other locations throughout the United States. A total of 1,176 relatives of our longitudinal panel members were tested. Of these 776 were adult offspring (465 daughters and 311 sons), and 400 were adult siblings (248 sisters and 152 brothers) of SLS participants. All subjects were tested on the basic cognitive battery. In addition they completed a family contact scale and family and work environment questionnaires as well as the standard SLS personal data form.

Data relevant to the present report on the target subjects (i.e., individuals who had previously been members of the SLS panel) were obtained during the 1991 longitudinal follow-up (data collection actually continued (from mid-1990 to mid-1992). Subsequent to matching target subjects and their relatives, we were able to identify 452 parent-offspring and 207 sibling pairs on whom complete data is available; or a total sample of 1,318 individuals. These consist of 85 father-son, 110 father-daughter, 96 mother-son, 161 mother-daughter, 28 brother-brother, 106 brother-sister, and 73 sister-sister pairings. The reduction in sample size occurred because of substantial attrition in the number of study members whose relatives we had been able to assess earlier; among the older

TABLE 5.1. Age and Sex Distribution of Study Participants

	Parents (Targets) (1991)			Offspring (Relatives) (1990)			Siblings (Targets) (1991)			Siblings (Relatives) (1990)		
Age Range	M	F	T	M	F	T	M	F	T	M	F	T
22 - 28	-	-	-	15	20	36	-	-	-	1	-	1
29 - 35	-	-	-	43	77	126	1	1	2	3	6	9
36 - 42	-	-	-	49	82	130	7	5	12	8	3	30
43 - 49	-	7	7	50	69	119	7	15	22	8	17	25
50 - 56	10	18	28	17	26	43	13	15	28	6	15	21
57 - 63	17	65	82	4	6	10	7	24	31	10	24	34
64 - 70	44	48	92	2	3	5	19	20	39	26	18	54
71 - 77	65	71	136	-	-	-	16	25	41	19	20	39
79 - 84	47	39	86	-	-	-	13	17	30	3	6	9
85 - 91	9	8	17	-	-	-	1	1	2	2	3	4
92 +	3	1	4	-	-	-	-	-	-	-	-	-
Total	181	271	452	195	267	452	84	123	207	77	130	207

study members attrition was due primarily to death or sensory and motor disabilities that precluded further assessment or questionnaire response.

Table 5.1 provides a breakdown of parents, offspring, and siblings by age and sex, using the 7-year cohorts conventionally employed in the SLS (cf. Schaie, 1983, 1988).

Average age of the parents was 70.26 years (SD = 9.24) and 39.94 years (SD = 8.64) for the offspring. The parents averaged 14.46 years of education (SD = 2.86) as compared to 15.56 years of education (SD = 2.41) for their children. Total family income averaged $24,681 for the parents and $26,841 for the offspring, respectively. Average number of children was 3.53 for the parental and 1.45 for the offspring generation.

Average ages for the siblings were 63.23 years (SD = 12.78) for the longitudinal study members and 61.06 years (SD = 13.16) for their relatives. The target siblings averaged 14.90 years of education (SD = 3.25) compared with 14.62 years of education (SD = 2.78) for their brothers or sisters. Average incomes were $26,416 for the longitudinal study members and $25,682 for their siblings. Average number of children were 3.09 for the longitudinal subjects and 2.69 for their siblings.

Marital status distribution and religious preferences for parents, offspring, and siblings are shown in Figures 5.2 and 5.3.

Measures

Family Environment

Moos and Moos (1986) constructed a 90-item true-and-false family environment scale measuring 10 different dimensions (each measured by nine items), three of which they described as relationship, five as personal growth, and the remaining two as system maintenance and change dimensions. The purpose of these scales was to provide an assessment instrument to examine environmental context of adaptation (Moos, 1985, 1987). We adapted eight of these scales for our purposes by selecting five items per scale and presenting each statement in Likert scale form (1 = strongly disagree; 2 = somewhat disagree; 3 = in between; 4 = somewhat agree; 5 = strongly agree). The eight dimensions included for our purpose and examples of statements scored in the positive direction on each dimension follow:

1. Cohesion   (Relationship)
   Example: "Family members really help and support one another."
2. Expressivity   (Relationship)
   Example: "We tell each other about our personal problems."
3. Conflict   (Relationship)
   Example: "Family members hardly ever lose their temper."
4. Achievement orientation   (Personal growth)
   Example: "We feel it is important to be the best at whatever we do."
5. Intellectual-cultural orientation   (Personal growth)
   Example: "We often talk about political and social problems."
6. Active-recreational orientation   (Personal growth)
   Example: "Friends often come over for dinner or to visit."

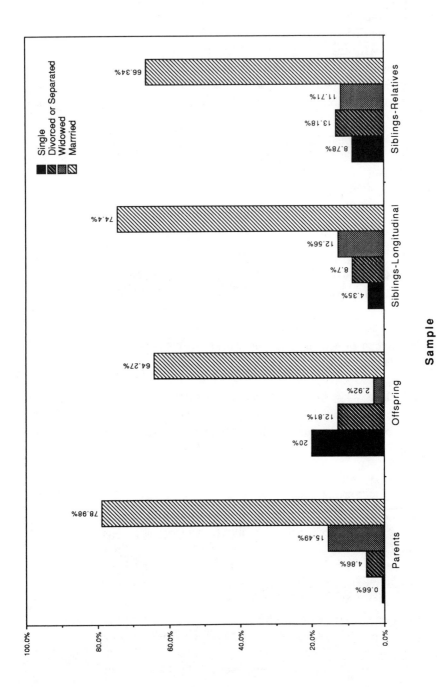

Figure 5.2.   Marital status distribution of parents, offspring, and siblings.

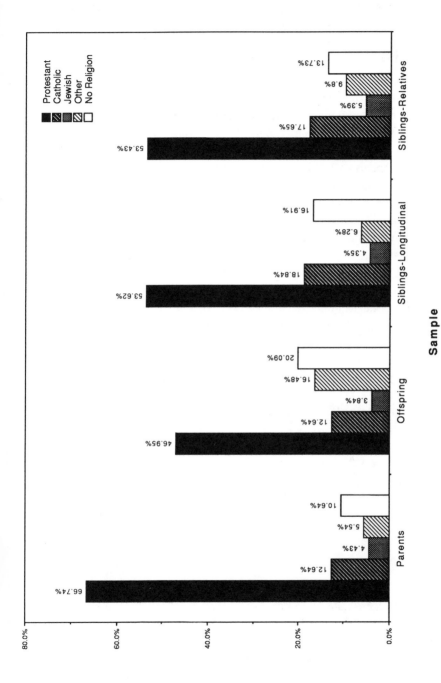

Figure 5.3.   Religious preference distribution of parents, offspring, and siblings.

7. Organization   (System maintenance)
   Example: "We are generally very neat and orderly."
8. Control   (System maintenance)
   Example: "There are set ways of doing things at home."

Two forms of the Family Environment Scale (FES) were constructed: The first asked that the respondents rate their family of origin (i.e., past tense statement with respect to the parental family); the second form requested the same information (in present tense) with respect to the current family. On each form respondents were also asked to indicate the membership of both their families of origin and their current families. They were then instructed to do the ratings with respect to the family grouping identified by them. In other words, for the parents this implied rating the "empty nest" family. In recognition of the fact that significant numbers of our young adult and older study participants lived by themselves, an alternative form was constructed that allowed defining the current family as those individuals (whether or not related by blood or marriage) that the respondent considered as his or her primary reference group and with whom the respondent interacted at least on a weekly basis.

A confirmatory factor analysis (using LISREL 7) was conducted on a random half of the sample of relatives for both forms to determine whether the retained items clustered on the factors described by Moos. The obtained fit (family of origin: $\chi^2(701) = 1,235.56$; $p < .001$; GFI = .842; RMS = .084. Current family: $\chi^2(701) = 1,254.48$; $p < .001$; GFI = .839; RMS = .089) was then confirmed on the second random half (family of origin: $\chi^2(701) = 1,266.05$; $p < .001$; GFI = .842; RMS = .090. Current family: $\chi^2(701) = 1,357.07$; $p < .001$; GFI = .829; RMS = .089). Factor intercorrelations for both scales are shown in Table 5.2.

Although we obtained a good fit for the primary dimensions, we were unable to reproduce the higher order structure postulated by Moos. Our findings will therefore be reported only with respect to Moos' primary dimensions.

Family Contact

As a measure of the intensity of family contact we asked respondents to indicate on a 5-point Likert scale the nature of their relationship (1 = close, 2 = somewhat close, 3 = in between, 4 = not close, 5 = not close at all), the number of years respondents and their relative had lived in the same household, and four 6-point Likert scales that assessed frequency of their physically visiting, talking on the telephone, writing letters, or obtaining news of their relative via a third

TABLE 5.2. Intercorrelation of Family Environment Scales (Family of Origin Above Diagonal, Current Family Below Diagonal)

	Cohesion	Express.	Conflict	Achievement Orientation	Intell. Cultural	Active- Recreational	Organiz.	Control
Cohesion		.860	.664	.372	.434	.524	.272	-.133
Expressivity	.837		.341	.339	.483	.515	.033	-.208
Conflict	.565	.323		.065	.161	.210	.256	-.286
Achievement- Orientation	.274	.239	.009		.430	.369	.333	.289
Intellectual- Cultural	.492	.562	.251	.234		.659	.056	-.130
Active-Recreational	.448	.453	.093	.445	.606		.138	-.038
Organization	.346	.235	.346	.234	.149	.186		.393
Control	-.013	-.121	-.155	.209	-.216	.006	.448	

party (1 = daily, 2 = every week, 3 = every month, 4 = every year, 5 = hardly ever, 6 = never). Item scores were reversed and summed to obtain a single contact score (a high score implying closeness and frequent contact).

RESULTS

We will first consider the similarity of perceptions in terms of intrapair correlations among parents and adult offspring and then examine the predictability of current family environments from knowledge of individuals' perception of their environment of origin, as well as their parent's perceptions. Similar data will be examined for sibling pairs. Next we consider the effect of perceived family environment on the frequency of contact among parent-offspring and sibling pairs. In a second section we consider the magnitude of (within-pair) intergenerational differences in perceptions of parental and current family environments.

Similarity of Family Environment Perceptions of Parents and Their Adult Offspring (Correlational Data)

Three sets of relationships can be considered: the correlations between family environment perceptions of the parents and offspring with respect to their family of origin and their current families, and the correlation of the offspring perception of their family of origin with their parent's perception of the parent's current family. The first two sets of relationships involve comparisons of the same life stage across generations, but representing different families for each generation. The third set of relationships is concerned with the perceived similarity of the family environment within the same family across generations. In comparing correlational patterns (magnitude of correlations) across generations, within life stages, and across different gender pairings, we employ a generalized maximum likelihood test (within LISREL VII) to test for statistical significance of differences between correlation patterns.

Family of Origin

For the total sample significant, but modest, correlations between parents and offspring where found for the dimensions of cohesion, expressivity, conflict, intellectual-cultural, organization and control (see Table 5.3). The highest overall correlation amounted to .294 for conflict. When analyzed separately by gender pairing, we note a significantly different pattern for the correlations for the father-daughter and mother-daughter combinations ($\chi^2[8] = 24.71$; $p < .01$). The relationships for cohesion and active-recreational orientation remain significant only for mothers and daughters, that for expressivity only between fathers and daughters, for intellectual-cultural orientation between mothers and their children (regardless of gender), and for organizational between fa-

TABLE 5.3. Correlation Between Parents and Offspring in their Perceptions of Family Environment in their *Family of Origin*

	Total Sample	Fathers/ Sons	Fathers/ Daughters	Mothers/ Sons	Mothers/ Daughters
Cohesion	.204***	.201	-.011	.191	.310***
Expressivity	.142*	.139	.268**	.088	.088
Conflict	.294***	.208*	.292**	.306**	.307***
Achievement Orientation	.093	.088	-.011	-.002	.206**
Intellectual-Cultural	.231***	.109	.177	.351***	.276***
Active-Recreational	.084	.043	.056	.036	.151*
Organization	.213***	.405***	.291***	.142	.119
Control	.151***	.230*	.244**	-.052	.154*

*$p < .05$; **$p < .01$; ***$p < .001$

thers and their children. The relationship for conflict holds for all gender pairings, whereas that for control holds for all except the mother-son pairings.

Current Family

Somewhat lower correlations are found when we compare our subjects' perceptions of their current families across the two generations. Overall, correlations

TABLE 5.4.   Correlation Between Parents and Offspring in their Perceptions of Family Environment in their *Current Family*

	Total Sample	Fathers/ Sons	Fathers/ Daughters	Mothers/ Sons	Mothers/ Daughters
Cohesion	.108*	.015	.106	.145	.147
Expressivity	.044	-.194	.038	.031	.172*
Conflict	.087	.094	.226*	.051	.023
Achievement Orientation	.098	-.083	-.047	.274**	.114
Intellectual- Cultural	.266***	.283**	.297**	.200*	.284***
Active- Recreational	.156**	.144	.090	.228*	.154*
Organization	.184**	.123	.178	.191	.233**
Control	.105*	-.092	.232*	.083	.131

*p <.05; **p <.01; ***p <.001

are significantly lower for the "current" correlations than the "origin" correlations for the fathers-sons ($X^2[8] = 17.71$; $p < .05$) and mothers-daughter ($X^2[8] = 12.46$; $p < .05$) combinations. However, here too significant overall correlations are observed for the dimensions of cohesion, intellectual-cultural, organization, and control (see Table 5.4). When gender pairings are considered, additional significant correlations are found for mothers and daughters on expressivity and for fathers and daughters on conflict. The relationship for achievement orientation remains significant only for mother-son pairings, for active-recreational orientation for mothers and their children (regardless of gender), for mothers and daughters on organization and for fathers and daughters on control. However, the correlational patterns do not differ significantly across pairings.

Similarity of Perceived Family Environment Across Generations

Here we inquire as to the magnitude of the relationship between the parents' current environment and their offsprings' perception of their family of origin. This is presumably the same family at different life stages, when the offspring were part of the parental family, and that same family is now in the post-parental phase. Even though the actual family composition has, of course, changed we found that correlations were substantially higher for this comparison, and statistically significant for the total sample for all dimensions (see Table 5.5). Statistically significant correlations were found also for all gender pairings for the intellectual-cultural, active-recreational, and organization and control dimensions. Significant correlations were found for same gender (father-son and mother-daughter) pairings for cohesion, and for all but mother-son pairings for conflict. Correlational patterns did not differ significantly by gender pairing. However, these correlations are significantly higher than those found for the family of origin ratings across the two generations ratings for the total sample ($\chi^2[8] = 31.38$; $p < .001$) as well as the father-son ($\chi^2[8] = 17.71$; $p < .05$, father-daughter ($\chi^2[8] = 15.51$; $p < .05$), mother-son ($\chi^2[8] = 22.88$; $p < .001$), and mother-daughter ($\chi^2[8] = 15.80$; $p < .05$) gender pairings. They are also significantly higher than the cross-generational correlations for their current families for the total sample ($\chi^2[8] = 30.87$; $p < .001$) and for the father-son ($\chi^2[8] = 29.95$; $p < .001$) gender pairing.

Similarity of Family Environment Perceptions of Siblings (Correlational Data)

In the case of the siblings comparisons were made within the same generation. However, it should be noted that for the siblings the family of origin ratings reflect perceptions of the same family at the same life stage, whereas ratings of the current family reflect membership in different families. Because of the small sample size for brother-brother pairings ($N = 28$) gender-specific data are reported only for the brother-sister and sister-sister pairings.

TABLE 5.5. Correlation Between Parents' Perception of their *Current Family* and Offsprings' Perception of their *Family of Origin*

	Total Sample	Fathers/ Sons	Fathers/ Daughters	Mothers/ Sons	Mothers/ Daughters
Cohesion	.207***	.305**	.178	.133	.242**
Expressivity	.101*	.007	.145	.072	.131
Conflict	.206***	.234*	.241*	.072	.230**
Achievement Orientation	.217***	.282**	.012	.257*	.263**
Intellectual- Cultural	.374***	.377***	.361***	.378***	.391***
Active- Recreational	.293***	.247*	.334***	.379***	.253***
Organization	.368***	.419***	.387***	.456***	.313***
Control	.194***	.228*	.185*	.225*	.184*

$*p < .05$; $**p < .01$; $***p < .001$

Family of Origin

Statistically significant correlations were found for all family dimensions, ranging from a low of .191 for achievement orientation to a high of .491 for intellectual-cultural. Correlational patterns did not differ significantly by gender pairings, and the correlational values remained significantly different from zero except for achievement orientation, which did not reach significance for the brother-sister pairs (see Table 5.6).

Current Family

The comparison of sibling perceptions of their current families yielded few significant correlations. Overall, low but significant correlations were found for the intellectual-cultural and organization dimensions. However, when broken by gender pairings, only the correlation between brothers and sisters for intellectual-cultural remained significant (see Table 5.7). Magnitudes of correlations for the perception of current families were significantly lower than for the family of origin for the total sample $(X^2[8] = 51.11; p < .001)$, as well as for the brother-sister $(X^2[8] = 30.96; p < .001)$ and sister-sister pairings $(X^2[8] = 21.87; p < .01)$.

Prediction of Offspring Perception of their Current Family Environment

We next consider to what extent parental perceptions of family environment, the offsprings' perception of the environment prevailing in their family and origin, as well as the extent of contact between offspring and parents impacts on the offsprings' perception of their current family environment. Table 5.8 provides the relevant β weights and multiple correlations. The magnitude of the relationship is highly significant, and between 20% to 25% of the variance in perceptions of current family environment can be accounted for. Note that the major significant predictor for each dimension of the current family environment turns out to be the corresponding dimension in the offsprings' perception of their family of origin. However, in each case there is one or more parental perception of their current or original family that contributes significantly to the variance in the offsprings' perception. Interestingly enough, however, frequency of contact with parents contributes little variance to these predictions (see Table 5.8).

Prediction of Contact Between Parents and Offspring

It would be interesting to know also whether perceptions of family environments of parents and offspring, both current and in their family of origin, influence their reports of frequency of intrapair contact. Reports of frequency of contact were provided by both parents and offspring. The offspring reported slightly more contacts than did their parents $(p < .05)$. The difference in reported contact by the two generations is greatest for the father-son pairings, but the greatest frequency of contact is reported by both parents and offspring for

TABLE 5.6. Correlation Between Siblings' Perception of their *Family of Origin*

	Total Sample	Brothers/Sisters	Sisters/Sisters
Cohesion	.390***	.427***	.370***
Expressivity	.251***	.277**	.220*
Conflict	.457***	.428***	.430***
Achievement Orientation	.169*	.119	.307**
Intellectual-Cultural	.491***	.486***	.473***
Active-Recreational	.366***	.301**	.381***
Organization	.414***	.430***	.489***
Control	.215**	.183*	.253*

*$p < .05$; **$p < .01$; ***$p < .001$

Note - Because of the small sample size, correlations are not reported for the brother/brother subset.

TABLE 5.7.   Correlation Between Siblings' Perception of their *Current Family*

	Total Sample	Brothers/Sisters	Sisters/Sisters
Cohesion	.072	-.013	..003
Expressivity	-.015	-.099	-.052
Conflict	.095	.098	.029
Achievement Orientation	.070	.059	.120
Intellectual-Cultural	.201**	.193*	.172
Active-Recreational	.099	.086	.103
Organization	.134*	.045	.146
Control	.015	.026	.028

*$p < .05$; **$p < .01$; ***$p < .001$

Note - Because of the small sample size, correlations are not reported for the brother/brother subset.

TABLE 5.8. Regression Analyses Predicting Offsprings' Perception of their Current Family Environment (β weights: $p < .05$)

	Cohesion	Express.	Conflict	Ach. Orient.	Intel. Cult.	Act. Recr.	Organ.	Control
Offspring Family of Origin								
Cohesion	.284						-.160	
Expressivity	.142		.367				.142	.167
Conflict				.383				-.157
Achievement Orientation					.271		-.130	
Intellectual-Cultural						.215		
Active-Recreational							.268	.302
Organization								
Control		.174						
Parent Family of Origin								
Cohesion		.169	-.154				-.169	
Expressivity								
Conflict						-.114		
Achievement Orientation								
Intellectual-Cultural								
Active-Recreational	.131		.134			.141	.110	
Organization								
Control								-.124
Parent Current Family								
Cohesion								
Expressivity								
Conflict		-.111					-.138	-.139
Achievement Orientation								
Intellectual-Cultural					.107			
Active-Recreational								
Organization								
Control								
Contact with Parent				.116		.101		
Multiple Correlation	**.392**	**.407**	**.434**	**.446**	**.431**	**.414**	**.478**	**.486**

the mother-daughter pairing. There is a significant correlation between contact reported by parents and offspring, but its magnitude ($r = .388$) is low enough to suggest that different aspects of family perception might influence contact as reported by parents and offspring. Frequency of specific types of contacts is provided in Figure 5.4.

Approximately 57% of the parents and 50% of the offspring describe the nature of their relationship as "very close." An additional 29% of the parents and 35% of the offspring describe it as "close." Nine percent of the parents and 11% of the offspring rated the relationship as "in between," whereas 3% of parent and offspring rated it as "somewhat close," and only 1.5% rated it as "not close at all."

Almost a fourth of the variance in contact can be predicted from perceptions of family environments. However, the only variable accounting for significant variance in common to parents and offspring is that of cohesion as rated for the parental family of origin (the grand-parental family for the offspring). The other significant predictors for the offspring reports of contact with parents are high cohesion in the offspring family of origin, high control in their current family, low achievement orientation in the parental family of origin, and low organization in the current parental family. By contrast, significant predictors for contact as reported by parents are low conflict and high active-recreational orientation in their families of origin, high cohesion and low expressivity in their current family, as well as high achievement and active-recreational orientation, low organization and high control in their offspring perception of the parental family (see Table 5.9).

Magnitude of Generational Differences in Perceptions of Family Environment

We now shift to the question as to differences in perceptions of family environment both within families across generations, and in the perception of differences between our study participants parental and current families. Because of the wide age range of our subjects, and to adjust for possible differences in the age span between individual parent-offspring pairs, we covaried on age of both parents and offspring. We used a MANCOVA design in which parental gender and offspring gender were the between-subject effects, generations (parents/offspring), and family stage (family of origin/current family) were treated as within-subject effects, with the family dimensions treated as dependent variables. Table 5.10 provides results of the overall MANCOVA which was then followed by univariate tests for the significant effects of interest. Main effects significant at or beyond the 5% level of confidence were obtained for gender of offspring,

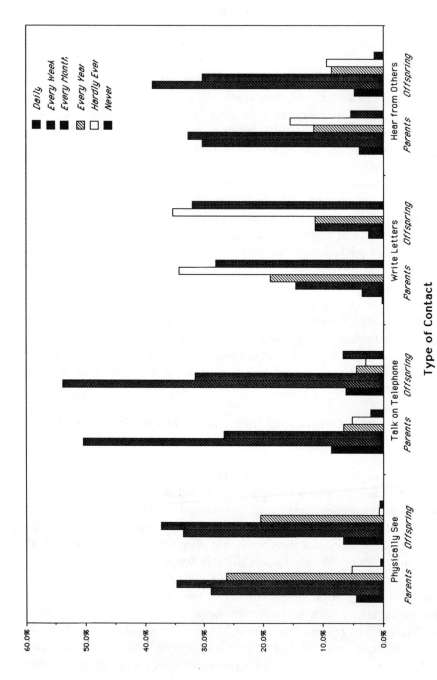

Figure 5.4. Frequency of contact between parents and offspring.

TABLE 5.9. Regression Analyses Predicting Parent-Offspring Contact (β weights: $p < .05$)

| | Contact as Perceived by | |
	Offspring	Parents
Parent Family of Origin		
Cohesion	.179	.251
Expressivity		
Conflict		-.148
Achievement Orientation	-.119	
Intellectual-Cultural		
Active-Recreational		.165
Organization		
Control		
Parent Current Family		
Cohesion		.159
Expressivity		-.146
Conflict		
Achievement Orientation		
Intellectual-Cultural		
Active-Recreational		
Organization	-.119	
Control		
Offspring Family of Origin		
Cohesion	.297	
Expressivity		
Conflict		
Achievement Orientation		
Intell ectual-Cultural		.115
Active-Recreational		.165
Organization		-.119
Control		.124
Offspring Current Family		
Cohesion		
Expressivity		
Conflict		
Achievement Orientation		
Intellectual-Cultural		
Active-Recreational		
Organization		
Control	.126	
Multiple Correlation	**.453**	**.451**

TABLE 5.10.   Multivariate Analysis of Variance of Family Environment Dimensions for Parental Gender, Offspring Gender, Generations and Life Stages

Effect	Rao's R
Parental Gender	.98
Offspring Gender	2.18*
Generations	32.91***
Family Stages	110.02***
Parental Gender x Offspring Gender	.72
Parental Gender x Generations	1.16
Parental Gender x Generations	1.91
Parental Gender x Family Stages	2.46**
Offspring Gender x Family Stages	1.52
Generations x Family Stages	8.47***
Parental Gender x Offspring Gender x Generations	.69
Parental Gender x Offspring Gender x Family Stages	.92
Parental Gender x Generations x Family Stages	2.46**
Offspring Gender x Generations x Family Stages 2.20*	
Parental Gender x Offspring Gender x Generations	
x Family Stages	1.25

*$p < .05$; **$p < .01$; ***$p < .001$; $df = 8,422$

generations, and family stage. Two-way interactions were significant for parental gender by family stage and for generations by family stage. Furthermore, there were significant three way interactions for parental gender by generations by life stage and for offspring gender by generations by life stage.

Univariate tests suggested that the main effect for offspring sex was significant only for the dimension of achievement orientation ($p < .01$), with men reporting a higher overall level of achievement orientation. The main effect for generations was significant for six dimensions ($p < .001$). The offspring reported lower overall levels of family cohesion, organization, and conflict, but greater achievement, intellect-cultural, and active-recreational orientation. The family stage main effects was also significant ($p < .001$) for all dimensions except achievement orientation. Higher levels of cohesion, expressivity, conflict, intellectual-cultural, and active-recreational orientation were reported for the current family, whereas a higher level of control was attributed to the family of origin.

The parental gender by family stage interaction was statistically significant for the cohesion ($p < .01$), conflict ($p < .05$), intellectual-cultural ($p < .01$), and organization ($p < .01$) dimensions. Mothers reported significantly lower cohesion and conflict for family of origin than for the current family. Their family of origin was also described as significantly lower in active-recreational orientation, and they reported greater control for the current family.

The generations by family stage interaction is of particular interest for our purposes. Here statistically significant effects were obtained for achievement orientation ($p < .001$), intellectual-cultural orientation ($p < .001$), and control ($p < .01$). Mean scores for these dimensions by generation and family stage are shown in Figure 5.5. Achievement orientation in the current family was rated significantly lower by the parents than the offspring. Not only is intellectual-cultural orientation rated lower for the family of origin, but it is rated lowest in the parents' family of origin. Level of control was reported to be greatest by the parents for their family of origin and about equally low for the current family of both generations.

Gender differences further complicate the findings with respect to generational/family stage differences in family perceptions. Significant triple interaction for parental gender by generations by family stage ($p < .01$) were found for the intellectual-cultural orientation, organization, and control. Intellectual-cultural orientation in their present family was perceived to be higher by mothers than by fathers; organization was perceived as greater in their current family by sons than by daughters; and control was seen to be greater in the current family by fathers than by mothers. A significant triple interaction for offspring gender by generations by family stage ($p < .001$) was found for expressivity. In the latter instance, daughters reported greater expressivity in their current family than did sons.

Cohort Differences in Perceptions of Family Environment

For a better understanding of possible shifts in intrafamily shifts in perceptions of family environments of successive cohorts, we repeated the preceding analyses

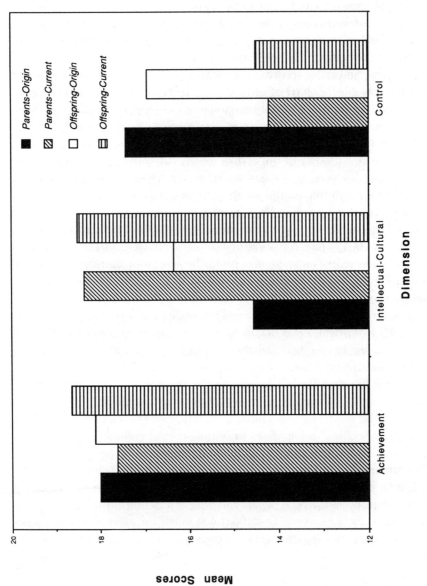

Figure 5.5. Interaction of perceived family environment by generation and life stage.

adding four levels of cohorts groupings. In terms of the years of birth of the off-spring these were those born before 1941, born between 1941 and 1947, 1948 and 1954, and between 1955 and 1968. Three significant interactions involving cohort grouping were found: cohort by family stage ($p < .01$), cohort by parental gender by family stage ($p < .05$), and cohort by generation by family stage ($p < .01$).

Significant univariate effects for the cohort by family stage interaction were found for cohesion ($p < .01$) and conflict ($p < .001$). Perceptions of both dimensions for the current family environment do not differ, but there is a linear decline for successive cohorts in perceptions of cohesion and conflict in the family of origin. With respect to the triple interaction of cohort by parental gender by family stage, significant univariate effects were found for expressivity ($p < .001$) and achievement orientation ($p < .05$). These effects seem to be accounted for primarily by significant drops in expressivity in the current family for the men in the most recent cohort with a concomitant significant increase for the women in that cohort. For achievement orientation, the effects reflect a slight but systematic drop for males in the family of origin and an increase for females in the current family. Finally, the triple interaction for cohort by generation by family stage was statistically significant ($p < .05$) for intellectual-cultural orientation and organization. The former effect reflects primarily a significant increase in intellectual-cultural orientation from the oldest to the youngest cohort within the family of origin. The latter reflects the fact that while there was a general decline in perceived family organization, this decline apparently reversed for the current families of the most recent cohort.

Magnitude of Differences in Family Perceptions Within Sibling Pairs

Differences in siblings' perceptions of family environment were analyzed with a MANCOVA design in which target and relative gender were the between effects, whereas target versus relative status and family stage (family of origin/current family) were treated as within effects, again with the family dimensions treated as dependent variables. Table 5.11 provides results of the overall MANCOVA which was followed by univariate tests for the significant effects of interest. Main effects significant at or beyond the 5% level of confidence were obtained for target versus relative status and family stage. A significant two-way interaction was found for target gender by status. None of the higher order interactions was statistically significant.

Univariate main effects for study status (i.e., whether the respondents were members of the longitudinal panel or their relatives were statistically significant for the dimensions of expressivity ($p < .01$), intellectual-cultural orientation

TABLE 5.11. Multivariate Analysis of Variance of Family Environment Dimensions for Taget Sibling Gender, Relative Sibling Gender, Target vs. Relative Status and Life Stages

Effect	Rao's R
Target Gender	1.32
Relative Gender	1.64
Status	2.96**
Family Stages	41.98***
Target Gender x Relative Gender	.95
Target Gender x Status	2.41*
Target Gender x Family Stages	.75
Relative Gender x Status	1.94
Relative Gender x Family Stages	.99
Status x Family Stages	1.70
Target Gender x Relative Gender x Status	.71
Target Gender x Relative Gender x Family Stages	1.88
Target Gender x Status x Family Stages	.98
Relative Gender x Status x Family Stages	1.00
Target Gender x Relative Gender x Status x Family Stages	1.65

*$p < .05$; **$p < .01$; ***$p < .001$; $df = 8,189$

($p < .05$), active-recreational orientation ($p < .01$), and control ($p < .01$). Our original study participants reported higher levels of expressivity, as well as intellectual-cultural, and active-recreational orientations across family of origin and current family than did their siblings. However, the relatives reported a higher overall level of control. As for the parent-offspring panel, siblings also reported significant differences in family environment between their family of origin and their current family for all dimensions. Higher levels of cohesion, expressivity, conflict, intellectual-cultural, and active-recreational orientation were reported for the current family, whereas achievement orientation, organization, and control were rated higher in the family of origin. The target gender by status orientation was only marginally significant for cohesion, with women from the longitudinal study reporting greater family cohesion than did the other groupings.

DISCUSSION AND CONCLUSIONS

Our past work has been concerned primarily with charting the course of intellectual competence across adulthood and to gain an understanding of the antecedent conditions that lead to so much individual variation in the maintenance of optimal levels of such competence. Search for these antecedents have led to systematic explorations of macroenvironmental and microenvironmental influences that might shape these individual differences (cf. e.g., Gribbin, Schaie, & Parham, 1980; Schaie & O'Hanlon, 1990; Schaie & Schooler, 1989). At the more psychological level they have also included inquiry into individuals' perceptions of their competence in mastering environmental challenges (cf. Schaie, Gonda, & Quayhagen, 1983; Scheidt & Schaie, 1978; Willis & Schaie, 1986). However, we have not previously dealt with the possible impact of our study participants' family environment on the maintenance of intellectual competence through adulthood.

The availability of a loyal panel of long-term research participants such as that in our longitudinal studies of adult competence simplifies the logistics of acquiring family data; hence, our successful effort to recruit good-size panels of adult offspring and siblings of our longitudinal study participants. However, when we began to consider the relevance of the SLS as a potential vehicle for behavior-genetic studies of family similarity it became apparent that although we had available to us extensive longitudinal data on cognitive performance, we had no direct measures of our study participants' family environments. Although one must always be careful in accepting the veracity of subjective data, particularly when it is retrospective in nature, there is substantial evidence of the utility of perceptions of behavioral dimensions (e.g., in the literature on personal efficacy in adults, e.g., Lachman, 1989), and we have previously obtained useful evidence on our own study participants' ability to retrospect on their prior performance in the cognitive area (Schaie, Willis, & O'Hanlon, 1994).

In earlier work with adolescent siblings, Plomin and Daniels (1987) had successfully employed a true-and-false derivative of the Moos and Moos (1986) family environment scales to assess perceptions of the common family environment. It seemed sensible, therefore, to employ these measures for our adult family studies. However, on closer review the materials in the original scales were deemed to be too lengthy, and we proceeded with the development of briefer forms that employed Likert scales and were also phrased in such a fashion as to be useful for the assessment of families of origin and current families. The psychometric work on these scales mentioned earlier suggested that we have maintained the dimensionality of the original family environment scales both for retrospective and current reports and have thus created appropriate instruments to obtain data relevant to the questions raised here.

What we have done then is to obtain evidence with respect to similarities and differences within and across generations in the perception of eight basic dimensions of family environment. Our data could have been arrayed in a variety of complex ways (for an alternative approach cf. Rossi, 1989). We elected to analyze data for our adult siblings with respect to within generation similarities and differences, and by studying parent-offspring pairs to determine these relations across generations. Moreover, for each of these analyses we contrast perceptions of the family of origin and current family (as a within subject variable). Because of the possibility of shifts in these relationships for successive cohorts, similar to those we have often reported for cognitive variables (cf. Schaie, 1990b), we also elected to include a cohort variable, classifying our offspring into those born before World War II, those born during the war years and immediately thereafter, and into the early and late baby boomers.

CONCLUSIONS

Our first and most dramatic conclusion is that there is a clear differentiation for parents, offspring, and siblings in the perceived level of all family dimensions between the family of origin and the current family. Obviously the distance in time was greater for the parents than for the offspring, a factor in part controlled by covarying on respondents' age. Nevertheless it seems clear that our respondents perceived shifts in the quality of family environments over their own life course. They see their current families as more cohesive and expressive, but also characterized by more conflict than was true for their families of origin. What these changes reflect, of course, may simply express generally greater openness and engagement in family interactions. More intensive family interactions may also be represented by the reported increase in intellectual-cultural and active-recreational orientation from the family of origin to the current family. Concomitant with these shifts as well is the overall perception of lower levels of perceived control, family organization, and achievement orientation. Perhaps these judgments are another way of the increasing complexity of modern American families (cf. Elder, 1981; Elder, Rudkin, & Conger, this volume; Hareven, 1982).

Combined with continuing reports of ever lower reported levels of social responsibility (cf. Schaie & Parham, 1974), this may well mean that the perceived role of the family is changing from that of a primary socialization agent (operating on behalf of the larger society) to a more effective support system for the needs of the individual family member. When our parent-offspring sample is broken down into four distinct cohort groups, we noted further that the shift in perceived family level occurred primarily for perceptions of the family of origin, with much greater stability for perceptions of the current family. This is reasonable because judgments of the current family occurred at one point in time, whereas judgments with respect to the family of origin necessarily reflected different secular periods for which successive cohorts described their early family experiences.

The second conclusion, with respect to within-family similarity in the perception of family environments is that siblings (and particularly sister-sister) pairs share substantial variance in the perception of their family of origin (i.e., the family that they shared in childhood and adolescence) over all family dimensions that we examined. However, this commonality does not extend to their perception of their current (nonshared) families. The only exception to this finding was a low correlation for intellectual cultural orientation and family organization. The reported similarity of early environments might support the contention that retrospective perceptions of families over a long time interval represent the validation of the veracity of these perceptions. Conversely, the shared variance may simply indicate currently shared (and perhaps idealized) perceptions about the childhood family. However, the lack of similarity between current environments might reflect the fact that siblings do not seem to seek out to replicate these early family environments.

Third, despite the lack of similarity of current family environments in siblings, we do find that the best predictor for the level of each dimension of the current family turns out to be the corresponding level reported by each person for their family of origin. Perhaps perceptions of the family environment of origin may be one of the factors entering into marital assortativity, even though such perceptions may differ for and may differentially affect the perceptions of current family environments by different siblings.

Fourth, supporting evidence for the continuity of family values and behaviors (cf. Bengtson, 1986) is provided by our finding of substantial correlations between the parents' description of their current family environment and their offsprings' description of their family of origin. Even though there is a substantial time gap in the period rated, these two ratings do refer to the same parental family unit. These relationships were particularly strong for the three dimensions most closely reflective of value orientations (achievement, intellectual-cultural, and active-recreational) and for family organization.

Fifth, differences in perceived family environment and the magnitude of similarity across generations will differ by gender pairing and by dimensions, although it is not surprising that the strongest relationships are observed within mother-daughter and sister-sister pairings, even though frequency of contact is only slightly greater than for other relationship combinations.

Sixth, we conclude that the intensity (frequency) of contact between parents and offspring has virtually no impact on the similarity of reported family environments. However, there were family environment dimensions (particularly level of cohesion) that could predict almost a fourth of the variance in the total family contact scores.

Finally, we suggest that the hierarchy of the magnitude of shared perceptions, from low correlations when describing nonshared environments, to moderately high correlations when describing commonly experienced environments provides at least indirect evidence for the contention that self-descriptions of family environments (perceptions) may well be useful indicators of the actually experienced environments.

We believe that in this chapter we have shown the viability of a system of describing family environments as they affect both within and across generation family similarity. As found earlier with respect to cognitive similarity, we were also able to show substantial shared variance with respect to the perceptions of the family of origin. This finding has important implications for behavior genetic studies, because it increases the plausibility of using retrospective perceptions as estimates of early shared environments. For the study of intergenerational continuity, our data support earlier literature (cf. Bengtson, 1975) that successive generations tend to evaluate their family environments in rather similar terms. Nevertheless, there is also strong evidence that perceived environments in the newly formed families of the offspring generation are not simply replications of their families of origin but may well represent the outcome of restructured family relations (cf. Green & Boxer, 1985). Hence, the perceived differences in family environments in the current families of successive generations, as well as the substantial differences reported within generations between the perceived environments in their families of origin and their current families extends the concept of developmental plasticity (Lerner, 1984) from the level of individual behavior to developmental plasticity in the value system ascribed to whole family units.

ACKNOWLEDGMENT

The research reported in this chapter is currently supported by Grant R37 AG08055 from the National Institute of Aging. We gratefully acknowledge the enthusiastic cooperation of members and staff of the Group Health Cooperative of Puget Sound. Thanks are due also to our coinvestigator Robert Plomin, and to Michael Cady, Jean Day, Walter Eden, Dean Melang, Cherill Perera, and Christine Roy, who ably assisted in the testing, and to Ann Gruber-Baldini, Ranjana Dutta, Heiner Maier, Scott Maitland, and Sherry Murr who assisted in the instrument development, data reduction, and analysis.

REFERENCES

Bengtson, V. L. (1975). Generation and family effects in value socialization. *American Sociological Review, 40*, 358–371.

Bengtson, V. L. (1986). Sociological perspective on aging, the family and the future. In M. Bergener (Ed.), *Perspectives on aging: The 1986 Sandoz lectures in gerontology.* New York: Academic Press.

Defries, J. C., Ashton, G. C., Johnson, R. C., Kusi, A. R., McClearn, G. E., Mi, M. P., Rashad, M. N., Vandenberg, S. G., & Wilson, J. R. (1976). Parent-offspring resemblance for specific cognitive abilities in two ethnic groups. *Nature, 261*, 131–133.

Elder, G. H., Jr. (1981). History of the family: The discovery of complexity. *Journal of Marriage and the Family, 43*, 489–519.

Green, A., L., & Boxer, A. M. (1985). Daughters and sons as young adults: Restructuring the ties that bind. In N. Data, A. Green, & H. Reese (Eds.), *Lifespan developmental psychology: Intergenerational relationships* (pp. 125–149). Hillsdale, NJ: Erlbaum.

Gribbin, K., Schaie, K. W., & Parham, I. A. (1980). Complexity of life style and maintenance of intellectual abilities. *Journal of Social Issues, 36*, 47–61.

Hareven, T. K. (1982). Family history at the crossroads. *Journal of Family History, 12*, ix–xxiii.

Jarvik, L. F., Blum, J. E., & Varma, A. O. (1971). Genetic components and intellectual functioning during senescence: A 20–year study of aging twins. *Behavior Genetics, 2*, 159–171.

Kallman, F. J., & Sander, G. (1949). Twin studies on senescence. *American Journal of Psychiatry, 106*, 29–36.

Lachman, M. E. (1989). Personality at the cross-roads: Beyond stability and change. In K. W. Schaie & C. Schooler (Eds.), *Social structure and aging: Psychological processes* (pp. 167–190). Hillsdale, NJ: Erlbaum.

Lerner, R. M. (1984). *On the nature of human plasticity.* New York: Cambridge University Press.

Moos, R. H. (1985). Context and coping: Toward a unifying conceptual framework. *American Journal of Community Psychology, 12*, 5–25.

Moos, R. H. (1987). *The Social Climate Scales: A user's guide.* Palo Alto, CA: Consulting Psychologists Press.

Moos, R. H., & Moos, B. (1986). *Family Environment Scale manual* (2nd ed). Palo Alto, CA: Consulting Psychologists Press.

Plomin, R. (1983). Developmental behavior genetics. *Child Development, 54*, 253–259.

Plomin, R. (1986). *Development, genetics, and psychology.* Hillsdale, NJ: Erlbaum.

Plomin, R., & Daniels, D. (1987). Why are two children in the same family so different from each other? *The Behavioral and Brain Sciences, 10,* 1–16.

Plomin, R., & McClearn, G. E. (1990). Human behavioral genetics of aging. In J. E. Birren & K. W. Schaie (Eds.), *Handbook of the psychology of aging* (3rd ed., pp. 67–78). New York: Academic Press.

Plomin, R., Pedersen, N. L., Nesselroade, J. R., & Bergeman, C. S. (1988). Genetic influence on childhood family environment perceived retrospectively from the last half of the life span. *Developmental Psychology, 24,* 738–745.

Rossi, A. S. (1989). A life-course approach to gender, aging and intergenerational relations. In K. W. Schaie & C. Schooler (Eds.), *Social structure and aging: Psychological processes* (pp. 207–229). Hillsdale, NJ: Erlbaum.

Rowe, D. C., & Plomin, R. (1981). The importance of nonshared (E1) environmental influences in behavioral development. *Developmental Psychology, 17,* 517–531.

Schaie, K. W. (1958). Rigidity-flexibility and intelligence: A cross-sectional study of the adult life-span from 20 to 70. *Psychological Monographs, 72,* No. 462 (Whole No. 9).

Schaie, K. W. (1983). The Seattle Longitudinal Study: A twenty-one year exploration of psychometric intelligence in adulthood. In K. W. Schaie (Ed.), *Longitudinal studies of adult psychological development* (pp. 64–135). New York: Guilford Press.

Schaie, K. W. (1988). Variability in cognitive function in the elderly: Implications for social participation. In A. Woodhead, M. Bender, & R. Leonard (Ed.), *Phenotypic variation in populations: Relevance to risk assessment* (pp. 191–212). New York: Plenum.

Schaie, K. W. (1989). The hazards of cognitive aging. *Gerontologist, 29,* 484–493.

Schaie, K. W. (1990a). Intellectual development in adulthood. In J. E. Birren & K. W. Schaie (Eds.), *Handbook of the psychology of aging* (3rd ed., pp. 291–310). New York: Academic Press.

Schaie, K. W. (1990b). Late life potential and cohort differences in mental abilities. In M. Perlmutter (Ed.), *Late life potentials* (pp. 43–61). Washington, DC: Gerontological Society of America.

Schaie, K. W., Gonda, J. N., & Quayhagen, M. (1983). The relationship between intellectual performance and perceived every-day competence across adulthood. In H. Löwe, U. Lehr, & J. E. Birren (Eds.), *Psychologische Probleme des Erwachsenenalters* [Psychological problems of adulthood] (pp. 43–67). Berlin: VEB Deutscher Verlag der Wissenschaften.

Schaie, K. W., & Hertzog, C. (1986). Toward a comprehensive model of adult intellectual development: Contributions of the Seattle Longitudinal Study. In R. J. Sternberg (Ed.), *Advances in human intelligence* (Vol. 3, pp. 79–118). Hillsdale, NJ: Erlbaum.

Schaie, K. W., Labouvie-Vief, G. (1974). Generational versus ontogenetic components of change in adult cognitive behavior: A fourteen year cross-sequential study. *Developmental Psychology, 10,* 151–156.

Schaie, K. W., & O'Hanlon, A. M. (1990). The influence of social-environmental factors in the maintenance of adult intelligence. In R. Schmitz-Scherzer, A. Kruse, & E. Olbrich (Eds.), *Altern – Ein lebenslanger Prozess der Sozialen Interaktion* [Aging – A lifelong process of social interaction] (pp. 55–66). Darmstadt: Steinkopf Verlag.

Schaie, K. W., & Parham, I. A. (1974). Social responsibility in adulthood: Ontogenetic and sociocultural change. *Journal of Personality and Social Psychology, 30,* 483–492.

Schaie, K. W., Plomin, R., Willis, S. L., Gruber-Baldini, A., & Dutta, R. (1992). Natural cohorts: Family similarity in adult cognition. In T. Sonderegger (Ed.), *Psychology and aging: Nebraska Symposium on Motivation, 1991* (pp. 205–243). Lincoln, NE: University of Nebraska Press.

Schaie, K. W., Plomin, R., Willis, S. L., Gruber-Baldini, A. L., Dutta, R., & Bayen, U. (1993). Family similarity in adult intellectual development. In J. J. F. Schroots (Ed.), *Aging, health and competence: The next generation of longitudinal research* (pp. 183–198). Amsterdam, The Netherlands: Elsevier.

Schaie, K. W., & Schooler, C. (Eds.) (1989). *Social structure and aging: Psychological processes.* Hillsdale, NJ: Erlbaum.

Schaie, K. W., & Strother, C. R. (1968). A cross-sequential study of age changes in cognitive behavior. *Psychological Bulletin, 70,* 671–680.

Schaie, K. W., Willis, S. L., & O'Hanlon, A. M. (1994). Perceived intellectual performance change over seven years. *Journal of Gerontology: Psychological Sciences, 49*(3).

Scheidt, R. J., & Schaie, K. W. (1978). A taxonomy of situations for the elderly population: Generating situational criteria. *Journal of Gerontology, 33,* 848–857.

Thurstone, L. L. (1938). *The primary mental abilities.* Chicago: University of Chicago Press.

Willis, S. L. (1989). Cohort differences in cognitive aging: A sample case. In K. W. Schaie & C. Schooler (Eds.), *Social structure and aging: Psychological processes* (pp. 94–112). Hillsdale, NJ: Erlbaum.

Willis, S. L., & Schaie, K. W. (1986). Practical intelligence in later adulthood. In R. J. Sternberg & R. K. Wagner (Eds.), *Practical intelligence: Origin of competence in the everyday world* (pp. 236–268). New York: Cambridge University Press.

Commentary: Generational Shifts in Family Environments: Perceived *and* Real?

Christopher Hertzog

I begin my comments on Schaie's chapter with a premise: We know surprisingly little about the causes of age-related changes in intelligence across the human life span. To be sure, there have been studies of age differences and age changes in intelligence for more than seven decades (see Jones, 1959; Schaie, 1983); although some controversies remain, the description of age-related patterns in fundamental dimensions of intelligence, as defined by traditional psychometric measures, has in large measure been accomplished. Why, then, has there been relatively slow progress in understanding the antecedents of intellectual growth and decline?

Part of the problem is that psychologists have devoted more energy to cognitive and intellectual variables, but, comparatively, relatively little attention to important classes of potential antecedent variables. Often, the explanations that psychologists interested in aging and intelligence offer for age changes in intelligence are actually what I consider attempts to refine and clarify the dependent variable—intelligence—in terms of basic cognitive operations and information-processing requirements for complex thinking. Salthouse's important work in the relationship of basic information processing resources and reasoning ability (see Salthouse, 1991) is an interesting and telling case in point. Explanations for age changes in complex reasoning are reduced to contributions of different classes of cognitive resources, like attention, working memory, and information-processing speed. Salthouse and others like him, including myself (e.g., Hertzog, 1989a) typically do not seek to investigate the antecedent causes of changes in these kinds of cognitive mechanisms, probably owing in part to the meta-theoretical assumption that the next layer of antecedent variables is to be pursued at other levels of explanation, like biological aging and age-related patterns of disease.

Certainly there are longitudinal studies examining some of the relationships between antecedent variables and intellectual change, including work from Schaie's SLS (e.g., Schaie, 1983). Most studies do not, however, do justice to the full range of important social variables that potentially shape the course of both intellectual growth and decline across the human life span (Baltes, 1993). Historically, these studies have focused more on health-related factors than on other classes of explanatory variables. The most notable exceptions to this generalization can be found in the work often presented in this continuing conference series (e.g., Schooler & Schaie, 1987), and certainly the SLS project itself is one of the more important exceptions.

Schaie's chapter begins the process of applying techniques from human behavior genetics to the study of intellectual level and change in his SLS. I am far from an expert in the analysis of family environments using these techniques, so I will not attempt to elaborate on the theoretical treatment provided by Schaie as background for the problem. The basic premise seems clear: To understand how variation in environments influences the initial growth and constrains patterns of change in adulthood, we need to measure the environmental variation. The family environment is one principal source of such variation, among others (such as the environments that lead to crystallization of life course trajectories in early adulthood; Mumford & Owens, 1985).

Schaie's initial analyses of the Moos Family Environment Scale (FES) in the SLS are interesting and provocative. The chapter contains several important findings: (a) demonstrated factorial validity of the scale, providing support for the conceptualization of dimensions of family environment that may be predictively useful in understanding intellectual change; (b) data on level of agreement regarding reported environmental circumstances between siblings and parents; and (c) cross-sectional patterns or trends in reported environmental circumstances. I will consider each of these briefly in turn.

FACTORIAL VALIDITY OF THE FES

Although presented in abbreviated form, the evidence that Schaie reports on the factor analyses of his revised version of the FES is important, because it supports the claim that differentiable dimensions of perceived family environments can be identified by confirmatory factor analysis. Having said that, the scale intercorrelations, reported in Table 5.2, are some cause for concern about whether all eight dimensions are sufficiently differentiated to use all subscales in future analyses predicting intellectual functioning from family environmental scales. For example, one would expect muticollinearity problems if both cohesion and expressivity were used as predictors, given that the two scales correlate .84 with each other. It would clearly be desirable to reduce the set of family environment measures further if that is possible, at least for some future analyses, but that reduction should reflect theoretically meaningful relationships.

Schaie mentions that he could not replicate Moos's model for higher order dimensions in the FES but provides no data about what an appropriate higher order structure might be. Solving this problem will be a necessary additional step before extensive use of the scales in predicting intelligence. Crude eyeballing of the correlations in Table 5.2 suggests rough correspondence of the scale correlations with the three factors suggested by Moos: relationship, personal growth, and system maintenance, but there are some important deviations of correlations from what would be expected if these three second-order dimensions fully accounted for the relationships. That is, the highest correlations are for scales within these three subsets, but there are also a few high correlations (e.g., the .56 correlation of expressivity with intellectual-culture) that are disproportionally larger than what would be expected if these three higher order factors accounted for all of the information contained in the scale correlations.

My own experience with this kind of hierarchical factor analysis suggests that there are two important and distinct issues to differentiate: (a) cross-scale contamination of item content, leading to embedded interrelationships between items that should, by theory, be associated with different subscales; and (b) specific additional interrelationships among first-order scale dimensions that are inconsistent with a pure higher order model. Hierarchical confirmatory item factor analysis is clearly superior to exploratory factor analysis precisely because one can directly model these sources of "perturbations" in the model in terms of two kinds of residual covariances (item specific, scale factor specific). Occasionally item factor structures have a clean, simple structure—an excellent example is the CES-D depression scale (e.g., Hertzog, Van Alstine, Usala, Hultsch, & Dixon, 1990). Unfortunately, it is probably more often the case that factor structure is quite a bit messier than would be expected from a literature based on exploratory factor analyses—as Blanchard-Fields, Suhrer-Roussel, and Hertzog (in press) recently discovered when we analyzed gender difference in the factor structure of the Bem Sex Role Inventory. Either way, hierarchical confirmatory factor analysis is the clear method of choice for identifying appropriate higher order structures among item factors (see Hertzog, 1989b). Schaie's use of this technique is therefore commendable. Gerontologists interested in using the revised FES will want to attend carefully to the details of Schaie's analysis of the new scale when they are available.

An additional construct validity issue that needs to be addressed in further analyses of the SLS data is the discriminant validity of family environment dimensions from other social address variables, including socioeconomic status and education. One could argue that the subscales that belong to the personal growth subset of Table 5.2 ought to relate highly to educational attainment and socioeconomic status, and it will be important to demonstrate, in the short run, that (a) these constructs are not merely alternative measures of these status variables, and, in the long run, that (b) the relationship to factors such as educational attainment can be attributed to processes of intergenerational transmission of values that shape behaviors leading to educational and social status attainment. One will also want to determine whether the family environment variables have any predictive value for intellectual attainment above and beyond the level of prediction from education and social status by themselves.

CONSISTENCIES AND INCONSISTENCIES IN PERCEIVED FAMILY ENVIRONMENT

Schaie presents a complex (even bewildering!) array of correlations that show relationships between ratings of family of origin and current family for parents and sibs in pairwise combinations. Schaie argues that the pattern of correlations is consistent with the argument that the self-reports, even though retrospective in nature, are valid. And, indeed, the pattern he finds suggests that common sources of variance influence some ratings and not others. Sibling correlations of rated family environment scales concerning one's current family are relatively modest (these are the different families of siblings). The same siblings show much higher correlations in rating family of origin (which is the same family). Likewise, parent ratings of current family correlate significantly, for at least some scales, with offspring ratings of family of origin.

Although this pattern does suggest some common sources of variance, there are two general points I would like to make here. First, many of the significant correlations are not actually all that high (see Tables 5.3 to 5.6). Second, there are multiple possible explanations for the pattern of agreement and disagreement across sets of correlations. In particular, one may get agreement because persons are rating objective characteristics of the family environment. Alternatively, one may get agreement because persons share perceptions of the family environment that are not necessarily accurate. Perceptions of family environments may reflect both subjective and objective reality. I will return to this point in a moment.

How do we explain the fact that most significant correlations between scales across the tables hover in the .2 to .4 range? One possible explanation is attenuation due to random measurement error in the FES, and it will be important at some point for Schaie to estimate disattenuated correlations to evaluate this possibility. However, there are also other factors that may limit the magnitude of the observed correlations. I will highlight a couple.

First, it does not appear that participants were provided with specific time frames within which to rate the family of origin. This leave open the possibility that the family of origin as rated by the parents represents a different functional epoch in the family's history than the epoch rated by a sibling. Family environments are probably not static entities, but shift as a function of parental roles outside the home (the professor with and without tenure comes immediately to mind), different constellations of children (in terms of number and ages), changes in relationships between family members as children progress through different developmental periods, and the like. The study as designed neither captures nor controls for these kinds of dynamic shifts in the family environment. For example, the child, especially in a multiple offspring family, may be thinking of the family at the point in history where the oldest child was 10 years old, but the parent is thinking of the same family unit when the oldest child was 20. To the extent that the family environment differed between these two epochs, agreement in rated environments would be reduced. Alternatively, of course, these ratings might be based on some global, aggregated sense of family taken across the entire epoch of family history, but it may be the case that parents and siblings views will diverge because of different developmental levels of the raters at a given point in historical time.

I should be careful here to point out that I'm not suggesting that the data collected by Schaie is necessarily invalid because it does not attend directly to the issue of dynamics in family development. Indeed, to the extent that certain aspects of family environment are highly stable over time, then there is little cost of the approach used in this study. The limited empirical correlations, in terms of empirical agreement, force us to consider this explanation, and a refinement of the method to consider the issue of the dynamics of family development may be necessary to triangulate optimally on aspects of family environment that may be important for assessing intellectual development.

Second, the study design involved an interesting definition of current family. For adults who lived by themselves, current family could be defined as those individuals constituting the primary reference group (or proximal social network). Although the motives for this approach are clear and justifiable, one wonders the extent to which the alternative definition of current family may have affected the correlations. One way to examine this issue is to assess the data without persons having no other cohabiting family members.

With respect to the issue of multiple interpretations of the patterns of correlations, consider the fact that siblings demonstrate a higher degree of concordance in rating the family of origin than do the parents and offspring. This may not be surprising if one pauses to consider that siblings often share perspectives on the family (both when they are children and later when they are adults) to which the parents have no access. Parents may be unaware of children's attitudes regarding the family context and vice versa. This reinforces the concept that the scales of the FES may validly reflect perceptions of family environments, and these perceptions may differ across family members.

Schaie acknowledges the fact that these self-reports may reflect perceptions, not "objective reality," about family environments and argues that such perceptions are useful. I totally agree. My colleagues and I have been interested for some time in the relationships of perceived memory ability to actual memory ability in older adults, in part because we believe that perceptions may be as important as objective abilities in determining some aspect of behavior in memory-demanding situations (Hertzog, Dixon, & Hultsch, 1990). In fact, much of our work has focused on demonstrating that measures of self-reported memory functioning may be construct-valid measures of individuals' beliefs about memory that are not necessarily accurate. Ultimately it will be important, however, for research in this area to differentiate between current beliefs about how the family environment was versus beliefs about the family environment during the formative years of the offspring. For an interesting demonstration that current ratings of past personal characteristics are influenced by present conditions and beliefs, see Ross (1989).

COHORT PATTERNS IN SELF-REPORTED FAMILY ENVIRONMENTS

Conversely, Schaie's interesting analyses of generational differences in family environments suggest to him that there have been cultural shifts in the nature of family environments. This set of results is indeed promising, because it sets up the argument that the differences in family environments do produce generational effects in social contexts that could, in principle, have an impact on generational differences in intellectual development. This is important, for I would argue that the perceived family environments are most relevant, and perhaps only relevant, to the study of adult intellectual development to the extent that they actually reflect (albeit imperfectly) either (a) objective characteristics of family environments that may have shaped individual development or (b) a child's perceptions of the family environment that could have actually influenced a child's intellectual development. I would further argue that the objective characteristics of the family environment are likely to be the more important set of potential influences. In any event, assessing and analyzing the nature of current, inaccurate perceptions of the past family environment might be crucial for some purposes (e.g., counseling individuals in dysfunctional marriages), but it is difficult to imagine how such perceptions could have altered the course of intellectual development. Thus one will be most interested in the FES data if subsequent work can provide additional evidence that rated family environments do reflect, at least to a moderate degree, the actual family environment.

Schaie is appropriately circumspect about the limits of interpreting self-reports of this kind, but he does offer some tentative interpretations of effects in terms of generational shifts in experienced family environments. I will not comment directly on the potential validity of Schaie's interpretations of these effects (e.g., greater openness and engagement in family interactions in recent history). It will be fascinating to see what additional inferences can, in principle, be drawn from the complex patterns of effects he reports, and the degree to which variation in family environments covaries with generational differences in intelligence.

To conclude, Schaie is to be congratulated for embarking on a major expansion of the set of antecedent variables that can now be addressed in the SLS. I, for one, look forward with great enthusiasm to the next series of analyses he mentions in his chapter. If we are to explain age and cohort effects in intelligence, we certainly must have the kind of thinking and empirical inquiry into classes of antecedent conditions that is reflected in this chapter. Schaie has taken a promising initial step in the direction of measuring the family context.

REFERENCES

Baltes, P. B. (1993). The aging mind: Potential and limits. *The Gerontologist, 33,* 580–594.

Blanchard-Fields, F., Suhrer-Roussel, L., & Hertzog, C. (in press). A confirmatory factor analysis of the Bem Sex Role Inventory: Old questions, new answers. *Sex Roles*.

Hertzog, C. (1989a). The influence of cognitive slowing on age differences in intelligence. *Developmental Psychology, 25,* 636–651.

Hertzog, C. (1989b). Using confirmatory factor analysis for scale development and validation. In M. P. Lawton & A. R. Herzog (Eds.), *Special research methods for gerontology* (pp. 281–306). New York: Baywood Press.

Hertzog, C., Dixon, R. A., & Hultsch, D. F. (1990). Metamemory in adulthood: Differentiating knowledge, belief, and behavior. In T. M. Hess (Ed.), *Aging and cognition: Knowledge organization and utilization* (pp. 161–212). Amsterdam: North Holland.

Hertzog, C., Van Alstine, J., Usala, P. D., Hultsch, D. F., & Dixon, R. A. (1990). Measurement properties of the Center for Epidemiological Studies of Depression Scale (CES-D) in older populations. *Psychological Assessment: A Journal of Consulting and Clinical Psychology, 2*, 64–72.

Jones, H. E. (1959). Intelligence and problem solving. In J. E. Birren (Ed.), *Handbook of aging and the individual* (pp. 700–738). Chicago, IL: University of Chicago Press.

Mumford, M. D., & Owens, W. A. (1985). Individuality in a developmental context: Some empirical and theoretical considerations. *Human Development, 27*, 84–108.

Ross, M. (1989). Relation of implicit theories to the construction of personal histories. *Psychological Review, 96*, 341–357.

Salthouse, T. A. (1991). *Theoretical perspectives on cognitive aging.* Hillsdale, NJ: Erlbaum.

Schaie, K. W. (Ed.). (1983). *Longitudinal studies of adult psychological development.* New York: Guilford Press.

Schooler, C. & Schaie, K. W. (1987). *Cognitive functioning and social structure over the life course.* New York: Academic Press.

Commentary:
The Life-Course Approach to Perceived Family Environments

John C. Henretta

The chapter by K. Warner Schaie and Sherry L. Willis on "Perceived Family Environments Across Generations" raises conceptually important questions concerning the extent to which shared family environments exist and the mechanisms that produce within-family uniformity or variation. This issue is also a central concern of sociologists who work in the life-course framework; hence, this discussion addresses sociological approaches to understanding similarities and differences in family environments as they are both experienced and perceived by family members across generations.

The life-course approach offers a conceptual account for three central issues. First, should we expect family members to reproduce their family of origin in their own families? Sociologists working in the status attainment tradition have long been interested in the intergenerational transmission of status and have found heterogeneity in outcome among family members. Family origin is only moderately constraining. In the life-course tradition, this moderate correlation arises from the nature of event linkages across time. Second, do family members of the same generation share the same environment in their family of origin? The answer focuses on the trajectory of events originating inside and outside the family that have variable effects, partly because of their timing and sequence in the lives of individual family members. Third, are there systematic time-based processes that create divergence between true and perceived environments? The life-course approach provides an account of subjective reconstruction of events that accompanies individual agency in the developmental process.

The distinctive sociological contribution is the life-course conceptualization of the intersection of family-based and institutionally based social structure that impinges on the individual and has variable effects in individual lives dependent on sequence and timing. Hence, family environment reports need to be anchored in time and a changing social and family context. In developing this idea, I first discuss the central ideas of the life-course framework relating to structural linkages within individuals and families. I then return to the questions outlined earlier and discuss the distinct life-course–related processes that may be relevant for understanding actual and perceived family environments.

LIFE-COURSE APPROACH TO INDIVIDUAL LIVES

The life-course approach to individual lives examines development and change by focusing on the age-graded timing, sequence, and character of events across interrelated domains of life. The approach embeds individual lives in their historical context by examining the effect of changing social structure on individuals. Population structure, the institutions of the state and workplace, and general sociocultural change (Featherman & Lerner, 1985; Henretta, 1992) produce changing age-graded social structures. Historical events, such as higher unemployment rates, are not experienced evenly (Elder & O'Rand, 1994); hence, the institutional life course may be experienced in highly variable ways.

A second source of life-course programs arises from individual agency. In this biographical perspective, individuals are active in their own lives. They interpret their actions and choose among structurally defined alternatives in a way that alters probabilities of events (Featherman & Lerner, 1985; Kohli, 1986a, 1986b). Combining these two approaches, development does not simply occur within a uniform social and historical context; rather, individual development and a variable social context interact over time in complex ways (Featherman, 1986).

The life-course perspective contains elements that are highly consequential for theory. The central aspect with theoretical import is focus on the effects of distal as well as proximal events. The linkage between past and present events is conceptualized as arising from event sequence, with the probability distribution of later events contingent on the pattern of earlier events. Event order and timing is important because earlier events both constrain probabilities of later events and affect their meaning and significance. This sequential, contingent approach is highly consistent with a relatively open view of development because continuity is produced by the linkages between events, not by permanent or fixed characteristics of individuals. Continuity over time arises from cumulative constraints of earlier transitions and from a nonrigid social structure that allows individuals to choose compatible transitions (Elder & O'Rand, 1994).

Both conceptual and empirical research within this tradition reinforces the openness of development. Conceptually, recent focus on the "deinstitutionalization" of the life-course in which state and workplace programs are less restrictive (Henretta, 1992) opens a greater field for individual action. Empirically, life-course research has demonstrated that the behavioral ordering of major individual transition events such as completion of schooling, marriage, starting work, and early family formation (e.g. Hogan, 1981; Rindfuss, Swicegood, & Rosenfeld, 1987) is highly variable. Findings such as these challenge oversocialized perspectives on life transitions (George & Gold, 1991).

The life-course view is a highly structural view of human lives in that continuity arises from linkages between events occurring at a particular individual and historical time. Hence, at least conceptually, the correlations between states at different times may be understood as resulting from microlevel linkages. The life-course approach shares many elements with the earlier status attainment approach in sociology because both examine the links between early and late life. The life-course approach goes beyond the correlational approach in its greater focus on the transitions, mechanisms, and timing of events that link states across time. Moreover, it is more focused on the historical context that alters the nature of age-graded transitions.

FAMILY AS A LINKING MECHANISM

For the individual, the family is an additional domain with an event sequence that is interrelated with other domains. Yet, the family is structurally complex because it ties together the interdependent life histories of its members (Elder, 1978). For example, research on retirement timing demonstrates the interconnection between work and family domains, with both proximal and distal family states creating links between husband's and wife's retirement timing (e.g., Henretta, O'Rand, & Chan, 1993).

The increasing length of life means family linkages must be conceptualized more broadly than just among spouses and their minor children since multiple generation families create patterns of reciprocal influence (Bengtson, Rosenthal, & Burton. 1990). An excellent example is work by Vern Bengtson and his colleagues (Glass, Bengtson, & Dunham, 1986) with three generation families in which they conceptualize attitudes as arising from individual states (e.g., employment) but with reciprocal effects across generations.

Simple focus on cohort demographic shifts is inadequate in understanding family cross-generational influence because within-cohort variability in mother's age at childbearing produces variability in existence of multiple-generation families (George & Gold, 1991) and likely affects family environment. Age at childbearing affects generational structure of the family, economic status of parents, and may affect parental values through age-graded involvement in occupational contexts (e.g., Kohn & Schooler, 1983) when children are young.

Family environments need not be constant over time. Events external or internal to the family occur at different times, affecting children of different ages in diverse ways. For example, an extended span of childbearing may alter the family economic status level experienced by later children. Many other family changes occur: children leave home; children or parents experience problems in their individual lives; grandparents enter or leave the household; the family experiences economic problems, or is reconstituted through divorce, death, and remarriage. Hence, the complex pattern of event timing will produce variation in the family experience of children in the same family.

Sociologists have long been interested in the intergenerational transmission of status in families. Correlational approaches usually show moderate correlations over time and across generations. This pattern implies an attenuation of the relationship from the origins of the first generation to the destination of the second (O'Rand, 1990) and implies divergence between family members. A simple empirical example is helpful in establishing this point. In one study of fraternal resemblance, observed correlations between brothers' attainments were about .400 for years of schooling and .265 for occupational status 18 years after high school graduation (Hauser & Mossel, 1985). Though siblings are anchored in the same family of origin, their relative status diverges over time.

The life-course approach provides a conceptual account of the linkages across generations and the attenuation of relationships over time. As within the life course of one individual, the mechanism is the sequential and contingent nature of transitions that link states across time, with great variability in the timing, order, and character of events resulting from variable effects of institutional schedules, family events, individual agency, and the "loose coupling" (Elder & O'Rand, 1994) between events.

Loose coupling hypothesizes a nonrigid social structure governing transitions in which timing and type of transition are only weakly predetermined. This characteristic is a social structural requisite for variation in family and institutional events or individual agency to produce variability in outcome. Social class boundaries provide a good example. Families may be roughly grouped into categories of social class that imply differing probabilities for specific transitions in domains such as educational attainment and occupational choice. The degree to which social class constrains transition probabilities is defined by the rigidity of social class boundaries. For example, in a caste-like social structure, one might expect high correlations between siblings' schooling and occupational levels—and, hence, their adult social environments including dimensions of family achievement motivation and intellectual-cultural orientation.

Because social structure in industrial societies is generally less rigid than caste-like social class, origins have weak to moderate links with destinations. An important application of this general perspective that combines effects of historical and family events is Glen Elder and his colleagues' work on intergenerational transmission of problem behavior (Elder, Caspi, & Downey, 1986). The authors find that problem behavior is transmitted to children, though the effects are moderate in size. The link between parent and child is the proximate environment of the child. Two findings from this research are particularly instructive to this explication of the life-course framework for studying family relationships. First, the relation between parent's and child's behavior is conditioned by both historical context and the intertwining of two parents' life histories. The long-term effects of family environment are contingent; for example, unemployment occurs unevenly, and its effects are mediated by parental resourcefulness. Second, the adult implications of childhood problem behavior are conditioned by occupational status in adulthood. These contingent linkages produce an attenuated link between parent's and child's problem behavior with increasing time.

APPLYING THE LIFE-COURSE PERSPECTIVE TO UNDERSTANDING FAMILY ENVIRONMENTS ACROSS GENERATIONS

What are the conceptual linkages in the life-course framework that might tie together perceived family environment over time? Perceptions are some mixture of "true" environment plus the effects of perceptual processes. Understanding them requires that we both focus on conceptual models for true environments and perceptions. The life-course perspective may be used to understand three issues: the level of correlation between siblings' current perceived environments, siblings' agreement on the environment of their family of origin, and the role of perceptual processes in determining perceived family environments.

Linkages Between Siblings' Current Environments

The data show fairly weak correlations between siblings' current perceived environments. In line with the earlier discussion of intergenerational transmission, the family of origin provides an anchor point. From this point, individual development proceeds through events in several domains including choice of schools, occupation, peer group, marital partner, and childbearing. The loose coupling between events ensures that individuals from the same family may drift apart as they make choices consistent with their developing temperament and goals within the context of a constraining social structure that offers varying opportunities to different family members. The life-course approach understands the low correlation between siblings' current family environments as resulting from this sequential, contingent movement between states. This conceptual account is consistent with the correlational model. For example, in a simple model in which the only link between siblings is their common family environment, a moderate correlation between environment and each child's characteristic implies a weak correlation between siblings.

The types of events that one might examine probably differ across the dimensions of family environment. The possible linkages across generations in intellectual-cultural environment might arise in the sequential and contingent transitions to school, peer group, college, as well as to adult peer group and mate selection. Given the relatively weak correlations, it is particularly important to ask whether they may arise simply from the broad social class context that is likely to be shared by siblings.

Though the data suggest they do not affect Schaie and Willis's findings, other factors potentially increase correlations. Individuals may not simply select transitions in line with their preferences, but they may interact with siblings differentially. Any tendency of family members to grow apart if they are dissimilar may be reflected in the panel members' willingness to provide particular children's names and the children's willingness to volunteer. The same processes of life-course contingent transitions discussed earlier leads to the expectation that friendship and contact among adult members of a family will be partly contingent on their having followed similar pathways through life, leading to more similar values—and, hence, environment. Schaie and Willis's analysis explores the possibly confounding selection factor between parents and children by measuring current contact. Among those who participated in the study, level of contact does not predict similarity between parents and children.

Agreement Among Siblings on the Family of Origin Environment

It is important to introduce both family and historical time into the examination of environments in the family of origin. Children in the same family share some aspects of environment, but as discussed earlier, external events may produce variability over time with diverse effects on different children. The variability in family environments over time is a question for empirical research, but it is unlikely that it can be captured in a retrospective design. Retrospective sociological research on the life-course usually focuses on events such as leaving school or getting married. These events may be dated using event calendars (Freedman, Thornton, Camburn, Alwin, & Young-DeMarco, 1988), though recall of less central life events involves relatively large amounts of error (Clogg, 1986).

Though siblings share families, Schaie and Willis make the point they do not necessarily share common environments. Families both change over time and are experienced differently by different persons as a result of these changes. The life-course framework provides a conceptual approach to understanding this environmental variability, and it is a compelling area for research.

Perceived Environments

Third, in focusing specifically on the measurement of perceived environment, it is important to consider the biographical processes implied in the life-course framework. These are central in producing intraindividual continuity and inter-individual heterogeneity. Individuals participate in their own development by choosing environments compatible or different from current ones, and they interpret the meaning and significance of earlier and current states (Kohli, 1986a, 1986b). Hence, the structure and timing of transitions are partly the result of individuals' intentions based on their views of themselves. Subjective constructions of current events and reconstructions of past events help make sense of one's previous life (Breytspraak, 1984); measuring perceived family environments implies measuring the outcome of this subjective process.

Processes of reminisce or reconstruction are often initiated by important life-course transitions (Breytspraak, 1984) that require interpretation. For example, in raising her own children, a woman constantly recalls and reinterprets interactions with parents. Current events affect past reconstructions, and may reduce agreement among family members on earlier shared environments. Conversely, as Schaie and Willis point out, the reconstruction process may be shared among siblings as family members attempt to understand their shared past. Clearly, the subjective reconstruction of events has potentially highly diverse effects on correlations among family members' perceptions.

CONCLUSIONS

Coming from different directions, psychologists in the life-span developmental tradition and sociologists in the life-course tradition have common interest in family environments. The life-course perspective provides one conceptual account of the processes producing correlations in perceived family environments across generations and leads to three conclusions. First, the level of correlation across generations results from the loose coupling of transitions that allows siblings to diverge. Second, different children in the same family experience variable environments in childhood because historical events mediated by family history produce variability in family environments over time. Third, perceptions of environments are influenced by processes of subjective reconstruction through which individuals construct and interpret the meaning of events.

REFERENCES

Bengtson, V. L., Rosenthal, C., & Burton, L. (1990). Families and aging: Diversity and heterogeneity. In R. H. Binstock & L. K. George (Eds.), *Handbook of aging and the social sciences* (pp. 263–287). New York: Academic Press.

Breytspraak, L. M. (1984). *The development of self in later life*. Boston: Little, Brown.

Clogg, C. C. (1986). Invoked by RATE. *American Journal of Sociology, 92*, 696–706.

Elder, G. H., Jr. (1978). Family history and the life course. In T. K. Hareven (Ed.), *Transitions: The family and the life course in historical perspective* (pp. 17–64). New York: Academic Press.

Elder, G. H., Jr., Caspi, A., & Downey, G. (1986). Problem behavior and family relationships: Life course and intergenerational themes. In A. B. Sorensen, F. E. Weinert, & L. R. Sherrod (Eds.), *Human development and the life course: Multidisciplinary perspectives* (pp. 293–342). Hillsdale, NJ: Erlbaum.

Elder, G. H., Jr., & O'Rand, A. M. (1994). Adult lives in a changing society. In K. Cook, G. Fine, & J. S. House (Eds.), *Sociological perspectives on social psychology*. Boston: Allyn Bacon.

Featherman, D. L. (1986). Biography, society, and history: Individual development as a population process. In A. B. Sorensen, F. E. Weinert, & L. R. Sherrod (Eds.), *Human development and the life course: Multidisciplinary perspectives* (pp. 99–152). Hillsdale, NJ: Erlbaum.

Featherman, D. L., & Lerner, R. M. (1985). Ontogenesis and sociogenesis: Problematics for theory and research about development and socialization across the lifespan. *American Sociological Review, 50*, 659–676.

Freedman, D., Thornton, A., Camburn, D., Alwin, D., & Young-DeMarco, L. (1988). The life history calendar: A technique for collecting retrospective data. *Sociological Methodology, 18*, 37–68.

George, L. K., & Gold, D. T. (1991). Life course perspectives on intergenerational and generational connections. *Marriage and Family Review, 16*, 67–88.

Glass, J., Bengtson, V. L., & Dunham, C. C. (1986). Attitude similarity in families: Socialization, status inheritance, or reciprocal influence. *American Sociological Review, 51*, 685–698.

Hauser, R. M., & Mossel, P. A. (1985). Fraternal resemblance in educational attainment and occupational status. *American Journal of Sociology, 91*, 650–673.

Henretta, J. C. (1992). Uniformity and diversity: Life course institutionalization and late-life work exit. *Sociological Quarterly, 33*, 265–279.

Henretta, J. C., O'Rand, A. M., & Chan, C. G. (1993). Joint role investments and synchronization of retirement: A sequential approach to couples' retirement timing. *Social Forces*, *71*, 981–1000.

Hogan, D. P. (1981). *Transitions and social change: The early lives of American men*. New York: Academic Press.

Kohli, M. (1986a). Social organization and the subjective construction of the life course. In A. B. Sorensen, F. E. Weinert, & L. R. Sherrod, (Eds.), *Human development and the life course: Multidisciplinary perspectives* (pp. 271–292). Hillsdale, NJ: Erlbaum.

Kohli, M. (1986b). The world we forgot: A historical review of the life course. In V. W. Marshall (Ed.), In *Later life: The social psychology of aging* (pp. 271–303). Beverly Hills: Sage.

Kohn, M. L., & Schooler, C. (1983). *Work and personality: An inquiry into the impact of social stratification*. Norwood, NJ: Ablex.

O'Rand, A. M. (1990). Stratification and the life course. In R. H. Binstock & L. K. George (Eds.), *Handbook of aging and the social sciences* (pp. 130–148). New York: Academic Press.

Rindfuss, R. R., Swicegood, C. G., & Rosenfeld, R. A. (1987). Disorder in the life course: How common and does it matter. *American Sociological Review*, *52*, 785–801.

CHAPTER 6

The "Intergenerational Stake" Hypothesis Revisited: Parent–Child Differences in Perceptions of Relationships 20 Years Later

Roseann Giarrusso
Michael Stallings
Vern L. Bengtson[1]

Why are parents and their adolescent children often so far apart in the views they have of their shared relationship? Why are survey descriptions of relationships *downward* in the generational chain — toward children — generally more positive than reports of relationships *upward* — toward parents? Do such differences in intergenerational perceptions change over time, with the maturation of children and parents? Or are parents consistently more positive than children over the life course and, if so, why?

Two decades ago, Bengtson and Kuypers (1971) proposed the "developmental stake hypothesis" in an effort to answer questions such as these. They were

227

attempting to explain surprising intergenerational contrasts they found in the descriptions of parent-child relationships in their data: middle-aged parents consistently reported higher levels of closeness and consensus in the parent-child relationship, relative to the reports of their children. They suggested that such systematic contrasts emerge because each generation has different developmental concerns, and in consequence each has a different "stake" in their intergenerational relationship. Parents, they hypothesized, are more concerned with the continuity of values they have found important in life, and with close relationships in the family they have founded—so they tend to minimize conflict and overstate solidarity with their offspring. Young adults, by contrast, are more motivated to establish autonomy from their parents in values and social relationships, and have less commitment to the parent-child relationship—so they tend to understate intergenerational solidarity and overstate intergenerational contrasts.

Thus, according to Bengtson and Kuypers' original hypothesis, contrasts in developmental needs explain differences in the "stake" each generation has in intergenerational cohesion, continuity, and conflict. Furthermore, these differences in developmental stake explain contrasts in opinions and orientations between the generations, independent of any specific issues that appear to be the focus. It is the stake of the older generation in continuity and transmission, in contrast to the stake of the younger generation in autonomy and innovation, that provides the fundamental mechanism for differences between parents and young adult children.

Two decades have passed since the notion of differential developmental stake between parents and children was first proposed to explain intergenerational differences. Since then, public preoccupation with the "generation gap" of the 1960s has given way to popular concerns about "elder care" in the 1990s. Developmental theories focusing on individual ontogeny have been supplemented by life-course perspectives emphasizing sociocontextual influences on development. So, in the context of these and other developments, how much—if anything—of the developmental stake hypothesis still seems relevant to explaining perceptions of parent-child relationships over time?

Since 1971, the "developmental stake" hypothesis has become referred to as the "generational stake" or, most recently, the "intergenerational stake." The change in terms (by members of our own research group, as well as by other investigators who have employed it as an explanation for empirically observed parent-child contrasts) acknowledges factors other than simple individual development levels that may account for cross-generational differences in perception. This reflects a more social-structural explanation, based on generational location itself as a variable: the differential social investment of parents and children in their joint relationship results in perceptual differences between the generations. In this chapter we use "intergenerational stake" as an inclusive term to refer to both the "developmental stake" (individual-level) and the "generational stake" (sociostructural-level) hypotheses. The new term better connotes the cross-generational nature of the phenomenon under consideration, and it reflects the fact that the intergenerational stake hypothesis incorporates two predictions: (a) parent's descriptions of parent-child relationships will generally be more positive than children's descriptions, and (b) differential investment as well as differential development may account for cross-generational biases in perception.

In this chapter our purpose is to examine the intergenerational stake hypothesis 20 years later, with data now available from our longitudinal study of grandparents, parents, and young adult children. We first discuss the conceptual and theoretical background of the analysis, noting results of several empirical replications of the original hypothesis and its expansion to include an exchange theoretical perspective. We note three crucial issues that should be examined with data: (a) tests of dyadic parent-child data in addition to individual-level perceptions; (b) tests of parent-child interactions over the full life course—including aging parents and middle-aged children; and (c) gender differences in intergenerational investments, none of which were considered in the initial formulation by Bengtson and Kuypers (1971). Second, we describe the methods and procedures we have used in tests of the intergenerational stake hypothesis, focusing on the longitudinal and multivariate designs that can now be employed. Third, we summarize findings of our analysis, noting that (a) much of the original intergenerational stake hypothesis appears supported by our longitudinal assessment, and (b) the dynamics behind the intergenerational stake phenomenon appear to be related to generational lineage position rather than individual life-course developmental stage. Fourth, we discuss some implications of these findings for future empirical assessment and theory development.

BACKGROUND OF THE PROBLEM: ARE THERE SYSTEMATIC BIASES IN PERCEPTIONS ACROSS GENERATIONS?

Since the 1970s scores of studies have been published concerning parent-child relationships; in most of these, intergenerational relationship variables have been assessed by asking the individual respondent about his or her evaluation concerning the degree of contact, support, or conflict with his or her parent or offspring. In only a few studies have similar questions been asked of the other intergenerational dyad member, parent or child, for corroboration or for contrast of the original respondent's report.

The intergenerational stake hypothesis suggests that such individual-level, self-report data characterizing family dyadic relationships may be significantly bi-ased. The implications of this are sobering, in terms of much of family research published today. There may be a critical flaw in most survey research about fam-ily intergenerational relationships to date—for example, the many published analyses based on the NSFH—in that the perceptions of one generation about the other are systematically colored by the respondents' motivational concerns *up* and *down* the family generational ladder.

What evidence exists supporting the intergenerational stake hypothesis about biases in perceptions of parent-child interaction? Which theory—individ-ual developmental or social exchange—provides a better explanation of the phe-nomenon? And how do considerations of aging and gender affect the hypothesis?

Previous Empirical Analyses of the Intergenerational Stake Hypothesis

In justifying the initial intergenerational stake hypothesis formulation, Bengtson and Kuypers (1971) summarized results comparing responses of 312 college students and their 371 middle-aged mothers and fathers on questions about in-tergenerational relations. They found that parents as a group consistently overes-timated the degree of parent-child closeness, understanding, and communica-tion, compared to children as a group. In addition they found that children reported more disagreement, but less frequent discussion, than their parents did regarding common topics of discussion. They attributed these generational dif-ferences to the motivational influence of different developmental life-course con-cerns characterizing each generation, and suggested that these systematically bias evaluations and definitions of their common relationship.

That the intergenerational stake hypothesis became recognized as a useful explanatory framework is indicated by the number of studies citing it to explain empirical findings (see e.g., Bond & Harvey, 1991; Callan & Noller, 1986; Cashmore & Goodnow, 1985; Chapman & Neal, 1990; Fisher, Reid, & Melen-dez, 1989; Holmbeck & Hill, 1988; Knipscheer & Bevers, 1985; Spitze & Lo-gan, 1991; Taylor, Chatters, & Jackson, in press; Talbott, 1990). However, sev-eral theoretical and empirical problems remained. First, Bengtson and Kuypers did not pursue additional empirical or theoretical support for the rationale be-hind the phenomenon. For example, they did not explicitly test the link be-tween psychosocial development and cross-generational differences in percep-tion. Second, the hypothesis was limited originally to youth and their middle-aged parents. Yet the intergenerational stake dynamic should logically be applicable later in the life course, for example, to adult children and their elderly parents. But this would require developmental tasks to be expanded to include those of older life-course phases, leading to further theoretical elaboration. Third, although Bengtson and Kuypers were concerned with the dynamics of parent-child dyads, in their data they did not match the responses of parents with children, reporting only aggregate generation-group contrasts. Without matching dyadic responses, it would be impossible to assess the magnitude of the intergenerational stake phenomenon directly or to investigate any of its correlates.

Subsequent analyses by other researchers addressed some of these problems. For example, Thompson, Clark, and Gunn (1985) tested the hypothesis with a dyadic sample of college students and their parents. Further, they tested the link between individual psychosocial development (in Erikson's [1950] conceptualization) and individuals' perceptions of intergenerational continuity. They asked children and parents to rate their own attitudes, as well as their perceptions of their parent's/child's attitudes, on eight issues and calculated the absolute difference between the two sets of scores. Children and parents also each completed a measure of psychosocial development. Results indicated that children indeed perceived greater differences in intergenerational continuity than did their parents. However, contrary to the intergenerational stake prediction, children who had successfully achieved "ego identity" and parents who had reached the "generativity" stage did not perceive greater amounts of intergenerational continuity than their less psychosocially mature counterparts. Thompson et al. (1985) limited their analysis to consensual solidarity indicators, leaving the relationship between psychosocial development levels and parent-child affectual solidarity untested. Further, they did not examine matched parent-child dyads and thus did not test the crucial link between parent-child perceptual differences and psychosocial development.

Gesser, Marshall, and Rosenthal (1985) applied the hypothesis to later stages of the life course, noting that issues of independence and value continuity remain agendas throughout adulthood: "Elderly parents continue to be concerned with value continuity while adult children continue to desire value systems and identities perceived as separate" (p. 10). Moreover, they suggested that the "mutual fear of anticipated parental dependence" also influences how elderly parents and adult children perceive closeness: "elderly parents emphasize closeness in an attempt to diffuse fear of anticipated dependence," while adult children "minimize closeness as a means of psychologically distancing themselves from a situation viewed as threatening" (p. 11). Despite the importance of this proposed theoretical elaboration, Gesser et al. did not explicitly analyze either the former or the elaborated theoretical explanations of the intergenerational stake phenomenon. Rather, they described evidence for the phenomenon across four of the six dimensions of family solidarity operationalized in Mangen,

Bengtson, and Landry (1986). They found that there was a significantly greater likelihood of parent's ratings of affectual, consensual, and associational solidarity to be higher than their child's. An exception was functional solidarity, the exchange of help and support, where children's ratings were higher than parents'. Although they improved upon the design of previous studies by matching the responses of parents and children rather than relying on generational group comparisons, they did not explore issues of magnitude in the observed parent-child differences. For example, parent–child perceptual differences of one unit were considered comparable to differences of six units.

The intergenerational stake hypothesis was also examined from the perspective of how members of one generation perceive their relationship with family members both up and down the generational line. Richards, Bengtson, and Miller (1989) examined how the middle-age "sandwich" generation comparatively evaluated their current relationship with young adult children and with elderly parents. This version of the hypothesis suggested that "relationships downward in the generational chain are phenomenologically more important, and therefore evaluated more positively, than relationships upward" (p. 351). They argued that this occurs because the middle generation tends to have a greater stake in the younger generation than in the older generation because of their greater psychological and socioeconomic investment in the younger generation. Their data supported the hypothesis and an interpretation more in line with exchange theory than developmental theory perspectives.

Theoretical Refinements to the Hypothesis

As suggested by the preceding review, the original Bengtson and Kuypers (1971) intergenerational stake formulation was in need of conceptual and theoretical revision. Subsequent analyses, although confirming several aspects of the phenomenon proposed, suggested that not one, but several, hypotheses should be identified for empirical testing, and that at least two theoretical perspectives are relevant as explanatory frameworks.

In revisiting the intergenerational stake hypothesis, it is necessary to be more explicit concerning the general theoretical perspectives relevant to its predictions. In particular, we must examine two sources of explanation: (a) developmental theory and (b) exchange theory.

Developmental Theory

The developmental or life-course approach to the explanation of parent-child differences focuses on changes in individual or family relationships over time (Elder, 1984; Hagestad, 1990; Kreppner & Lerner, 1989; Lerner, 1982, 1984;

Knapp, 1975; Treas & Bengtson, 1987; Troll & Bengtson, 1979). As members develop and age they experience a series of adjustments in life th to death. The family is viewed as a group of interacting persons. At e of life new challenges or developmental tasks emerge, and through re-interaction the family attempts to deal with the changing needs of the members. The classic Erikson (1950) theory focuses on psychosocial de-ntal tasks, whereas other versions of the theory focus on biological and developmental tasks. Dealing adequately with the developmental task of r stage will influence the individual's success at later tasks. Some tasks or ay be more difficult than others. Conflicts are more likely to arise be-arents and children at certain stages.

e stage during which conflict is likely to arise is adolescence. During their y stage" of individual development, adolescents are trying to achieve inde-ce. At the same time, parents are entering middle age and seeking the g of life by looking to the younger generation. They view their children nsions of themselves. Thus adolescents fear losing their identities in their s with their parents; consequently this leads to a period of storm and Holmbeck & Hill, 1988). Some studies indicate that both parents and n perceive improvement in their relationship as children pass from adoles-to adulthood (Baruch & Barnett, 1983; Green & Boxer, 1985; Sullivan & n, 1980). As children marry and begin families of their own, intergenera-relationships improve (Angress, 1975; Bengtson & Black, 1973; Fischer, Wilen, 1979).

he child's developmental transition from adolescence to adulthood often leads period of stability in perceptions of the parent-child relationship. But in-nerational conflict can arise again as the parents undergo the role transitions of life. A growing body of research on parent-child relationships in later life has ined the "burden" middle-age children experience while caring for an elderly t (Brody, 1981, 1985; Poulschock & Deimling, 1986; Stoller, 1983; Zarit, ver, & Bach-Peterson, 1980). Many of these studies have found a negative relationship between parental dependency or poor health and the quality of the parent-child relationship (Baruch & Barnett, 1983; Johnson, 1978; Johnson & Bursk, 1971; Mindel & Wright, 1982). And data presented by Silverstein and Bengtson (1991) suggest a particularly dramatic consequence of an aged parent's perceptions of unsatisfying relations with their middle-aged child: higher mortality risks.

Exchange Theory

Social exchange explanations focus on the rewards and costs individuals obtain through social interaction, based on the assumption that individuals try to maximize their rewards and minimize their costs (Blau, 1964; Emerson, 1981; Homans, 1974; Thibaut & Kelley, 1959). The exchange model has been applied to close relationships (Sprecher, 1986), and it has received increasing attention in the gerontological literature to explain parent-child relationships (Suitor & Pillemer, 1988).

The exchange between parents and children is not, to be sure, balanced. By virtue of their lineage position in the family, parents invest more in their children than their children invest in them (Hagestad, 1981). Parents and children may perceive the emotional distance between them differently because of this asymmetry in investment. Asymmetry in investment leads to feelings of inequity and a motivation to reduce those feelings. Individuals can restore *actual* equity by altering their own investments or they can restore *psychological* equity by changing their perceptions of their own or their partners' investment (Walster, Walster, & Berscheid, 1978). Because it is difficult for parents to terminate their relationship with their children (another possible response to inequity), parents restore equity by perceiving their relationship with their child as closer than their child perceives the relationship.

Propositions derived from exchange theory may be unclear about whether investment accumulates over time, even with day-to-day fluctuations. If investment does accumulate, the stake in the younger generation may increase as individuals of different generations share more and more years of life and age together.

Need for a Longitudinal Research Perspective

Neither of these two major theories—individual developmental or social exchange—has been explored as explanations for the intergenerational stake phenomenon; each of these theories suggests different long-term predictions. Longitudinal data are required to provide an adequate test of these competing explanations. For example, developmental theory would suggest that the intergenerational stake phenomenon occurs early and late in the family life cycle. By contrast, exchange theory would predict that the phenomenon should hold across time, not just early and late in the family life course.

It is possible that both theoretical explanations of the phenomenon are correct: They may be complementary rather than competing. It is necessary to examine intergenerational stake phenomenon over time to determine if its magnitude covaries with developmental or life stage issues. Cross-sectionally, at each point in time, parents may report higher affectual solidarity for their children than their children report about them, as exchange theory would suggest. However, over time the degree of parent–child differences in affectual solidarity may

change in response to varying ontogenetic issues being faced by different family members, as predicted by developmental theory. Consequently, the magnitude of the intergenerational stake phenomenon may be greatest early in the family life cycle when the family is dealing with the independence of adolescent children and the continuity concerns of middle-aged parents, and late in the family life cycle when the family is dealing with the dependence of parents moving into advanced ages.

Figure 6.1 diagrams what four competing theoretical predictions might look like over the adult life course, with hypothetical data. The solid line represents parents' affection for their children, and the broken line represents children's affection for their parents. First, if there were no evidence of the intergenerational stake phenomenon, there would be no difference in the levels of the affection for parents and children (see Figure 6.1a). But second, if exchange theory were supported, parent's affection for children would be greater than children's affection for parents across time because parent's investment in their joint relationship is always greater than the child's. Hence, the solid line would be above the broken line, across the family life cycle, but the distance between the lines at any point in time would be about the same (see Figure 6.1b). Third, if developmental theory predictions alone were supported, parent's affection for children would be greater than children's affection for parents early and late in the family life cycle. That is, the solid line would be above the broken line *only* during adolescence, when children are dealing with autonomy concerns and parents with intergenerational continuity concerns, and later life, when children and parents are dealing with parental dependency concerns. The lines would be at the same level during the middle of the family life cycle (see Figure 6.1c). Fourth, by contrast, if both the developmental and exchange theories were correct, then the solid line would always be above the broken line, but there would be a greater divergence between the lines early and late in the family life course (see Figure 6.1d).

Importance of Gender Differences in Intergenerational Relationships

It is likely that the intergenerational stake phenomenon does not apply equally to men and women. Rossi (1993) has noted several reasons why women might have a greater investment in intergenerational relationships than men. First, women not only have a biological role in childbearing and nursing, they also still function as the primary family caretakers later in life. Second, differential socialization experiences result in motherhood assuming a more central role in the lives of women, than fatherhood in the lives of men. Similarly, women are socialized to be more expressive than men and are more likely to serve as kin

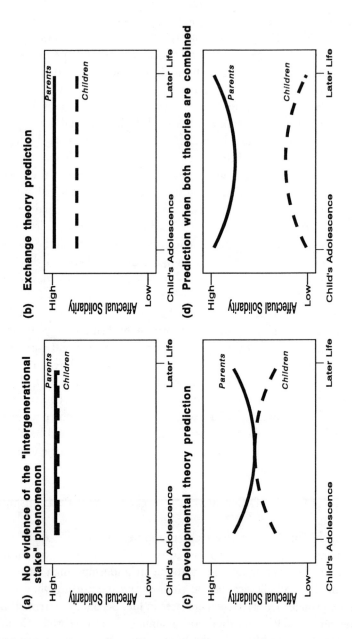

Figure 6.1. Predicted patterns of parent–child affecual solidarity over the family life cycle

keeper in the family. Third, women have a greater economic need for interdependence with other family members because they make lower wages than men, are responsible for children after divorce, and often suffer reduced savings in later life after the illness and death of their husbands.

Because of these gender-based differences, it is prudent to examine the intergenerational stake phenomenon separately for males and females, in terms of both developmental and exchange theoretical frameworks. It could be that the intergenerational stake hypothesis is supported for women but not men.

Hypotheses to be Tested

Thus, four specific hypotheses can be derived from the preceding discussion. The first hypothesis is based on exchange theory and predicts consistency in the intergenerational stake phenomenon over time:

H1 Because parents' investment in children is greater than children's investment in parents, parents will feel closer to their children than their children will feel to them, across the family life course.

The second hypothesis is based on developmental theory; it predicts variations over the life course in the intergenerational stake phenomenon:

H2 Parents will feel closer to their children than their children will feel to them *early* in the family life course (when families are dealing with adolescent independence and parental concern for intergenerational continuity in values) and *late* in the family life course (when families are dealing with parental dependence).

H1 and H2 are not mutually exclusive; both could be correct. If so — if exchange theory and developmental theory are complementary explanations for the intergenerational stake phenomenon — then the prediction would be that while parents will consistently have higher investment than children in their relationship, there will be variation in the magnitude of the phenomenon in response to the developmental issues noted previously,

H3 Parents will always feel closer to their children than their children will feel to them, but differences in parent-child affectual solidarity will be greatest early and late in the family life course.

The fourth hypothesis suggests variations in the magnitude of the intergenerational stake phenomenon based on gender rather than developmental/life-course issues.

H4 Women's investment in children being greater than men's, parent-child differences in affectual solidarity will be greatest for mother-child than for father-child dyads.

METHODS AND PROCEDURES: ANALYZING POSSIBLE CROSS-GENERATIONAL PERCEPTUAL BIASES ACROSS 20 YEARS OF TIME

Sample

Data for this analysis are based on participants in the USC Longitudinal Study of Generations, now measured across 20 years. The original 1971 (Time-1) sample included 2044 individual respondents, members of over 300 three-generation families. These family members were subsequently measured again in 1985 (Time-2), 1988 (Time-3), and most recently in 1991 (Time-4). Because of federal funding constraints the intervals between measurements are not equal: There was a 14-year interval between Time-1 and Time-2, and there are 3-year intervals between the three subsequent measurement periods. Of the original 2,044 respondents, 820 completed surveys across all four waves of measurement.

The original 1971 sample was drawn from a population of 840,000 members from a Los Angeles area prepaid health care plan, which primarily served labor unions (see Bengtson, 1975). To obtain a representative sample of adult three-generation families in this population, a screening questionnaire was sent to a random sample (1 in 6) of all male subscribers 55 years of age or older, who had a dependent enrolled in the plan. To be eligible for inclusion in the sampling frame, the male subscriber had to have a living child and at least one grandchild between the ages of 16 and 26. At Time-1 eligible families were mailed a 26-page survey, first to all grandchildren (G3s; mean age, 19), then to their parents (G2s; mean age, 44), and finally to the grandparents (G1s; mean age, 67). This ordering allowed a random assignment of one "study child" per generation: to each of the G2s (parents of the G3s) and then to the G1s (who were parents of the G2s). Data were subsequently collected from all siblings in each generation, as well as their spouses.

The longitudinal sample that resulted consists of predominantly white, working and middle class families, reflecting the bias of the HMO's membership at that time. Twenty years later, the mean ages for the three generations in the Time-4 (1991) survey were 83, 64, and 39 years for the G1s, G2s, and G3s, respectively (a fourth generation, the great-grandchildren of the original G1s, was also added at Time-4, but these data are not reported here). The ratio of female to male respondents by Time-4 was approximately 1.5 to 1.0, but the mean ages for the two sexes were not significantly different within the generation groups. Table 6.1 shows the age and gender distributions for each wave of the longitudinal design between 1971 and 1991 for the cross-sectional and longitudinal samples.

To investigate variations in the intergenerational stake phenomenon over time, the sample for this analysis was restricted to G2-G3 parent-child dyads in which both members of the dyad had participated at all four measurement waves and had complete data on the affectual solidarity items. Our inclusion criteria resulted in a sample of 77 father-child dyads and 121 mother-child dyads assessed over 20 years. G1-G2 parent-child dyads are not analyzed in this report; because of attrition through death of the older G1s, especially G1 males, there was not sufficient data available for complete dyads at all four measurement periods to make meaningful comparisons.

This longitudinal design of respondents from all four measurement periods allows for comprehensive comparisons across two decades of time; however, it also resulted in a reduction in the number of G2-G3 parent-child dyads available for analysis. In any longitudinal study one must test for possible attrition bias: whether there are differences on the dependent variable of interest between those remaining in the study over time and those who drop out. Analyses comparing longitudinal respondents to "dropouts" revealed no significant differences between the two groups in their Time-1 ratings of affectual solidarity toward parents or children. These analyses suggest there was no systematic bias because of attrition of respondents regarding affectual solidarity.

Analysis Plan

There were two components to the examination of the intergenerational stake hypothesis using matched parent-child dyads: (a) an analysis of the pattern of means and (b) regression analyses. In the analysis of means, time of measurement was used as a proxy for developmental issues confronted during the family life cycle. In the regression analyses, developmental concerns were measured more directly with indicators of adolescent autonomy, parental concern for intergenerational value continuity, and parental dependence. All analyses were conducted separately for mother-child and father-child dyads to investigate whether there were any gender differences.

Measures

Intergenerational Stake Phenomenon: Parent-Child Differences in Affectual Solidarity

Affectual solidarity was assessed as the mean of responses (1 = not at all; 6 = very much/a great deal) to six survey questionnaire items: (a) Taking everything into consideration, how close do you feel is the relationship between you

TABLE 6.1. Cross-Sectional and Longitudinal Sample

	Cross-Sectional								Longitudinal Sample	
	Time-1 1971		Time-2 1985		Time-3 1988		Time-4 1991			
	N	Age	N	Age	N	Age	N	Age	N	Age
G1:										
Male	266	68	91	79	64	81	44	83	34	84
Female	250	66	130	77	111	79	93	83	76	83
G2:										
Male	322	46	243	59	241	61	204	65	147	65
Female	379	42	313	56	327	59	291	62	220	62
G3:										
Male	385	20	226	33	313	36	297	40	122	40
Female	442	19	328	33	427	35	400	39	221	39

and your "study" child (or your mother/father) at this point in your life? (b) How is communication between yourself and this child (or your mother/father)—exchanging ideas or talking about things that really concern you at this point in your life? (c) In general, how similar are your opinions and values about life to those of your "study" child (or your mother/father) at this point in time? (d) Overall, how well do you and this child (or your mother/father) get along together at this point in your life? (e) How well do you feel you understand this "study" child (or your mother/father)? (f) How well do you feel this "study" child (or your mother/father) understands you? Reliability and validity information on this scale are reported in Mangen, Bengtson, and Landry (1988).

Developmental Concerns: Indirect Measures

At Time-1, most of the children in the sample were adolescents and most of the parents were middle-age. Therefore, it was assumed that most parents and children would be dealing with the developmental concerns related to that stage of life: children would be confronting issues of autonomy and parents would be grappling with concerns over intergenerational continuity of values. It was also assumed that by Time-4 parents and children would be beginning to face issues of parental dependency because of parent's advanced age and declining health. Thus, time of measurement was used as an indirect measure of developmental concerns of parents and children across the life course.

Developmental Concerns: Direct Measures

An alternative way to examine Hypothesis 2 was to use more direct measures of developmental concerns rather than assume that time of measurement could serve as an adequate proxy. Although there is an advantage to using more direct measures, the disadvantage is that the measures are not repeated across time (or are not measured at the ideal time) making the interpretation of the results suggestive rather than conclusive:

The *adolescent autonomy* indicators were measured at Time-1. They included responses to (a) a single item reflecting the perception of the generation gap in the family between children and parents on a 6-point scale (1 = no gap; 6 = very wide gap); and (b) the mean response on eight items (Cronbach's alpha = 0.75) assessing attitudes toward youth rebellious behaviors (1 = formally punished; 4 = left alone): a teenager who runs away from home; a teenager who continually argues with his parents; a teenager who smokes cigarettes in public; a teenage girl who hitchhikes; a person who smokes marijuana; a teenager who skips school; a teenager who drinks liquor; and a teenage boy who throws a rock through a window. The mean for perceived generation gap in the family was 2.92 (SD = 1.14), and the mean for rebellious behaviors was 3.02 (SD = 0.48).

Parental concern with intergenerational continuity in values ideally would have been measured at Time-1 rather than at Time-2. However, it was felt that this Time-2 variable could still provide some information about developmental theory. Four questions were asked: "Some parents feel it is important for their adult children to share the same values in life as they do. How important is it to you that you and your study child agree in the following areas?" That is, have similar (a) religious beliefs, (b) political beliefs, (c) views on the roles of husbands and wives, and (d) views on the importance of family ties over other relationships? Each question was answered on a scale from "(1) not at all important" to "(5) extremely important." Parental concern for intergenerational continuity in values represents the average of these four items (Cronbach's $\alpha = 0.75$); the mean was 2.62 (SD = 0.87).

Indicators of *parental dependence in old age* were measured at Time-4. They included (1) the number of chronic illnesses or disabilities of parents from a list of 15 items that included such things as heart disease, memory problems, respiratory problems, digestive problems, etc. as reported by (a) the parents and (b) by their children; and (2) an index of six types of help and support provided by the child to the parent, as reported by both (a) the parent and (b) the child (1 = yes, 0 = no). The latter measure was comprised of three types of instrumental help and support—household chores, transportation/shopping, or help when mother/father is sick—and three types of emotional help and support—information and advice, emotional support, or discussion of life decisions. The number of health problems reported by mothers ranged from 0 to 7 (mode = 1) while the number reported by fathers ranged from 0 to 8 (mode = 2). Children reported 0 to 7 health problems for their mothers (mode = 1) and 0 to 8 health problems for their fathers (mode = 0). Fathers and mothers both reported being helped by their children with 0 to 6 categories of help and support (mode = 0). Children reported helping their fathers with 0 to 5 categories (mode = 0) and their mothers with 0 to 6 (mode = 0) categories of help and support.

RESULTS

Comparisons of Means: Matched Parent-Child Dyads

Following the recommendation of Bernhardson (1975), we made mean comparisons directly, rather than perform omnibus repeated measures analyses. We used modified *t*-tests, using a procedure to control for Type I error inflation (Rom, 1990) over "subsets" of mean comparisons that involved comparing mean affection towards children over time; or comparing sex differences at each time point. Thus, α was not controlled at .05 for the entire number of t-tests, only within reasonable blocks of hypotheses. Paired t-tests were used for all comparisons between groups.

Hypotheses 1 and 2

Hypothesis 1 predicted that parents would feel closer to their children than their children would feel toward them, across the family life course, whereas Hypothesis 2 predicted this would be true only at early and late in the family life course. To test these hypotheses, mean levels of parents' and children's affectual solidarity were compared across time. If, at each time point, parents' affectual solidarity was significantly greater than their children's, this was taken as evidence of the consistency of the intergenerational stake phenomenon as predicted by Hypothesis 1. If parents' affectual solidarity was significantly greater than their children's only at Time-1 and Time-4, this was taken as evidence of variation in the phenomenon as predicted by Hypothesis 2.

Figure 6.2 shows the mean levels of affectual solidarity for parents' and children's reports over time, reported separately for father-child dyads and mother-child dyads. The solid lines represent the parents' perceptions of closeness and the broken lines the children's perspective.

The top portion of Figure 6.2 compares the affectual solidarity of fathers towards their children with that of children toward their fathers. On a 6-point scale, the means for fathers' affectual solidarity ranged from 4.26 to 4.50; the means for children's affectual solidarity toward their fathers was lower, ranging from 3.93 to 4.23. T-tests of these scores were significant at each time point. This suggests support for Hypothesis 1: fathers' affectual solidarity was consistently, and significantly, greater than their children's.

The bottom portion of Figure 6.2 compares the affectual solidarity of mothers toward their children with that of children toward their mothers. The means for mothers' scores on affectual solidarity for their children ranged from 4.53 to 4.67; children's mean scores on affectual solidarity toward their mothers ranged from 4.15 to 4.35. Thus, results for mother-child dyads also indicate support for Hypothesis 1: means for mothers' affectual solidarity for their children were consistently, and significantly, higher than their children's at each time point.

Thus, parent-child differences in affectual solidarity did not follow the pattern suggested by developmental theory as represented in Hypothesis 2.

Hypothesis 3

Based on a combination of exchange and developmental theory, Hypothesis 3 predicted that the intergenerational stake phenomenon would appear at each

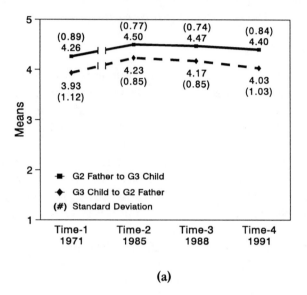

(a)

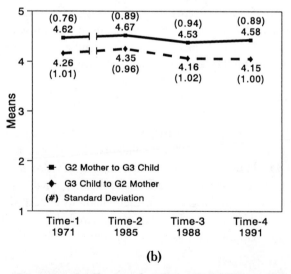

(b)

Figure 6.2.   G2 parents' affection for their G3 children and children's affection for them over time. (a) Father–child dyads (*N* = 77): mean levels of affection. (b) Mother–child dyads (*N* = 121): mean levels of affection.

time point but the magnitude of cross-generational differences in affectual solidarity would be greatest early in the family life course, when families were dealing with adolescent independence and parental concern for intergenerational continuity in values, and late in the family life course, when families were dealing with parental dependence.

To test Hypothesis 3, children's affectual solidarity for their parents was subtracted from parents' affectual solidarity for their children, creating a "dyadic difference score." The dyadic difference score was an indicator of the magnitude of the intergenerational stake phenomenon. Consistency in the intergenerational stake phenomenon across time, combined with an increase in the magnitude of the phenomenon at Time-1 and Time-4, would support Hypothesis 3.

Table 6.2 shows the mean dyadic difference scores were positive at all time points—indicating in a slightly different way from Figure 6.2—that the parent's affection for the child was greater than the child's affection for the parent at all time points. Table 6.2 also shows that the magnitude of the dyadic difference scores were only moderate, ranging from .27 to .36 for father-child dyads and from .32 to .43 for mother-child dyads. However, contrary to Hypothesis 3, there were no significant differences over time in the magnitude of the intergenerational stake phenomenon. Rather, the magnitude was stable across the 20 years for both father-child and mother-child dyads.

Hypothesis 4

Hypothesis 4 predicted gender differences for parents in the magnitude of the intergenerational stake phenomenon. It was thought that parent-child differences in affectual solidarity would be greater in mother-child than in father-child dyads, based on the assumption that women's investment in children is greater than men's. The results in Table 6.2 failed to reveal support for the Hypothesis 4: there were no significant differences in the magnitude of dyadic difference scores of father-child as compared with mother-child dyads at any time point. That is, the magnitude of the intergenerational stake phenomenon was not greater for mother-child than for father-child dyads.

Regression Analyses: Predictors of the Intergenerational Stake Phenomenon

The first component of our analyses—the comparisons of means—established the existence of the intergenerational stake phenomenon across the family life course and indicated that the magnitude of the phenomenon was not greatest early and late in the family life course.

Although the magnitude of the intergenerational stake phenomenon was

TABLE 6.2. The Magnitude of the Intergenerational Stake Phenomenon over Time: Mean Levels of Parent–Child Differences in Affectual Solidarity

	Time-1		Time-2		Time-3		Time-4	
	Mean	S.D.	Mean	S.D.	Mean	S.D.	Mean	S.D.
Father–Child	.33	(1.12)	.27	(0.81)	.30	(0.85)	.36	(0.88)
Mother–Child	.36	(0.95)	.32	(0.95)	.37	(0.85)	.43	(0.94)

found to be consistent over the life course, the distributions of the dyadic differences scores reported below show variations among parent-child dyads not indicated by an examination of means. Moreover, the analyses of means were based on the assumption that time of measurement served as an adequate proxy for developmental concerns. For these reasons, a second component was added to our analyses: regression analyses were conducted in an attempt to predict variation in the magnitude of the intergenerational stake phenomenon from more direct measures of developmental concerns than time of measurement. The regression analyses provide an additional test of whether developmental theory is complementary to exchange theory as an explanation of the intergenerational stake phenomenon.

Hypothesis 3 proposed that adolescent independence and parental concerns for value continuity would be related to the magnitude of the intergenerational stake phenomenon early in the family life cycle; parental dependence would be related to the magnitude of the phenomenon late in the family life cycle. Thus, these developmental concerns are predicted to be related to the intergenerational stake phenomenon within time, not across time.

Distributions of Dyadic Difference Scores

Table 6.3 shows the distributions of dyadic difference scores for each measurement period. The data here reflect the percentages of dyads (rather than the frequencies) having positive or negative dyadic difference scores. The dyadic difference scores were divided into three categories based on the sign and magnitude of the parent-child difference in affectual solidarity: (a) *consistent* with the intergenerational stake hypothesis—differences in the positive direction indicating greater affection by parents for children than the reverse, (b) *no parent-child difference*—differences in either the positive ($+.5$) or negative ($-.5$) direction not large enough to indicate a meaningful difference between parents and children, and (3) *inconsistent* with the intergenerational stake hypothesis—differences in the negative direction indicating greater affection by children for parents than the reverse.

In examining the distributions of these scores over time, Table 6.3 shows that, at any one time point: (a) 38% to 51% of the parent-child dyads indicated greater parental affection (.5-units or more) towards children than child affection toward parents; (b) 31% to 39% of the dyads had difference scores between $\pm .5$ units, indicating substantial agreement in affectual solidarity between parents and children; and (c) 15% to 28% of the dyads showed a pattern inconsistent with the intergenerational stake hypothesis. These distributions suggest that

TABLE 6.3. Distributions of Dyadic Difference Scores: Percent Consistent and Inconsistent with the Intergenerational Stake Hypothesis at Each Time Point

Pattern of Dyadic Difference Score	Magnitude of Dyadic Difference Score	Father-Child Dyads (N=77)				Mother-Child Dyads (N=121)			
		T1	T2	T3	T4	T1	T2	T3	T4
Consistent with Intergenerational Stake Hypothesis	≥ +2.0	10%	1%	1%	4%	5%	4%	5%	6%
	1.5	5	6	6	3	12	7	7	7
	1.0	13	17	19	17	9	12	12	16
	0.5	9	19	17	21	15	24	21	22
No Parent-Child Difference	LT 0.5 and GT -0.5	34	35	34	39	39	38	31	33
Inconsistent with Intergenerational Stake Hypothesis	-0.5	14	16	14	9	13	10	18	7
	-1.0	13	3	4	6	7	3	4	7
	≤ -1.5	1	3	4	1	1	2	1	2

there was considerable variability among parent-child dyads in the magnitude of the intergenerational stake phenomenon.

Adolescent Autonomy

Adolescent autonomy was measured at Time-1. Dyadic difference scores from Time-1 were regressed on the two indicators of adolescent autonomy, separately for father-child and mother-child dyads. The regression analyses in Table 6.4 indicate that parent-child differences in affectual solidarity were predictable from indicators of youth autonomy at Time-1 when the children were adolescents. The overall equation predicting father-child dyadic difference scores was significant, although children's perception of a generation gap was the only measure of adolescent autonomy accounting for a significant unique proportion of variance. The pattern of results for mother-child dyads was the same. Only children's perception of a large generation gap was related to larger positive dyadic difference scores for mother-child pairs.

Before it can be determined whether Hypothesis 3 is supported, it is necessary to also examine whether adolescent autonomy predicts parent-child differences in affectual solidarity across time, as reported subsequently.

Parental Concern for Intergenerational Continuity

As with adolescent autonomy, parental concern for intergenerational continuity in values was measured only at one time point (Time-2). Adolescent autonomy and parental concern for value continuity were both used to predict dyadic difference scores at Time-2, Time-3, and Time-4. Table 6.5 shows the results of separate regressions of the dyadic differences scores on the youth independence and parental concern for value continuity, for father-child and mother-child dyads.

Results in Table 6.5 indicate that by Time-2, adolescent autonomy was not predictive of parent-child differences in affectual solidarity for either father-child or mother-child dyads. Further, parental concern for intergenerational continuity was not a significant predictor of dyadic differences in affectual solidarity within Time-2.

However, there are indications of differences by gender. By Time-3 and Time-4 both adolescent autonomy and parental continuity significantly predicted parent-child differences in affectual solidarity for father-child dyads but not for mother-child dyads. The greater the children's concern for independence during adolescence, the greater was the difference in affectual solidarity between themselves and their fathers when the children reached adulthood. Similarly, the greater the fathers' concern for intergenerational continuity in values, the greater

TABLE 6.4. Correlates of Intergenerational Stake at Time 1: Prediction of Variation in Dyadic Difference Scores from Adolescent Autonomy

Predictors	Father-Child Dyads (N=77)	Mother-Child Dyads (N=121)
Attitude Towards Teenage Rebellion	-.02	.11
Perception of Generation Gap in Relationship	.43***	.31**
d_F	2, 63	2, 101
overall F-ratio	6.93	7.14
p-value <	.002	.001
adj R^2	.15	.11

*** p < .001
** p < .01
* p < .05

Note: Standardized b weights

TABLE 6.5. Correlates of Intergenerational Stake at Time-2, Time-3, and Time-4: Prediction of Variation in Dyadic Difference Scores from Adolescent Autonomy and Parental Concern for Continuity

Predictors	Father-Child Dyads (N=77)			Mother-Child Dyads (N=121)		
	T2	T3	T4	T2	T3	T4
T1 Child Variables:						
Attitudes Towards Teenage Rebellion	-.02	.10	.18	.02	.06	.03
Perception of Generation Gap in Relationship	.29*	.25*	.25*	.08	.17	.18
T2 Parent Variables:						
Concern for Continuity	.08	.39**	.27*	.09	.03	.08
d_F	3, 61	3, 61	3, 61	3, 100	3, 100	3, 100
overall F-ratio	1.77	5.33	4.25	0.41	1.18	1.26
p value <	NS	.01	.01	NS	NS	NS
adj R^2	.03	.17	.13	-.02	.01	.01

*** $p < .001$
** $p < .01$
* $p < .05$

Note: Standardized b weights

the dyadic differences in affectual solidarity between themselves and their children later in the family life course. Thus, this aspect of Hypothesis 3 – regarding the early stages of the family life cycle – was not supported for father-child dyads. Both adolescent autonomy and parental concern for intergenerational continuity in values predicted the magnitude of cross-generational differences in affectual solidarity across time, rather than just during the adolescent years of the child, as developmental theory would have predicted.

This was not, however, true for mother-child dyads in this sample. For mother-child dyads, neither adolescent autonomy nor parental concern for intergenerational continuity significantly predicted dyadic difference scores from Time-2, Time-3, or Time-4. These results suggest limited support for Hypothesis 3 regarding the early stages of the family life cycle for mother-child dyads.

Parental Dependence

Table 6.6 shows the extent to which parental dependence at Time-4 (when the parents are beginning to reach older adulthood – mean age at this time is 64 years) was predictive of dyadic difference scores in affectual solidarity at Time-4. Four variables were regressed on the dyadic difference scores: (a) children's reports of the number chronic illnesses their parents have, (b) children's reports of the amount of help and support they provide their parents, (c) parents' reports of the number of chronic illnesses they have, and (d) parents' reports of the amount of help and support their children provide.

Table 6.6 presents the results for both father-child and mother-child dyads. Neither the children's nor the parents' reports of parental dependence significantly predicted the difference in parent-child affectual solidarity for either father-child or mother-child dyads at Time-4. Thus, this aspect of Hypothesis 3 – regarding the late stages of the family cycle – was not supported.

DISCUSSION

The "developmental stake hypothesis" was suggested two decades ago in an attempt to explain why youth and parents differed so much in their descriptions of their joint parent-child relationship (Bengtson & Kuypers, 1971). The hypothesis was that parents, because of their desire to maintain continuity between the generations, tended to overestimate affectual solidarity between themselves and their children; and that children, because of their desire for independence, tended to underestimate levels of affectual solidarity. Later, the hypothesis was expanded to include another explanation of cross-generational differences in perception – the differential investment of parents and children in their joint relationship because of their contrasting position in the cycle of generations. The

TABLE 6.6. Correlates of Intergenerational Stake at Time-4: Prediction of Variation in Dyadic Difference Scores from Parental Dependence

Predictors	T4 Father-Child Dyadic Difference Scores	T4 Mother-Child Dyadic Difference Scores
T4 Child Variables:		
G3's Report of G2's Chronic Illnesses	.23	.11
G3's Report of Help and Support Provided to G2	-.13	-.17
T4 Parent Variables:		
G2's Report of Chronic Illnesses	-.24	-.16
G2's Report of Help Received	.11	.12
d_F	4, 67	4, 105
overall F-ratio	1.04	1.31
p value <	NS	NS
adj R^2	.00	.01

*** p < .001
** p < .01
* p < .05

Note: Standardized b weights

expansion of the hypothesis led to a change in name to the "intergenerational stake hypothesis." Over the last two decades, the intergenerational stake hypothesis has been frequently referenced by other family researchers in explaining their findings on intergenerational relations.

Longitudinal data from a 20-year study with four time points allowed us to examine the intergenerational stake phenomenon in matched parent-child dyads. Moreover, the data provided an opportunity to examine two more general theoretical explanations of the phenomenon implicit in previous work—developmental theory and exchange theory—as well as some extensions. Four hypotheses were tested using two modes of analysis: a comparison of means across time and regression analyses.

Table 6.7 summarizes the results of the hypothesis tests. Subsequently, we discuss (a) the consistency and magnitude of the intergenerational stake phenomenon across the family life course, and the implications these findings have for developmental theory and exchange theory; (b) whether there are gender differences in the intergenerational stake phenomenon; and (c) directions for future research.

Consistency and Magnitude of the Intergenerational Stake Phenomenon

Exchange theory and developmental theory each provided different predictions for the pattern of the intergenerational stake phenomenon over the family life course. Hypothesis 1, based on exchange theory, predicted that the intergenerational stake phenomenon would occur across time, because parents have more invested in their children than their children have in them. In contrast, Hypothesis 2, based on developmental theory, postulated that the intergenerational stake phenomenon would manifest itself only early in the family life cycle when nuclear families confront adolescent autonomy and parental concerns for intergenerational continuity, and late in the family life cycle when families confront issues of elder parental dependence. Hypothesis 3 was based on the possibility that both theories were correct. It predicted that the intergenerational stake phenomenon would appear consistently across time, but that its magnitude would be greatest early and late in the family life cycle in response to developmental concerns.

The comparisons of means over time supported Hypothesis 1 rather than Hypothesis 2. As exchange theory predicted, fathers' and mothers' affectual solidarity for their children was greater than was children's affectual solidarity for their parents at all four time points. These findings go beyond previous research in that they establish the existence of the intergenerational stake phenomenon in parent-child dyads across time. Thus, we can conclude that *the intergenerational*

TABLE 6.7.   Summary of Results

H1	Because parents' investment in children is greater than children's investment in parents, parents will feel closer to their children than their children will feel to them, across the family life course.
	Supported.
H2	Parents will feel closer to their children than their children will feel to them early in the family life course (when families are dealing with adolescent independence and parental concern for intergenerational continuity in values) and late in the family life course (when families are dealing with parental dependence).
	Not supported.
H3	Parents will always feel closer to their children than their children will feel to them, but differences in parent-child affectual solidarity will be greatest early and late in the family life course.
	Not supported:
	(1) The analyses of means reveal that the magnitude of the intergenerational stake phenomenon does not covary with time points representing developmental concerns.
	(2) The regression analyses using more direct measures of developmental concerns reveal conflicting results for fathers and mothers: results for fathers show no support for developmental theory while results for mothers are inconclusive.
H4	Women's investment in children being greater than men's, parent-child differences in affectual solidarity will be greatest for mother-child than for father-child dyads.
	Not supported.

stake phenomenon is not limited to adolescent children and their middle-age parents; rather, it extends across the life course as children enter adulthood and parents enter advanced ages, as exchange theory would predict.

Further, contrary to Hypothesis 3, the consistency of mean parent-child differences across the life course suggests that the magnitude of cross-generational differences does not covary with developmental or life stage issues. That is, the intergenerational stake phenomenon was not significantly greater early and late in the family life cycle than it was at other times, as would be suggested by developmental theory. Although the magnitude of parent-child differences in affectual solidarity was only moderate, it showed a stable pattern across a twenty year period. Thus, *the link between levels of psychosocial development and the intergenerational stake was not supported.*

These results are consistent with those of Thompson, Clark, and Gunn (1985) who explicitly tested the link between psychosocial development and individual perceptions of cross-generational differences. They did not find a relationship between scores on a psychosocial development scale and perceived parent-child continuity in attitudes. However, their analyses were cross-sectional and limited to consensual solidarity; they did not test the link between psychosocial development and emotional continuity. Our research focused on parent-child differences in affectual solidarity. Like Thompson et al. (1985), we did not find a relationship between psychosocial development and cross-generational differences in perceptions, though we used time of measurement as a proxy for developmental concerns.

Our regression analyses, using more direct measures of developmental concerns than time of measurement, also suggest that parent-child differences in affectual solidarity are not the result of development.

Adolescent Autonomy and Parental Concern for Intergenerational Continuity in Values

Contrary to prediction, adolescent autonomy was found to significantly predict (with the exception of Time-2) the variability in the magnitude of the intergenerational stake phenomenon across the family life course for father–child dyads. That is, the greater children's independence during adolescence, the greater the difference in affectual solidarity between fathers and children, not only during adolescence, but also after children reached adulthood (average age of 39) and fathers reached advanced ages (average age of 64).

Continuity concerns of the father also significantly predicted variability in the magnitude of the intergenerational stake phenomenon across more than one time period. The greater the fathers' concern for continuity with the younger generation (measured only at Time-2), the greater the difference in affectual solidarity between fathers and children across 6 years (from Time-2 to Time-3 and Time-4).

In contrast, for mother–child dyads the intergenerational stake phenomenon was moderated by autonomy only while children were adolescents and was not moderated by parental concern for value continuity at any time.

These results suggest that adolescent autonomy and parental concern for value continuity may be lineage and gender issues rather than developmental issues. If autonomy and continuity were developmental concerns, they would, by definition, be related to the intergenerational stake phenomenon only during the time children were adolescents and parents were middle aged. However, both continued to predict the magnitude of the intergenerational stake phenomenon past this time for father–child dyads and, therefore, appear to be lifelong rather than developmental. These findings support earlier assumptions by Troll (1982): Children's concern for independence from their parents appears to be lifelong—children seem to be "trapped" in a struggle to establish autonomy, at least with their fathers.

Parental Dependence

The original intergenerational stake hypothesis was limited to youth and their middle-aged parents. It was hypothesized that the intergenerational stake phenomenon would be applicable to adult children and their elderly parents as long as the developmental tasks were expanded to include those of older life-course phases. Although Gesser, Marshall, and Rosenthal (1985) applied the intergenerational stake hypothesis to adult children and their elderly parents, they did not test this theoretical elaboration.

The regression analyses show that, contrary to developmental theory, parental dependence did not moderate the intergenerational stake phenomenon when parents were approaching advanced ages (mean age of 64). These results suggest that the dynamics behind the intergenerational stake phenomenon are the same for adult children and their elderly parents as for adolescent children and their middle-age parents; parental dependence does not seem to influence it. Therefore, *the intergenerational stake hypothesis appears applicable to adult children and their elderly parents without any theoretical elaboration to include developmental tasks of older life-course phases.*

However, it is possible that age 64 is not old enough for dependence issues to play a significant role. (Unfortunately, there was an insufficient number of older G1-G2 dyads with complete data to investigate this with older parents). Future waves of data where the G2 parents are of more advanced ages would be needed to rule out this alternative explanation.

Thus, taken as a whole, the regression results for father–child dyads show no support for developmental theory either early or late in the family life cycle. The results for mother–child dyads are inconclusive: There was support for developmental theory early in the family life cycle but no support for the late stage in the family life cycle.

The regression analyses, as well as the analyses of means, suggest that parent-child differences in affectual solidarity result from differential investment because of lineage position (parent vs. child) rather than developmental stage. Thus, exchange theory seems to provide a better explanation of our findings than does developmental theory: parents have a greater investment in their children than their children have in them, regardless of their developmental stage in the family life cycle.

Gender Differences in the Intergenerational Stake Phenomenon

Hypothesis 4 posited that the magnitude of the intergenerational stake phenomenon would be greater for mother-child dyads than for father-child dyads because of mothers' greater investment in children. Contrary to this prediction, there were no significant gender differences in the magnitude of the intergenerational stake phenomenon across 20 years.

However, post hoc analyses revealed a significant gender difference when parental affectual solidarity for children was considered independently of children's affectual solidarity for parents: Mother's affectual solidarity for children was significantly greater than father's when children were adolescents (Time-1). (Mothers' and fathers' affectual solidarity for children was comparable at all other time points.) However, the greater affectual solidarity of mothers at this time did not increase the magnitude of intergenerational stake phenomenon because it was offset by children's greater affectual solidarity for their mothers compared to their fathers. Additional post hoc analyses indicated that, across all time points, children reported significantly greater affectual solidarity for their mothers than for their fathers.[2]

Thus, unexpectedly, there were gender differences for children, looking upward, but not for parents, looking downward across generations. Therefore, the influence of gender on the magnitude of the intergenerational stake phenomenon may stem more from the differential investment of children in their fathers and mothers, than in the differential investments of fathers and mothers in their children.

However, gender differences in the intergenerational stake phenomenon may occur earlier in the family life cycle than we were able to examine with these data. The greatest difference in fathers' and mothers' investment in children is most likely to be found in families with young children, when the role of women as the primary caretakers is most profound. Further, it is likely that the gender of the child would interact with the gender of the parent. Rossi and Rossi (1990) suggest that a special bond exists between mothers and daughters. Future research should examine gender differences in the intergenerational stake phenomenon in families with younger children and should also consider the gender of the child as well as the gender of the parent. Unfortunately, there were not enough parent-child dyads with complete data in this study to break the dyads down by both the gender of the parents and the gender of the children.

Conclusion: Why the Intergenerational Stake Hypothesis Is (Mostly) Valid and How This May Affect Family Research and Theory

In summary, what these findings suggest is that the intergenerational stake phenomenon appears to be robust, if only moderate in magnitude. Investment of affect downward in the generational chain appears to be greater than investment of affect upward. There *is* a systematic bias in interpersonal perceptions regarding family relationships, and this bias can be seen along generational lines across the family life cycle.

Although our results suggest overall support for the intergenerational stake hypothesis, they also indicate some necessary revisions to the original theoretical statement. For example, evidence suggests that the intergenerational stake phenomenon is *not* the result of individuals' progression through developmental stages. This can be concluded because (a) the intergenerational stake phenomenon was manifest across time—parents' mean level of affectual solidarity for children was always greater than children's mean level of affectual solidarity for parents; and (b) the magnitude of the phenomenon was stable and did not covary with developmental concerns including adolescent autonomy, middle-age parental concern for intergenerational value continuity, and elderly parental dependence. Autonomy and continuity appear to be lifelong concerns for fathers and their children. Thus, the dynamics behind the bias in cross-generational perceptions appear to be related to lineage position rather than to psychosocial development, as originally postulated.

The intergenerational stake phenomenon suggests a caution for those of us who base our research about the family on large-scale surveys: There may be a critical flaw in individual-level, self-report data on intergenerational relationships. The perceptions of one generation about the other appear to be significantly biased by the respondents' contrasting motivational concerns *up* and *down* the family generational ladder. As researchers we unwittingly exacerbate this perceptual bias if we allow only one generation's report to characterize family interaction—as is done in most surveys. An effort should be made in future research on the family to include the perspectives of all family members in question.

These findings suggest several directions for future analyses of intergenerational stake phenomenon. First, it is of interest to assess how far down the generational chain the investment of affectual solidarity extends. We are currently analyzing the extent to which grandparents also have a greater stake in their grandchildren than grandchildren have in them. Second, future studies should examine whether "comparison levels for alternatives" (Thibaut & Kelley, 1959) influence the intergenerational stake. For example, it is possible that parents with many children have less of a stake in any one child than parents with a single child. In addition, it is possible that a parent's stake in their children may increase after the parent divorces or becomes widowed. Third, it would be interesting to examine whether there are ethnic or cultural differences in the intergenerational stake phenomenon. Perhaps the intergenerational stake phenomenon does not exist in less youth-oriented or less individualistic cultures (cultures where the family unit takes primacy over individual family members).

NOTES

[1]With the assistance of Matthew Jendian, Du Feng, and Bi-ling Shieh.

[2]Note that the means (child to father: $X_1 = 3.95$, $X_2 = 4.19$, $X_3 = 4.07$, $X_4 = 3.95$; child to mother: $X_1 = 4.21$, $X_2 = 4.46$, $X_3 = 4.24$, $X_4 = 4.19$) on these comparisons differ slightly from those displayed in Figure 6.2 because they must necessarily be limited to only those children reporting affection for both mothers and fathers.

REFERENCES

Angress, S. (1975). *Intergenerational relations and value congruence between young adults and their mothers*. Unpublished doctoral dissertation, University of Chicago.

Baruch, G., & Barnett, R. C. (1983). Adult daughters' relationships with their mothers. *Journal of Marriage and the Family, 45*, 601–606.

Bengtson, V. L. (1975). Generation and family effects in value socialization. *American Sociological Review, 40*, 358–371.

Bengtson, V. L., & Black, K. D. (1973). Inter-generational relations and continuities in socialization. In P. Baltes & K. W. Schaie (Eds.), *Life-span developmental psychology: Personality and socialization* (pp. 207–234). New York: Academic Press.

Bengtson, V. L., & Kuypers, J. A. (1971). Generational difference and the "developmental stake." *Aging and Human Development, 2*, 249–260.

Bernhardson, C. (1975). Type I error rates when multiple comparison procedures follow a significant F-test of ANOVA. *Biometrics, 31*, 229–232.

Blau, P. (1964). *Exchange and power in social life*. New York: Wiley.

Bond, J. B., & Harvey, C. D. H. (1991). Ethnicity and intergenerational perceptions of family solidarity. *Intergenerational Journal of Aging and Human Development, 33*, 33–44.

Brody, E. M. (1981). "Women in the middle" and family help to older people. *The Gerontologist, 21*, 471–480.

Brody, E. M. (1985). Parent care as a normative family stress. *The Gerontologist, 25*, 19–29.

Callan, V. J., & Noller, P. (1986). Perceptions of communicative relationships in families with adolescents. *Journal of Marriage and the Family, 48*, 813–820.

Cashmore, J. A., & Goodnow, J. J. (1985). Agreement between generations: A two-process approach. *Child Development, 56*, 493–501.

Chapman, N. J., & Neal, M. B. (1990). The effects of intergenerational experiences on adolescents and older adults. *The Gerontologist, 30*, 825–832.

Elder, G. H., Jr. (1984). Families, kin, and the life course: A sociological perspective. In R. Parke (Ed.), *Advances in child development research: The family* (pp. 80–136). Chicago: University of Chicago Press.

Emerson, R. M. (1981). Social exchange theory. In M. Rosenberg & R. Turner (Eds.), *Social psychology: Sociological perspectives*. New York: Basic Books.

Erikson, E. H. (1950). *Childhood and society*. New York: Norton.

Fischer, L. R. (1981). Transitions in the mother-daughter relationship. *Journal of Marriage and the Family, 43*, 613–622.

Fisher, C. B., Reid, J. D., & Melendez, M. (1989). Conflict in families and friendships of later life. *Family Relations, 38*, 83–89.

Gesser, G. L., Marshall, V. W., & Rosenthal, C. J. (1985, October). Developmental stake and the perception of intergenerational solidarity in the older family context: The extended generational stake hypothesis. Revised version of A test of the generational stake hypothesis with an older Canadian sample. Paper presented to Canadian Association on Gerontology meetings, Hamilton, Ontario.

Green, A. L., & Boxer, A. M. (1985). Daughters and sons as young adults: Restructuring the ties that bind. In N. Datan, A. Green, & H. Reese (Eds.), *Life-span developmental psychology: Intergenerational relationships* (pp. 125–149). Hillsdale, NJ: Erlbaum.

Hagestad, G. O. (1981). Problems and promises in the social psychology of intergenerational relations. In R. W. Fogel, E. Hatfield, S. B. Kiesler, & E. Shanas (Eds.), *Aging: Stability and change in the family* (pp. 11–47). New York: Academic Press.

Hagestad, G. O. (1990). Social perspectives on the life course. In R. Binstock & L. George (Eds.), *Handbook of aging and the social sciences* (3rd ed., pp. 151–168). San Diego: Academic Press.

Holmbeck, G. N., & Hill, J. P. (1988). Storm and stress beliefs about adolescence: Prevalence, self-reported antecedents, and effects of an undergraduate course. *Journal of Youth and Adolescence, 17*, 285–306.

Homans, G. (1974). *Social behavior: Its elementary forms*. New York: Harcourt Brace Jovanovich.

Johnson, E. S. (1978). "Good" relationships between older mothers and their daughters: A causal model. *The Gerontologist, 18*, 301–306.

Johnson, E. S., & Bursk, B. J. (1971). Relationships between the elderly and their adult children. *The Gerontologist, 17*, 90–96.

Knipscheer, K., & Bevers, A. (1985). Older parents and their middle-aged children:

Symmetry or asymmetry in their relationship. *Canadian Journal on Aging, 4,* 145–159.

Kreppner, K., & Lerner, R. M. (Eds.). (1989). *Family systems and life-span development.* Hillsdale, NJ: Erlbaum.

Lerner, R. M. (1982). Children and adolescents as producers of their own development. *Development Review, 2,* 342–370.

Lerner, R. M. (1984). *On the nature of human plasticity.* New York: Cambridge University Press.

Lerner, R. M., & Knapp, J. R. (1975). Actual and perceived intergenerational attitudes of late adolescents and their parents. *Journal of Youth and Adolescence, 4,* 17–36.

Mangen, D. J., Bengtson, V. L., & Landry, P. H. (1988). *Measurement of intergenerational relations.* Beverly Hills: Sage.

Mindel, C., & Wright, R. (1982). Satisfaction in multigenerational households. *Journal of Gerontology, 37,* 483–489.

Poulschock, S. W., & Deimling, G. (1986). Families caring for elders in residence: Issues in the measurement of burden. In L. Troll (Ed.), *Family issues in current gerontology* (pp. 226–245). New York: Springer.

Richards, L. N., Bengtson, V. L., & Miller, R. B. (1989). The "generation in the middle": Perceptions of adults' intergenerational relationships. In K. Kreppner & R. M. Lerner (Eds.), *Family systems and life-span development* (pp. 341–366). Hillsdale, NJ: Erlbaum.

Rom, D. M. (1990). A sequential rejection test procedure based on a modified Bonferroni inequality. *Biometrika, 77,* 663–666.

Rossi, A. S. (1993). Intergenerational relations: Gender, norms, and behavior. In V. L. Bengtson & W. A. Achenbaum (Eds.), *The changing contract across generations.* Hawthorne, NY: Aldine.

Rossi, A. S., & Rossi, P. H. (1990). *Of human bonding: Parent-child relationships across the life course.* New York: Aldine De Gruyter.

Silverstein, M., & Bengtson, V. L. (1991). Do close parent-child relations reduce the mortality risk of older parents? A test of the direct and buffering effects of intergenerational affection. *The Journal of Health and Social Behavior, 32,* 382–395.

Spitze, G., & Logan, J. R. (1991). Sibling structure and intergenerational relations. *Journal of Marriage and the Family, 53,* 871–884.

Sprecher, S. (1986). The relation between inequity and emotions in close relationships. *Social Psychology Quarterly, 49,* 309–321.

Stoller, E. P. (1983). Parental caregiving by adult children. *Journal of Marriage and the Family, 45,* 851–858.

Suitor, J. J., & Pillemer, K. (1988). Explaining intergenerational conflict when adult children and elderly parents live together. *Journal of Marriage and the Family, 50,* 1037–1047.

Sullivan, K., & Sullivan, A. (1980). Adolescent-parent separation. *Developmental Psychology, 16,* 93–99.

Talbott, M. M. (1990). The negative side of the relationship between older widows and their adult children: The mothers' perspective. *The Gerontologist, 30,* 595–603.

Taylor, R. J., Chatters, L. M., & Jackson, J. S. (1993). A profile of family relations among three-generation black families. *Family Relations*.

Thibaut, J., & Kelley, H. (1959). *The psychology of groups*. New York: Wiley.

Thompson, L., Clark, K., & Gunn, W. (1985). Developmental stage and perceptions of intergenerational continuity. *Journal of Marriage and the Family, 47*, 913–920.

Treas, J., & Bengtson, V. L. (1987). Family in later years. In M. Sussman & S. Steinmetz (Eds.), *Handbook on marriage and the family* (pp. 625–648). New York: Plenum.

Troll, L. E. (November, 1982). Family life in middle and old age: The generation gap. In F. M. Berardo (Ed.), *The annals of the American academy of political and social science: Middle and later life transitions* (pp. 38–46). Beverly Hills, CA: Sage Publishers.

Troll, L., & Bengtson, V. L. (1979). Generations in the family. In W. Burr, R. Hill, I. Reiss, & I. Nye (Eds.), *Theories about the family* (Vol. 1, pp. 127–161). New York: The Free Press.

Walster, E., Walster, G. W., & Berscheid, E. (1978). *Equity: Theory and research*. Boston: Allyn & Bacon.

Wilen, J. B. (1979). *Changing relationships among grandparents, parents, and their young adult children*. Paper presented at the annual meeting of the Gerontological Society of America, Washington, DC.

Zarit, S. H., Reever, E., & Bach-Peterson, J. (1980). Relatives of the impaired elderly: Correlates of feelings of burden. *The Gerontologist, 20*, 649–655.

Commentary:
Wanted: Alternative Theory
and Analysis Modes

Alice S. Rossi

I was very pleased to serve as a discussant of the Giarrusso et al. (this volume) paper at the Penn State Conference, because I have been indebted to Vern Bengtson for important input to my own thinking about intergenerational relationships and kinship structure. The central constructs that guided the University of Southern California (USC) Longitudinal Study of Generations informed my own design of a study of parent–child relationships, reported in *Of Human Bonding* (Rossi & Rossi, 1990). Included among them are the *dimensions* of intergenerational and lineage solidarity (i.e., affective closeness, social interaction, help exchange, and normative consensus). I was further persuaded by Bengtson of the importance of obtaining data from *both* partners of the parent–child dyad.

The design and analysis of the USC study has differed from my own in several key respects, and because they are relevant to the themes I will discuss in this commentary, I mention them here. For one, gender was a central construct in my analysis of intergenerational relations, whereas in most previous reports from the USC study, little attention was given to gender: reference is made to "parents," "children," and "grandparents" rather than to mothers and fathers, daughters and sons, grandmothers and grandfathers. It was refreshing to note that gender is given more attention in the present paper based on the USC data, although only partially so, because the authors specify only gender of the G2 parents, not of their G3 children.

A second difference between us is my emphasis on the critical importance of the past history of the parent–child dyad. What happens to us as children and to our parents when they are young adults rearing us continues for many decades to shape the relationship between us, and even more deeply, our own self-concept; indeed, there is probably no other human relationship that has as profound an impact on us as the relationship to our parents when we were growing up. Even during the years following the death of our parents, we carry their internalized voices within us. My study confirmed the expectation that early family life continues to show effects on contemporary parent-child relationships, *net* of any array of intervening life circumstances or developmental turning points in the lives of either parents or children. Such findings come as no surprise to clinicians or developmental psychologists, nor to those who reflect on the lingering impact in their own biographies of their early family life. As seen later, I think studies of intergenerational relations that do not include measures of the early family structure and the quality of relationships experienced in childhood suffer from a slimness of interpretive depth, and invite the application of inappropriate explanatory theories.

Times have changed greatly since the early 1970s when the USC study was initiated. A major rationale for generational studies in that early period was to affirm or refute the common assumption of a significant "gap" of values and lifestyle between the generations. Issues of "equity" or "justice" or "stake" between the generations were rarely invoked and played little role in study designs. That they have become more dominant a focus of both public and social science debate in recent years, reflects growing public concern about the high financial drain that attends an aging society, especially health care and social security costs for the elderly. An implicit policy issue beneath much public funding of research on intergenerational relations is the extent to which families and lineages would be willing or able to reabsorb some of the financial and human costs of caring for the elderly if and when public funds for such purposes were reduced. Indeed, one of the interesting and important policy questions concerning the "intergenerational stake" thesis is not addressed in the Giarrusso et al. chapter—that is, if parents are more invested emotionally and socially in children than children are in their parents, does this mean adult children would be unwilling to assume greater responsibility for parent care?

THE USC PAPER ON INTERGENERATIONAL STAKE

The USC paper is a revision of the one prepared for the Penn State Conference in October 1992, which formed the basis of my own earlier paper. The current draft is different from its earlier version, in part in response to my criticism of it. Thus the central construct has been changed from "generational stake" (surely a misnomer, because the state is in the relationship between proximate generations) to "intergenerational stake." Second, as mentioned earlier, the paper gives more attention to gender. Third, more use is made of the longitudinal data set instead of just the 1971 initial wave of the study. Fourth, the authors dropped what I considered an inappropriate comparison of the G1-G2 relationship with the G2-G3 relationship, and have instead given primary emphasis to individual pairs of G2 parents and G3 adult children, with data from each partner obtained at the four waves of the 20-year longitudinal study.

Despite these improvements, the revised chapter is unfortunately weak and unconvincing on a number of counts, and it is to these that I now turn.

Measurement of the Major Dependent Variable: Affectual Solidarity

Fundamental to any empirical analysis is clarity of the constructs and adequacy of the measures that operationalize them. I found it surprising in the extreme that the authors defined their major dependent variable, Affectual solidarity, as they do. Affectual solidarity was carefully assessed and reported in the methodological volume on the USC study edited by Mangen, Bengtson, and Landry (1988). In the chapter on affectual solidarity, they report a 10-item Long Form and a 5-item Short Form scale of this construct, the major difference being that the short form is limited to 5 self-ratings and the long form adds 5 equivalent attribution items (e.g., a self-report on closeness of the relationship felt by a child and an attribution item on the closeness felt by the parent toward the child as perceived by the child). The five indicators of affectual solidarity were items on trust, fairness, respect, affection, and understanding.

But the 6-item measurement of affectual solidarity in the chapter under discussion is neither the long- nor the short-form scale. One of the 6 items is an attribution (my parent/child understands me), and 5 are self-reports. Only 3 of the 6 items were from the long form (two on understanding, one the self-report of closeness). Apparently the items on "communicating well" and "getting along with" did not meet their eigenvalue criterion when all possible affective items were factor analyzed. Most surprising, however, is the inclusion in the measure of affectual solidarity of an item, not on affectual solidarity but consensual solidarity (i.e., a rating on perceived similarity of opinions and values about life). Affective closeness between parents and children is rooted in their past together; sociopolitical values and opinions are more likely to be influenced by cohort and historical factors, and ought to be handled as a separate construct dimension of intergenerational solidarity. (In my own study, a comparable measure of value consensus showed only modest correlations with affective closeness, weaker in data obtained from parents than in the data obtained from children.)

Despite this conceptual blurring of the major variable, the chapter claims, after listing the 6 items for the major scale, that the "reliability and validity information on this scale are reported in Mangen, Bengtson, and Landry (1988)." This is simply not the case. My point here is not that an analyst is forever bound to rely on scales constructed at an earlier time period in a research project; rather, there is some responsibility to justify departure from earlier published reports on the grounds of either more recent measurement testing, or the requirements of a particular analysis topic. Furthermore, my point carries substantive as well as methodological importance, because one of the central hypotheses explored in the chapter centers on the effect of parental concern for value transmission in the family on affection between parents and children. There can be no clean test of this hypothesis when the measure of affection is contaminated with an item that is conceptually indistinguishable from the independent predictor variables. This is an invitation to tautological, spurious results.

Theoretical Interpretive Framework

The major analytic effort in the chapter by Giarrusso et al. (this volume) is to test which of two theoretical interpretations is most adequate as explanations for the tendency of parents to be more deeply invested emotionally in their relationship to their children than the children are invested emotionally in their relationship to their parents—the asymmetry at the heart of the "intergenerational stake" thesis. Thus they counterpose a developmental with an exchange theoretical interpretation of the differential stake hypothesis. But I found the assumptions underlying both of these interpretive possibilities murky and misleading. I shall discuss each in turn.

Developmental Theory

The authors report that in previous research based on samples of adolescents and their parents, the major interpretation for the affective asymmetry was the developmental pressure on adolescents to break away from parental dependency and to chart their own path into adulthood with values of their own in a kind of child-initiated weaning process. If this interpretation is correct, the authors argue, then the asymmetry should disappear when children are well along in years. This makes highly appropriate data from later waves in the USC longitudinal study, because the G3 children of G2 parents move from an average age of 19 at Time-1 to 33 at Time-2 and 39 at Time-4. In a similar analytic mode, the authors suggest that the parents themselves confront their own developmental tasks, seeking meaning in life by looking to their children in their middle years, and coping with their own declining strength and health in old age.

There are several problems with this formulation and the empirical mode by which the authors attempt to test them. I do not understand why they believe something can not be "developmental" if it is not unique to one life phase. Once children acquire a loving trust in the world as preschoolers, that trust is not lost when they confront issues of identity as adolescents; they carry the trust forward in time as they deal with issues relevant to later stages of life. So, too, once adolescents become autonomous and differ from their parents in lifestyle or sociopolitical values, this difference is carried forward in time, not dropped when they confront intimacy or generativity issues. As results from the European Value Studies have shown, the critical life phase when basic political and social values are acquired is late adolescence and early adulthood, values that then persist across the remainder of the life course, with distinct and persistent value profiles that continue to differentiate birth cohorts as they age (Lestheaghe, 1983; Lestheaghe & Surkyn, 1988).

Whether political and social value differences between parents and children persist over time. and how this difference impacts on intergenerational affectual solidarity is an interesting question, for which one might well find answers in the USC data set, but that is not pursued in the chapter. To do so would require developing measures at Time-1 of the variance in values in a variety of areas (e.g., politics, religious affiliation, and religiosity) of pairs of parents and children; testing how this value difference relates to affective closeness at Time-1; and then tracing whether the correlation between value differences and affection declines over the subsequent measurement points in the 20 year time span of the study. What the authors do, instead, is merely to measure the difference in affect scores of parents and children *at each period* and to explore on an aggregate level, whether that difference diminishes or increases as a function of earlier attitudes. In the analysis on the level of individual dyads, the predictor variables for the most part do not concern the actual behavior of the children, but general attitudes toward rebellious behavior of adolescents and the perceived generation "gap" in the family. Far more useful, and I assume possible with their own data, would be to create direct measures of religious or political value similarity and difference between pairs of parents and children at Time-1 and to trace the persistence and impact of such differences on affective closeness at later stages of life.

A second serious lack of clarity in the developmental framework of the chapter is the assumption that midlife adults *as parents* confront, for the first time, concern for seeking "meaning in life" and look to their children to provide such meaning. I can only assume they are trying to apply some Eriksonian idea of midlife generativity to their data. The Erikson construct of generativity seems to have a life of its own, often cited, rarely researched, and with no evidence of just when during the life course it is likely to develop. Most parents, I would submit, find meaning in their lives through their children from a very early phase in their childbearing and rearing; it is not something particular to parents in late midlife. In midlife, children may take on *additional* meaning, if other life hopes and dreams dim, for example, when men reach some plateau of earnings or begin to question whether the work they do is really making as much of a contribution to themselves and society as their family roles provide. If anything, the feeling that our children (and grandchildren) represent our hold on immortality may increase in salience in old age, when life runs down and our own demise is imminent.

But the only available measure of the presumed meaning-in-life seeking the authors link to midlife is a Time-2 measure on how concerned they are as parents that their "adult children share the same values in life as they do." This is *not* an appropriate measure of the construct of generativity, nor is there any reason to believe that there is some special developmental salience of this question to parents in late midlife (at Time-2, the average age of G2 parents is 59 and the G3 children are 33). Parental effort to transmit their own values to their children is long since past. If anything, by late midlife parents have accommodated to whatever value or lifestyle differences there are between themselves and their children. It is not shared values that are at issue for most late midlife parents, but how well the children are doing in their own lives in terms of status, health, happiness, and well-being, and doing an adequate job of producing and rearing grandchildren.

There is also a more fundamental question concerning affectual solidarity that is not confronted and hence not analyzed in the chapter. The level of affective closeness between parents and children is highly likely to be very stable over time, with only modest impact of later life events on the closeness between them. If development is indeed epigenetic, as many developmental psychologists claim, then neglect or rejection in childhood will permanently impair the affection between parent and child, just as an intact, loving home in childhood will permanently mark the level of affection between parent and child from that point forward. As Kierkegard reminded us, we have to live life "forward" but can only understand it "backward." For a social scientist concerned with intergenerational relations, this means contemporary relations between the generations are rooted in the biographies of the partners to such relationships. I take this to mean that any test of later life events on the quality of a parent–child relationship must use an earlier index of the affective quality of the relationship as a control; whether a later life event affects the affective closeness should be tested, *net* of the earlier level of affection between the generations. Hence, for example, to test whether parental ill health in late life affects the closeness between parent and child should involve a *control* on the affection *before* the ill health struck. Empirically this might involve a measure of change in health status of a parent between, say Time-2 and Time-3, (or a dummy variable to identify those whose health deteriorated significantly between waves) and a regression of the health change measure *and the Time-2 closeness measure* on the Time-3 measure of closeness. Only in this way could one test whether impaired health effects a *significant change* in affective closeness, and whether this change holds just for the children's ratings, the parents' ratings, or both.

The same mode of analysis could be attempted concerning critical life events that took place during the long 14-year interval between Time-1 (1971) and Time-2 (1985) of the USC study. In that interval, many G3 children acquired much more education than their parents whereas others attained only the same level of schooling as their parents (a measure of social mobility between the generations, with all manner of likely consequences in terms of value and lifestyle change); some children will have married and produced grandchildren, whereas others may still be single or childless. These likely demographic transitions invite an analysis that could show what changes, if any, occur in the affective closeness reported at Time-2 in the G2-G3 parent-child relationship as a function of intervening critical life transitions of the child, *net* of the level of affective closeness (or difference score as used in the paper) at Time-1. This would test the thesis, often talked about in family sociology literature but rarely empirically demonstrated, that becoming parents themselves triggers greater affective closeness between adult children and their parents. You could also test the impact of differential rates of social mobility on the affective closeness of the parent-child relationship by following the same analysis mode.

Two general points in these critical comments and the alternative analysis modes I have suggested are that (a) there is a far richer potential for analysis and theoretical contributions of the USC data set than the restricted revisit to the "intergenerational stake" thesis permits, and (b) the mode of analysis followed by the USC authors is not adequate to the task of testing any developmentally grounded set of moderators of the generational asymmetry in parent-child affective closeness.

Exchange Theory

The second of the two interpretations the authors explore is "exchange theory." No clear definition or exposition of exchange theory is given anywhere in the chapter, and we are left to infer what is intended from very varied allusions. The first time exchange theory is cited is in connection with the Richards, Bengtson and Miller (1989) chapter that reported G2 subjects (the "sandwich" generation) had closer ties *down* the generational ladder to G3 children than *up* the ladder to their G1 parents. The interpretation offered is that the middle generation has a "stronger stake in the younger generation than in the older generation due to their greater investment in the younger generation, which is more in line with exchange theory rather than developmental theory." The concept of "stake" surely hinges on "investment," which makes the statement tautological. But no specification is given for why the pattern found is consistent with an "exchange" theory, nor *which* exchange theory they have in mind. Nowhere in the chapter do they clarify this issue. No reference is made to the "principle of least interest" (Dowd, 1980), for example, that argues that power in a relationship is in the hands of the partner *least* involved in the relationship because the "cost" of impairing or severing the relationship is less than it is for the partner with greater involvement. The implicitly economic reasoning involved here is the claim that "the investment or social exchange approach focuses on the rewards and costs individuals obtain through social interaction, and is based on the assumption that individuals try to maximize their rewards and minimize their costs."

Because the exchange between parents and children is not balanced but asymmetrical, they further argue that this "leads to feelings of inequity and a motivation to reduce those feelings" by either restoring "actual" equity or "psychological" equity by changing their perceptions of their own or their partners' investment. Here the authors are applying exchange theory from studies of friendship and courting couples to the parent–child relationship. I consider the assumption that parent–child relations are analogous to friendship or courting relationships inappropriate. In the latter cases, relationships may indeed be renegotiated toward greater reciprocity of investment, or they will terminate. Such termination is also available to long-married couples by divorce when asymmetry in giving and getting becomes severely one-sided. But one cannot and does not divorce a parent or a child in contemporary Western societies, though the equivalent of a divorce may occur under pathological conditions through neglect, rejection, or abuse. I am simply not able to follow the authors' reasoning that "parents restore equity by perceiving their relationship with their child as closer than their child perceives the relationship." If you start with the finding that at Time-1, parents are closer to children than children are to them—the basic asymmetry in the first place—how is "equity restored" by *increasing* the asymmetry at later stages of life? Reciprocity is a major assumption of exchange theory, so how can one conclude as the authors do, after finding that asymmetry of affectual solidarity holds at all four time points in the 20-year USC study, that exchange theory is a better explanation of the "intergenerational stake hypothesis" than developmental theory?

In the next section, I confront exchange theory directly, and will argue that its application to parent-child relationships is misplaced and misleading.

EXCHANGE THEORY: PROMISE OR DEADEND IN INTERGENERATIONAL THEORY?

With the waning in popularity of functionalist theory in sociology in the 1970s and of Marxism in the 1980s, the discipline underwent a period of groping for new theoretical paradigms, with some sociologists moving toward social psychological theories (e.g., symbolic interaction) and others toward rational decision-making models in economics, of which exchange theory is one example. Thus we find sociologist Michael Hannan praising economist Gary Becker's exchange theory on intimate relationships for "cutting through the romantic mist that so often blinds social scientists" (Hannan, 1982, p. 68). Rationality may well be the mark of many decisions adults make: in seeking some match between interests and skills in occupational choice, in job selection that weighs job security against health benefits, in how much to spend on holiday gifts during a recession. It is quite another matter, however, to impute rationality to other aspects of human life, particularly to domains heavily influenced by strong social norms and deep emotions. Yet it came as a surprise to one trio of sociologists who hypothesized that marital satisfaction would be highest when couples attempt an equal contribution to household management and leisure time use; however, they found a *negative* correlation between the extent of egalitarian sharing and subjective ratings of marital satisfaction (Murstein, Cerrato, & MacDonald, 1977)—a flat contradiction of an exchange model proscription for a happy marriage.

The same point applies to parents and children, the most intensely affect laden of all family relationships, and at no time more so than in contemporary society. Today's parents now invest more time and money in rearing children than ever before in history, because ever higher levels of educational attainment have been deemed necessary to assure adequate status and financial security for our children. It is likely that over the past century, a good 10 years has been added to child dependency on parents, either because of graduate and professional training that for many young adults is not complete until late in their 20s, or because the economy is so poor that late adolescents and young adults face high unemployment rates when they leave school and parents continue to at least partially support them.

Despite this heavy investment in children for longer periods contemporary parents do *not* expect reciprocation in their declining years by residing with children or taking personal caregiving by their children for granted, and certainly they hope to avoid any financial dependence on children. Medicare, Social Security, private pension plans, and their own savings, they hope and expect will carry them through the remaining years of their lives. In fact, far from expecting great help from their children, Paul Cleary and Mark Schlesinger report (from a national survey sponsored by the American Association of Retired Persons) that elderly adults endorse the view that parents should try to save money and property to pass on as an inheritance to their children (Cleary, personal communication, February 22, 1991).

Most elderly parents today do not in fact represent a "burden" even in personal caregiving from their children. Glenna Spitze and John Logan report (1990) modest contributions of time to any kind of parent care—a *modal* pattern of between 3 and 4 hours a week. Nor is the typical middle aged "sandwich" generation of women caught between dependent age children and elderly parents, despite the claims of researchers (Brody, 1981, 1985) that the "empty nest is a myth" and middle-aged women are experiencing anxiety and emotional exhaustion from caring for both children and parents. The "overburdened middle aged woman" is as much a myth as was the "midlife crisis" so fashionable a decade ago (Hunter & Sundel, 1989). Spitze and Logan (1990) show, for example, that across 5-year age groups from 40 to 65 the proportion of women who are employed full time, provide 3 or more hours a week of help to a parent, and have a child (of any age) still living at home ranges from 0% to 8%. By the time elderly parents are in their 70s and 80s, their daughters are not "dependents" of their parents; many such daughters are even beyond childrearing themselves. In fact, for many middle-aged women with mothers in declining health, their own daughters are a source of comfort and help to them, not a further drain on their time and energy.

In addition, multiple roles are no necessary prescription for psychological and physical stress; they can in fact have positive, *buffering* effects because stress in one role is less overwhelming if gratification is experienced in other roles (Baruch, Barnett, & Rivers, 1982; Baruch, Biener, & Barnett, 1985; Stoller & Pugliesi, 1989).

Middle-aged adults may be "time-needy," but compared with their ancestors, they are hardly exhausted physically: We engage largely in sedentary occupations in a service and information based economy, work 35 to 40 hour work weeks, have small families, and compact homes with numerous labor-saving appliances, a profile with low potential for exhaustion compared with 70-hour work weeks of rural folk in the past, with numerous pregnancies, five or six children to rear, and physically exhausting labor to process food and make clothing.

My reservations concerning the appropriateness of economic exchange models is not limited to the sociological study of intergenerational relations. There is growing recognition even within economics itself, that rational decision-making models are not adequate to explain firm variation in productivity or profits. Robert Frank shows that rationality as an organization premise is far less powerful a predictor of productivity and efficiency of firms than a model that includes such socioemotionally based variables as loyalty, trust, and love (Frank, 1988). Satisfaction in intimate, ongoing, emotionally laden relationships derives, after all, from irrational love, which prompts a partner to want to do more for the other than the partner gives. Most midlife parents, I submit, are fully rewarded if and when their children grow into healthy, mature adults who invest in their own children as their parents did in them. Indeed, many midlife parents experience what I call *frustrated altruism*, because they wish to make gifts of substance or money their grown children do not wish or refuse to accept out of pride in fending for themselves—which may be why so many of these frustrated parents take special pleasure with the birth of grandchildren, gifts to whom are more acceptable to their children. Obligations and sentiments may flow down the generations and into a future we cannot know, with our descendants representing a feeble hold on immortality. I have seen no evidence to support any notion that asymmetry in intergenerational affection, interaction, or exchange of help is experienced by those involved in the parent–child relationship as lacking in equity or justice, to say nothing of psychological maneuvering to "restore equity" in the balance of affection between the generations.

Gender and Intergenerational Relations

Space limitations permit only a few comments on the analysis of gender in the chapter.

First, I do not think gender can be adequately analyzed in any intergenerational relations study unless it is specified for *both* sides of the parent–child relationship. The authors claim they can not do so because there would be insufficient cases were gender of G3 children specified as it is for G2 parents. This assumes it was necessary to restrict the entire analysis to the *full* longitudinal sample (i.e., just those G2 and G3 subjects who responded to all four waves of the study). I see no reason for such a restriction, in light of the fact that only 6 years intervene between Time-2 and Time-4. Had they been as persuaded as I am that gender specification needs to be done for both generations, they could easily have backed up to Time-3 and dropped Time-4 data. After all, there is no notable change in development terms between G2 parents of 62 compared to 65, or G3 children of 36 compared to 39.

Second, I would predict a number of interesting lines of analysis might have been attempted were gender fully specified. Clearly, with intervals of only 3 years between each of the last 3 waves of the study, they must have cases of divorce among the children, or a death among the parents. This would have permitted an interesting analysis of the impact of such changes in marital status on the affectual solidarity between parents and children, following the same analytical model I suggested to tap the impact of parental ill health in an earlier section of this commentary.

From my own analysis of intergenerational relations, it became clear that the mother–daughter relationship is pivotal to the structure of the kindred and the ties that hold families together in a socially embedded way. *Women are the unsung heroines of social integration:* As childrearers, caregivers, and kin keepers, women provide the glue that holds families and lineages together. In the highly urban societies of the 1990s with high social valuation of individualism, fragile ties to neighbors, and declining loyalties to the larger community, this fundamental axis of social integration takes on greater social and political significance than ever before.

CONCLUSIONS

Sociologists and gerontologists would do well to seek other theoretical models than a niggardly exchange model of rational men seeking "equity," and to consider seriously altruism and empathy as primary motivators of family behavior. I submit that these are the sentiments that stoke solidarity in society generally, and nowhere more so than in intergenerational relations. The "intergenerational stake" hypothesis has been revisited in the chapter by Giarrusso et al. (this volume), but it was not a successful visit. I urge these researchers to go back to their very rich data set with a new set of questions for which they have adequate measures, instead of conducting what can only be called "secondary analysis" because the developmental and exchange theories that dominate the empirical analysis in this chapter played no role in the basic design of the study, with the consequence that there were no appropriate measures of the "moderator" variables for the hypotheses they tried to test.

REFERENCES

Baruch, G. K., Barnett, R., & Rivers, C. (1982). *Lifeprints: New patterns of love and work for today's women.* New York: McGraw-Hill.

Baruch, G. K., Biener, L., & Barnett, R. C. (1985). *Women and gender in research on stress* (Working paper). Wellesley, MA: Center for Research on Women.

Becker, G. (1981). *A treatise on the family.* Boston: Harvard University Press.

Brody, E. (1981). "Women in the middle" and family help to older people. *The Gerontologist, 21,* 471–479.

Brody, E. (1985). Parent care as a normative family stress. *The Gerontologist, 25,* 19–29.

Dowd, J. J. (1980). *Stratification among the aged*. Monterey, CA: Brooks/Cole.

Frank, R. H. (1988). *Passions within reason: The strategic role of the emotions*. New York: Norton.

Hannan, M. (1982). Families, markets and social structures: An essay on Becker's treatise on the family. *Journal of Economic Literature, 20,* 65–72.

Hunter, S., & Sundel, M. (Eds.). (1989). *Midlife myths: Issues, findings and practice implications*. Newbury Park, CA: Sage.

Lesthaeghe, R. (1983). A century of demographic and cultural change in Western Europe: An exploration of underlying dimensions. *Population and Development Review, 9,* 413–435.

Lesthaeghe, R., & Surkyn, N. (1988). Cultural dynamics and economic theories of fertility change. *Population and Development Review, 14,* 1–45.

Mangen, D. J., Bengtson, V. L., & Landry, P. H. (Eds.). (1988). *Measurement of intergenerational relations*. Newbury Park, CA: Sage.

Murstein, B., Cerrato, M., & MacDonald, M., (1977). A theory and investigation of the effect of exchange-orientation on marriage and friendship. *Journal of Marriage and the Family, 39,* 543–548.

Richards, L. N., Bengtson, V. L., & Miller, R. B. (1989). The "generation in the middle": Perceptions of adults' intergenerational relationships. In K. Kreppner & R. M. Lerner (Eds.), *Family systems and life-span development* (pp. 341–366). Hillsdale, NJ: Erlbaum.

Rossi, A. S. & Rossi, P. H. (1990). *Of human bonding: Parent-child relations across the life course*. Hawthorne, NY: Aldine de Gruyter.

Spitze, G., & Logan, J. (1990). More evidence on women (and men) in the middle. *Research on Aging, 12,* 182–198.

Stoller, E. P., & Pugliesi, K. L. (1989). Other roles of caregivers: Competing responsibilities or supportive resources. *Journal of Gerontology: Social Sciences, 44,* S231–S238.

Commentary: A Finding in Search of an Interpretation: Discussion of "The Intergenerational Stake Hypothesis Revisited"

Victor W. Marshall

When, more than two decades ago, Bengtson and Kuypers (1971) noted some generational differences, and tried to explain them with a "developmental stake hypothesis," they established for subsequent inquiry one of a very small number of interesting and original research questions in the social psychology of intergenerational relationships; yet very few scholars have followed up on the research question and the developmental stake hypothesis. Having been one of those few, I welcome the opportunity to participate in this discussion. As my fellow discussant, Alice Rossi notes in this volume, the current discussion deals with two versions of the current conference paper, and our conference reactions to both of them and to each other's comments. The liveliness of the discussion might indicate the importance of the research question. My observations in this commentary are influenced by this process, and directed to selected issues concerning research on the "developmental stake hypothesis" and its successors over the years.

There has been an evolution of the developmental stake hypothesis to become the generational stake hypothesis (first mentioned by Bengtson, 1979) and now the intergenerational stake hypothesis. This evolution reflects changing times and evolving theoretical commitments and developments. The "generation gap" was important in popular culture in 1971, and developmental theory was more central to gerontology then than it is now. Two decades ago our methodological and statistical tools and expectations were not so highly developed. The scope of the research problem has varied since 1971. While the initial paper dealt with a small range of intergenerational solidarity phenomena (perceptions of social distance between the generations, perceptions of family discussion and disagreement, the actual extent of disagreement on eleven topics, and the amount of discussion between the generations), subsequent work has expanded the repertoire to include all the intergenerational solidarity dimensions.

Over the same period, our conception of intergenerational familial relationships has been formalized, notably through Bengtson and Schrader's (1982) codification of dimensions of "family solidarity"; and interest has risen in the extent to which the various solidarity dimensions are related. Simultaneously, other perspectives on, and insights into, the aging and family area have addressed issues that have been largely ignored by those seeking to understand family solidarity— and this is an issue I will turn to later in these remarks.

The chapter by Giarrusso, Stallings, and Bengtson (this volume) is mistitled. It does not "revisit" the "intergenerational stake hypothesis." The chapter briefly describes an empirical finding—that descriptions of generational relations downward are generally reported to be more favorable than descriptions of generational relationships upward. It then reviews some hypotheses, beginning with the developmental stake hypothesis, which have tried to explain these differences. Finally, it presents data on a highly selected aspect of the basic empirical finding, for only one dimension of intergenerational solidarity, the affective, and makes new contributions to explanation. In doing so, the chapter does not revisit an old hypothesis. Rather, it revisits in a quite narrow way an old (two decades old) empirical finding.

In these remarks I briefly critique the theorizing about this empirical question, particularly when it is extended to the later years, and then suggest that the ways in which this question has been addressed have contributed little to our understanding of what actually transpires in generational relations. I am less concerned than Rossi with specific methodological criticism but as concerned with theoretical issues. However, the content of my concerns differs from hers.

INITIAL AND SUBSEQUENT FORMULATIONS OF THE PROBLEM

The hypothesis was initially grounded in the developmental psychology of Erikson. Bengtson, and Kuypers suggested that differences in the reports of middle-aged parents and their children emerge because each generation has unique developmental concerns and a unique "stake" in the relationship. Middle-aged parents, for example, are concerned with the continuity of their values: they wish to see their values transmitted to their children. Perception is held to be shaped by want. They, therefore, report levels of closeness and consensus on values that are higher than the levels reported by their children. On the other hand, young adults are motivated to establish autonomy from their parents in values and social relationships. To admit to feelings of closeness and similarity of values would threaten their feelings of autonomy, so they perceive and report less closeness and less consensus than their parents report.

Thompson, Clark, and Gunn (1985), with the same generational groupings, found only limited support for the hypothesis, but the work of the USC group, under Bengtson's leadership, has confirmed, with increasing rigor and detail, the general finding that parents of any age see their relationship to their children as closer or stronger than the children see it. It is why this so that continues to be puzzling.

Troll (1982) argued that the generational stake hypothesis should apply to old parents and their children as well as at to the younger generations: "Old parents, feeling the end of their own life nearing and wanting to believe that the goals they fought for during their life will endure, tend to minimize the differences in values and characteristics between them and their children. Their offspring, still feeling there is time for them—they have the evidence of another generation living ahead of them—tend to emphasize their uniqueness more than their commonality with those who precede them" (Troll, 1982, p. 41). By this reasoning, the middle generation would be simultaneously biasing its perceptions toward dissensus with its parents and toward consensus with its children. Troll did not directly test the applicability of the generational stake hypothesis in later life, but she grounded her argument in a review of related studies of aging and family life.

Besides Troll, other scholars, including Bengtson himself (Gesser, 1986; Gesser, Marshall, & Rosenthal, 1985; Knipscheer & Bevers, 1985; Mangen, Bengtson, & Landry, 1988) tried to apply the developmental stake hypothesis to other generations—hence, the developmental stake hypothesis became the "generational stake hypothesis."

Knipscheer & Bevers (1985) tested the hypothesis with 74 older parent–middle-aged children pairs in Holland. On several items concerning political and religious values and the nature of the parent-child relationship, they found high objective disagreement, lower perceived disagreement than objective disagreement, and lower perceived disagreement reported by parents than by adult children. The latter confirms the general finding which the developmental/generational/intergenerational stake hypothesis seeks to explain. The explanation they offer claims to affirm the "developmental stake hypothesis" but interprets this not in terms of developmental theory but rather the "principle of least interest" as based in exchange theory (Dowd, 1980).

Knipscheer and Bevers (1985) stress that there is little perceived disagreement between the generations, and they attribute this to a "meta-orientation" of valuing the relationship. This important point reminds us that the developmental stake hypothesis in its various forms seeks to understand "variations on a theme," that is, the slight but largely consistent *differences* in levels of solidarity attributions between the generations over and above the simple fact that intergenerational solidarity is, generally speaking, quite high. Thus, what leaps from the charts and tables of the paper under discussion is not the difference between the generations but the similarities; yet the intellectual problem selected is to explain the differences.

I turn now to work done by Gesser, Rosenthal and myself (Gesser, 1986; Gesser, Marshall, & Rosenthal, 1985), that is relevant to the second major hypothesis of the paper under discussion. We drew heavily on Bengtson's measurement, indeed Bengtson served as a consultant for the study, so that we are able to make inferences within the same conceptual and measurement assumptions as he has used. We did not wed ourselves to a developmental interpretation, particularly to the quest for autonomy by the young, because we studied middle-aged children and their aged parents. We removed the discussion from the realm of developmental theory and suggested that mutual fear of anticipated parental dependence adds an additional dynamic to the parent–child relationship in later life.

We matched responses of a random sample of 188 parents aged 65 or older with those of a specific child, rather than simply making group comparisons of parents and of children. (Some parents were double-or triple-counted in relation to two or three children. There are thus 188 children but only 100 parents in the sample). The distributions of responses of parents and adult children on a single indicator of affectional solidarity ("how close do you feel is the relationship between you and your child/parent?"), are both highly skewed, with only 1.6% of parents and 8.6% of children opting for the "not close" and "not too close" options on a 5-point scale. Skew is similar though not nearly so strong on a single indicator of consensual solidarity tapping perceived agreement in "your ideas and opinions about the things you consider really important in life." The strongest finding, then, is that family solidarity, particularly affectional solidarity, is generally high. Second, perceived consensus is not necessarily a prerequisite for perceived positive affect. Third, both distributions also show that parents estimate greater solidarity than do children, confirming the general fact which the developmental/generational/intergenerational stake hypothesis seeks to explain.

A matched pairs or dyadic analysis shows the percentage of dyads in which the parent reports greater solidarity, the same amount, or less, than the matched child reports. There is a significant difference with respect to feelings of closeness, or affective solidarity, in the direction confirming a greater parental "stake" in the relationship; and there is a strong tendency with respect to consensual solidarity as well. As the Giarrusso et al. (this volume), paper points out in discussing our work, the only exception we found to the overreporting of solidary by the parental or older generation was with respect to functional solidarity. Children reported giving more assistance to their parents than the parents reported receiving.

It is likely that parental concerns for continuity begin before people have children and endure until they die, for a variety of developmental reasons including generativity issues (Erikson, 1963; Bengtson & Kuypers, 1971), and a quest for symbolic immortality (Levinson et al., 1978, p. 218; Lifton, 1971; Marshall, 1980, p. 87). Beyond that, both parents and children may be seen, as the parents become older, to be fearful of dependency on the part of the parent. Older parents may emphasize closeness in an attempt to diffuse fear of their anticipated dependence—"My children and I do things for each other, but it is because we are close and agree on important matters, not because I need help." Adult children, while generally affectively close to their parents, may slightly minimize their closeness in an attempt to distance themselves from a situation viewed as threatening. Consensus was measured too abstractly to support a strong argument, but it may be that older parents value consensus, particularly around norms of filial obligation, in anticipation of future dependency.

The chapter by Giarrusso et al., this volume, correctly notes that we offered but did not test the dependency hypothesis. Our data, especially the fact that the older generation report less functional solidarity than is reported by their children, are consistent with it. This latest analysis of the USC data found that "parental dependence did not moderate the intergenerational stake phenomenon when parents were approaching advanced ages." I would question that finding. First, because of sample size problems, the G2 sample was selected as the older generation, and its mean age was just 65 for men and 62 for women. This can hardly be taken as a generation for whom dependency concerns should be prominent, given that significant health changes generally occur at much later ages (a point acknowledged by Giarrusso et al., this volume). Moreover, the children of these people, with mean ages of 39 for males and 38 for females, are still about a decade away from the point at which the likelihood of their being implicated in serious caregiving responsibilities would be strong. In addition, the measures of parental dependence are weak. The first measure is a summary score of number of chronic illnesses; however, the relationship between chronic illness and dependency is not strong. A measure based on activities of daily living, and instrumental activities of daily living, would have been far superior. However, in this age group, very few respondents would score as dependent on those measures. The second measure of parental dependency is presumably based on help provided by both parents and children on ADL and IADL type items. However, the relationship between help received and help required is also not strong (people get help with chores whether or not they need it). These sampling and measurement limitations are so strong as to leave open the possibility that intergenerational stake is indeed mediated by dependency and dependency concerns.

CRITICAL ASSESSMENT OF THIS RESEARCH AREA

The line of research following the lead of the 1971 developmental stake paper has been intriguing and, I think, fruitful. It has certainly intrigued me. But my frustrations in this area are not relieved by the chapter under discussion. These are frustrations related to the broader state of scholarship in social gerontology and family studies.

What Is the Hypothesis?

It seems clear that there is no single hypothesis, but several. These are not all developmental, nor should they be. It is questionable whether young adults become trapped in the developmental quest for autonomy as Troll suggests they do, and that this continues to be the major motivation for exaggerating claims to be different in values from or not too affectively close to their parents. Developmental theories generally stress a quest for autonomy in adolescence and early adulthood, but in a life course perspective other developmental challenges or tasks are higher in priority.

What ties this research area together is the quest to answer one question, which is, in a specific application, the opening line of the latest paper: "Why is it that parents and their adolescent children differ frequently so much in the descriptions they give of their joint relationship?" The more general question simply drops the delimiter to adolescent children and seeks to understand the "why" of what has proven to be a lifelong difference in intergenerational descriptions.

The 1971 paper was most clear in stating a hypothesis concerning autonomy and generativity concerns of adolescents and their middle-aged parents, in a developmental theory context. A second hypothesis, much less clearly articulated, related to "fear of loss" (Bengtson & Kuypers, 1971, p. 249). The fear of loss hypothesis pitted the fear of loss of continuity of a middle-aged generation afraid of losing its children (in an era of student revolt and widespread, age-stratified cultural change) against the fear of loss of the "freedom to be me" of a younger generation allegedly rebelling against oppressive authority.

Neither of the two explanatory hypotheses advanced in the 1971 paper proved to be fully adequate to explain the different descriptions of intergenerational relationships given by the young and their middle-aged parents. Thompson, Clark and Gunn (1985), as the current chapter notes, confirmed the differences in how the generations perceive the relationship but did not confirm a developmental explanation in an explicit attempt to do so. Work by many scholars, including Bengtson (e.g., 1986) has shown considerable agreement in values across the generations (viewed as cohorts or within lineages), and over the 20 years since the initial developmental stake paper, the notion of the "generation gap" has greatly diminished in popular consciousness.

Other explanatory factors enter into this research tradition, including mutual fear of anticipated dependency of the older generation (Gesser et al., 1985), the "principle of least interest" (Knipscheer & Bevers, 1985) and the greater investment of the middle generation in their children than in their parents (Richards, Bengtson, & Miller, 1989; and the current chapter). The latter two suggestions are viewed as applications from exchange theory. We do not have a developmental stake hypothesis, a generational stake hypothesis, or an intergenerational stake hypothesis. We have a growing collection of hypotheses about a research question.

What Is "Stake" and How Should We Investigate It?

What is "stake"? In the developmental formulation, stake may be a developmental "press" based on bio(?)psychosocial needs of the individual. In the exchange theory formulation, stake may be a motivational factor rooted in conceptions of equity, on the assumption, as the current paper puts it, "that individuals try to maximize their rewards and minimize their costs." The chapter raises some important questions about the so-far limited adequacy of exchange and equity theory to explain intergenerational stake phenomena. In particular, it notes that exchange theory does not adequately deal with how investments accumulate or persist over time. I would add that an economic approach such as that of Gary Becker (1981, pp. 197–198) stresses the importance of altruistic behavior in families while also claiming to explain the fact that parents give more to children than the reverse as a function of the greater efficiency of giving generationally downward than upward.

By explicitly tying the intergenerational stake hypothesis to exchange and equity theory, this latest paper opens up new theoretical prospects from which, perhaps, a partial solution to the basic research question may be found. I would certainly not join Rossi in dismissing such a promising line of inquiry. She is not correct, for example, in asserting that it is tautological to argue that the middle generation has a stronger stake in the younger generation because of its greater investment in it. Stake might be based on investment or on something else—anticipated likelihood of return on investment, or psychological "inflationary" or "deflationary" factors or, more likely, contingencies that range far beyond dyadic relationships in families. But if an explanation for the different perceptions of the generations of intergenerational solidarity is to be found, then a more phenomenological approach may be needed, and this in turn may lead us away from the research designs we have been using toward an approach that is less predicated on the properties of individuals (of which their sense of fairness or stake would be examples), than on the systemic, qualitative properties of families.

In a recent article addressing the research tradition of family solidarity that we are discussing, Sprey (1991) suggests that

> *Why*, and *how* individual attributes conjointly may lead to a more, or less, stable familial process remains unexplored and unexplained in this [solidarity] context. The possibility, for example, that certain family members may truly like one another but may also, for some reason, neglect a sibling or parent simply does not fit into an explanatory framework in which mental states are linked to specific types of behavior.

Sprey cites Bengtson and Roberts (1988, p. 18) to the effect that the theory of family solidarity "may have been too abstract too soon. That is, the proper foundation had not been established for the interpretation of higher-order characteristics of families." But conceptions of equity and fairness in families, as well as questions of the investment of parents and children in one another (developmentally or in other psychological terms) are most probably rooted fundamentally in the structure, processes and sentiments of "whole" families and not of individuals or dyads. To explore such conceptions may therefore call for a different methodology not so closely tied to methodological individualism.

What Happened to the Drama?

Revisiting the 1971 paper on the developmental stake and the other major works which followed from it, I am struck by a change in style. The 1971 paper spoke of "drama in the continuing succession of one generation by another" and of "threat in intergenerational exchanges" (Bengtson & Kuypers, 1971, p. 250). Arguing that there are two processes, the "fear of loss mythology" and the "developmental stake mythology," Bengtson and Kuypers (1971, p. 250) "submit that these mythologies contribute substantially to the experience of anxiety in the drama of generations." They conclude that "the question naturally arises, after having argued for the sources of fear in the generational drama, of how to reduce the defensive, protective, and what seems to be the self-defeating conflict between generations" (p. 258). The language is of anxiety, fear, loss, threat, self-defeat, and conflict. Such is decidedly not the language of the latest paper. The language is more technical, more precise; the data are more abstractly packaged. The blood and guts, the emotions, the conflict are not there. What happened to the "drama in the continuing succession of one generation by another?"

The paper invokes the life course perspective, which I too consider to be an advance; yet Morgan (1985, p. 179) has argued that there are dangers with the life course approach, one of which "is the danger that . . . it may become a technique. Since much of the material with which life course analysis deals is so readily quantifiable and amenable to statistical manipulation of quite advanced kinds, there is the danger that method may triumph over meaning."

The disparity in style between the first and most recent papers leads me to ask what a dramaturgical analyst, such as Goffman, would make of the subject matter. The first paper on the developmental stake hypothesis mentioned fear as an element of intergenerational family life. Moss and Moss (1988) have written about "fearing" as a theme when generations reunite, occasions that fall under the category of "family rituals." Reunion, they note, is a process rather than an event, with symbolic aspects. Family reunions evoke a sense of anticipation and, when over, memories and a renewed sense of connection. They often evoke nostalgia and a shared revisit to the past which has the potential to rewrite family history. They are also occasions in which participants are careful to guard what they say and to avoid open conflict (as Troll, 1982 also mentioned), and where, in Goffman's terms, the behavior is "strategic," where processes of showing "deference and demeanor" are involved in the maintenance of identity, and where family members can be seen as engaged in "teamwork" to successfully bring off an encounter.

There is an "intergenerational stake" in evidence in family reunions, though the Mosses do not conceptualize it along the lines of the intergenerational stake hypothesis. They see each generation as wanting to reaffirm the self and as wanting to reaffirm the other: "Many persons wish to see the other as competent, in part as a reflection of the need to confirm their own self-image. Each may in some ways look to the other as a standard for judging the self, thus allowing for reciprocal mirroring . . . and reciprocal modelling" (Moss & Moss, 1988, p. 658).

We thus find in work such as that of Moss and Moss a more dramaturgical analysis of intergenerational relationships, giving a rich picture of the main finding of all the research on the developmental/generational/intergenerational stake: that the generations do have a stake in one another, and that they work hard to maintain solidarity.

CONCLUSIONS

Over 20 years, the developmental stake hypothesis has been taken up by fewer researchers than I should like to have seen address it. The evolution of the research problem has been left largely in the hands of Bengtson and many colleagues at The University of Southern California. They have nurtured the research question well, and it has changed over the decades.

Perhaps the question of why the generations perceive their relationship differently has been ignored by many because the differences in perception are overlain on generally strong patterns of intergenerational solidarity. This research question deals with "variations on a theme," a theme of strong intergenerational solidarity. Additional questions about gender differences in differences in developmental/generational/intergenerational stake become variations on variations on a theme. We may end up with quite a symphony if we can manage the orchestration. Conversely, all this variation may obscure or divert attention away from the main theme.

The chapter is most successful in demonstrating the importance of an explanation of the intergenerational stake problem based not only on developmental theory principles but on exchange and equity principles. In turn, this direction opens up new theoretical possibilities in the application of equity theory and the economic approach to family life, directions that could well keep the research question alive for another two decades at least. The chapter is, I think, too quick to dismiss dependency concerns as implicated in the generational stake phenomenon.

As the research on this question has progressed, research technology has improved and our sense of statistical technology and longitudinal design has improved. As the research has become more sophisticated it has perhaps lost something of the flavor of family and intergenerational life. In my view, a sustained attack on this research question involving qualitative research methodologies, and taking a more holistic view of family life, would prove enlightening.

ACKNOWLEDGMENTS

This chapter draws on research funded by the Social Science and Humanities Research Council of Canada through grant no. 492-79-0076R1 in support of the Generational Relations and Succession Project (V. Marshall, C. Rosenthal, and J. Synge); a grant from the Gerontology Research Council of Ontario (Marshall and Rosenthal); and a bursary from the same to the late Gina Gesser. Current support of CARNET: The Canadian Aging Research Network (funded by the Network of Centres of Excellence Program, Science and Technology Canada) and of the Centre for Studies of Aging, University of Toronto is also gratefully appreciated.

REFERENCES

Becker, G. S. (1981). *A treatise on the family*. Boston: Harvard University Press.

Bengtson, V. L. (1979). Research perspectives on intergenerational interaction. In P. Ragan (Ed.), *Aging Parents* (pp. 37–57). Los Angeles: University of Southern California Press.

Bengtson, V. L. (1986). Comparative perspectives on the microsociology of aging: Methodological problems and theoretical issues. In V. W. Marshall (Ed.), *Later life: The social psychology of aging*. Beverly Hills: Sage.

Bengtson, V. L., & Kuypers, J. A. (1971). Generational difference and the developmental stake. *Aging and Human Development, 2*, 249–260.

Bengtson, V. L., & Roberts, R. E. L. (1988, November). Parent-child solidarity in aging families: An exercise in theory construction. Paper presented at the Theory Construction and Methodology Workshop of the National Council on Family Relations, Philadelphia.

Bengtson, V. L., & Schrader, S. (1982). Parent-child relations. In D. J. Mangen, & W. A. Peterson (Eds.), *Research instruments in social gerontology: Vol. 2. Social roles and social participation* (pp. 115–185). Minneapolis: University of Minnesota Press.

Dowd, J. J. (1980). *Stratification Among the Aged*. Monterey, CA: Brooks/Cole.

Erikson, E. H. (1963). *Childhood and society*, 2nd ed. New York: W. W. Norton & Co.

Gesser, G. (1986). *An Application of the Developmental Stake Hypothesis to the Older Family Context*. Unpublished M.Sc. thesis in Community Health, University of Toronto.

Gesser, G. L., Marshall, V. W., & Rosenthal, C. J. (1985, November). A Test of the Generational Stake Hypothesis. Paper presented at the 14th Annual Meeting of the Canadian Association on Gerontology, Hamilton, Ontario.

Knipscheer, K., & Bevers, A. (1985). Older parents and their middle-aged children: Symmetry or asymmetry in their relationship. *Canadian Journal on Aging, 4*, 145–159.

Levinson, D. J., Darrow, C. M., Klein, E. B., Levinson, M. H., & McKee, B. (1978). *The seasons of a man's life*. New York: Knopf.

Lifton, R. J. (Ed.). (1971). *History and human survival*. New York: Vintage.

Mangen, D., Bengtson, V. L., & Landry, P. H., Jr. (Eds.). (1988). *Measurement of intergenerational relations*. Newbury Park, CA: Sage.

Marshall, V. W. (1980). *Last chapters: A sociology of aging and dying*. Monterey, CA: Brooks/Cole.

Morgan, D. H. J. (1985). *The family, politics and social theory*. London: Routledge & Kegan Paul.

Moss, M. S., & Moss, S. Z. (1988). Reunion between elderly parents and their distant children. *American Behavioral Scientist, 31,* 654–668.

Richards, L. N., Bengtson, V. L., & Miller, R. B. (1989). The "generation in the middle": Perceptions of adults' intergenerational relationships. In K. Kreppner & R. M. Lerner (Eds.), *Family Systems and Life-Span Development* (pp. 341–366). Hillsdale, NJ: Erlbaum.

Sprey, J. (1991). Studying adult children and their parents. *Marriage and Family Review, 16,* 221–235.

Thompson, L., Clark, K., & Gunn, W. (1985). Developmental Stage and Perceptions of Intergenerational Continuity. *Journal of Marriage and the Family, 47,* 913–920.

Troll, L. E. (1982, November). Family life in middle and old age: The generation gap. *Annals of the American Academy of Political and Social Science, 464,* 38–46.

Commentary:
A Response to Rossi

Roseann Giarrusso
Matthew Jendian
Du Feng
Bi-ling Shieh
Vern L. Bengtson

I n her role as discussant, Rossi presents five basic criticisms of chapter 6. First, she objects to our measurement of affectual solidarity. Second, she suggests that we do not have adequate measures to test the intergenerational stake hypothesis. Third, Rossi states that testing any explanation of the intergenerational stake phenomenon requires an alternative analysis mode—one that would control for earlier levels of parent–child affectual solidarity. Fourth, she claims that the application of exchange theory to parent–child relationships is inappropriate. Fifth, Rossi notes that the gender of the child as well as the gender of the parent must be considered in any analysis of parent–child relations and scolds us for not doing so.

In discussing our chapter, Rossi makes some valid and important points. We agree with her on most of her methodological recommendations and appreciate the thoroughness of her critique. However, although her points are well taken, in the end her suggestions do not end up making much of a substantive difference. Even when we address her concerns in our analyses, our findings and interpretations do not change considerably. We discuss each of her concerns in turn.

RESPONSE TO CRITICISM 1: MEASUREMENT OF AFFECTUAL SOLIDARITY

Rossi criticizes our selection of items to measure affectual solidarity because they do not reflect either the 10-item Long Form or the 5-item Short Form reported by Mangen, Bengtson, and Landry (1988). Rossi incorrectly states that (a) three of the 6 items we used were from the Long Form (only the two items on understanding were from the Long Form; the self-report of closeness was *not* part of the Long Form), and (b) that the items "communicating well" and "getting along with" were excluded from our measure of affectual solidarity—they were not.

We did mistakenly make reference to Mangen et al. (1988) in discussing the validity and reliability of our 6-item scale. Actually we had performed our own independent analyses of the reliability and validity of the 6-item scale. These analyses revealed that for each of the four waves of measurement the 6 items loaded more than adequately on the same factor as well as formed a reliable scale (α's were between .88 and .93 for each time point).

As Rossi points out, an analyst is not bound to rely on previously constructed scales as long as they justify their reasons for departure. Contrary to Rossi's accusation, we departed from the scales reported in Mangen et al. *not* because certain items "did not meet . . . [our] . . . eigenvalue criterion" but rather because our research question required an examination of affectual solidarity over time. Consequently, we were limited to those solidarity items measured at all four time points: only 6 items were measured longitudinally.

However, we agree with Rossi that the "similarity" item, despite its compatibility with the other items on empirical grounds, is conceptually different and should not have been included in the scale. Therefore, we recomputed analyses reported in the chapter using only the 5 items. The analyses revealed that this shortened version of the scale was still valid and reliable. Further, the pattern of results reported in Figure 6.2 and Tables 6.2 to 6.6 remained unchanged.

RESPONSE TO CRITICISM 2: INADEQUATE MEASURES

Rossi argues that instead of revisiting the intergenerational stake hypothesis (which provides developmental and exchange theory interpretations of cross-generational perceptual biases), we should have pursued other questions for which we have "more adequate measures." The alternative theoretical explanations of the intergenerational stake phenomenon she suggests we pursue (such as whether critical life events—becoming a parent, the marriage or divorce of a child, etc.—influence affectual closeness) *are* interesting and warrant study. In fact, the influence of child attainment of adult social roles on parent–child affectual solidarity has already been examined in much earlier work (Bengtson & Black, 1973). However, we felt the need to follow other paths of inquiry, and felt that there had been enough interest shown in the "intergenerational stake hypothesis" to justify doing exploratory analyses with the data at hand (the hypothesis has been cited in 82 published articles and books).

Our goal was to investigate whether developmental theory or exchange theory provided a better explanation of the "intergeneration stake" phenomenon over time because these were the two theoretical explanations implicit in previous work. A longitudinal design provided the best test of the two theories since each made different long-term predictions. The USC Longitudinal Study of Generations provided an opportunity to use four waves of data over a span of twenty years. Our analysis had two components: (a) an analysis of the pattern of means using time of measurement as a proxy for developmental concerns, and (b) regression analyses using more direct measures of developmental concerns— adolescent autonomy, parental concern for intergenerational continuity in values, and elderly parental dependence.

Rossi criticizes us for "merely" measuring the difference in parent–child affectual solidarity over a twenty year period and then later exploring whether those differences increase or decrease as a function of earlier moderator variables, arguing that we do not have adequate measures of the moderator variables we tried to test. Rossi puts too much emphasis on the second component of our analysis and does not give us enough credit for the first. The aggregate means analyses *alone* provide useful information about the two theoretical approaches, exchange and developmental, without going any further into the analysis of the predictor or moderator variables. We do not mean to suggest that our study is a definitive test of either theory; the results are suggestive rather than definitive. However, the analyses of the pattern of means provides an interesting exploration of the two theories under consideration.

As for the regression analyses, they focus on developmental theory as opposed to exchange theory, because developmental theory was the theoretical explanation put forth in the original paper (Bengtson & Kuypers, 1971). (It would have been too ambitious to test predictors suggested by exchange theory in the same chapter.) Therefore, criticism 2, regarding inadequate measures, actually applies only to our test of developmental theory in the regression analyses. Although our measures of developmental concerns were not ideal, they were adequate for our purposes.

Although the original "intergenerational stake hypothesis" was influenced by Eriksonian (1950) theory of development, the purpose of the chapter was to test the "intergenerational stake hypothesis," not Erikson's theory. Therefore, we did not measure resolution of particular stages (e.g., identity, intimacy, and generativity) or psychosocial maturity, but rather *dominant concerns* that children and parents confront while progressing through these developmental stages. We looked at whether individual differences in adolescent autonomy, parental concern for value continuity, or elderly parental dependence predicted the magnitude of parent–child dyad differences in affectual solidarity within and across time. Not all children and parents in the sample are in the same place with regard to their concerns over autonomy, intergenerational continuity in values, or parental dependence. Some have not yet confronted these issues, some are in the midst of grappling with them, and some have already dealt with then – either adequately or inadequately.

RESPONSE TO CRITICISM 3: MODE OF ANALYSIS

Rossi was correct in criticizing us for not taking into account earlier levels of parent–child differences in affectual solidarity in our analyses of individual differences. When parent–child affectual solidarity is relatively stable over time, as we found it is, the influence of variables measured early in the family life course on parent–child affectual solidarity later in the family life course could be a function of the indirect influence of earlier levels of parent–child solidarity rather than a direct effect of the moderator variables.

We redid the analyses presented in Table 6.5 of the chapter (using the 5-item affectual solidarity scale), this time controlling for differences in parent–child affectual solidarity from Time-1. Once we controlled for earlier differences, neither adolescent autonomy nor parental concern for continuity in values significantly predicted the magnitude of parent–child differences in affectual solidarity that occurred later in the family life cycle. Thus, children's concern for independence from their fathers does *not* appear to be lifelong as we had thought.

We had concluded that adolescent concern for autonomy from parents and parental concern for intergenerational value continuity were lineage issues because we had erroneously thought they predicted parent–child differences in affectual solidarity across the family life course. We reasoned that if these concerns were developmental, they should have been dominant only during early stages of the family life course when it would have been normative to be dealing with these issues. Developmental means that individuals progress through certain stages in a set sequence on a schedule that is normative. We figured, for example, that by middle-age, adult children would have moved on to a different stage and a different dominant concern more developmentally appropriate than autonomy from their parents. We thought that if these concerns were still predicting parent–child differences in affectual solidarity later in the life course that this was an indication that autonomy and continuity issues were built into the role of parent and child.

Rossi's criticism with regard to the importance of controlling for early levels of parent–child differences in affectual solidarity also applies to our analysis of parental dependency appearing in Table 6.6. Rossi suggests that we should have regressed *change* in health and parent–child differences in affectual solidarity at Time-2 on parent–child differences in affectual solidarity at Time-3. We assume she meant the reverse, that is, regress parent–child differences in affectual solidarity at Time-3 on the change in parent health measure controlling for the previous level of parent-child differences in affectual solidarity (since one regresses the dependent variable (DV) on the independent variable (IV)). In fact, we did follow her suggestion. However, we had to use a slightly different set of predictors because neither instrumental help and support, nor children's report of parental illnesses, was measured in earlier waves. Therefore, we substituted emotional help and support for instrumental help and support, and used only parent's report of illness.

We created three measures of change in parental dependence between Time-2 and Time-4, the increase or decrease in (a) the number of chronic illnesses reported by the parent, (b) the amount of help and support the parent reported receiving, and (c) the amount of help and support the children reported giving. We regressed parent-child differences in affectual solidarity at Time-4 on these measures of change in parental dependence, controlling for differences in parent-child affectual solidarity at Time-2. The results of this further analysis did not change the findings from our previous analysis. That is, none of the measures of change in parental dependence predicted the magnitude of parent-child differences in affectual solidarity (5-item scale).

Thus, taken as a whole, we still think that our results provide little support for developmental theory. Only one measure of autonomy predicted parent-child differences in affectual solidarity early in the family life course and none of the measures of change in parental dependence (controlling for differences in parent-child affectual solidarity from Time-1) predicted parent-child differences late in the family life course. Thus, the conclusions we drew remain basically unchanged.

RESPONSE TO CRITICISM 4: EXCHANGE THEORY

Rossi states that "no clear definition or exposition of exchange theory is given anywhere in the chapter." We had assumed that most readers would already be familiar with exchange theory. We should, perhaps, have emphasized that we are using *social* exchange theory as opposed to economic exchange theory, which Rossi so roundly attacks.

There are various versions of exchange theory from a variety of disciplines, including anthropology, psychology, sociology, and economics. Although there are minor differences among them, all versions focus on the rewards individuals obtain through social interaction. Further, they are all based on three core assumptions: (a) individuals act in a way which increases their rewards (i.e., they behave rationally); (b) the value of rewards decreases with satiation; and (c) rewards obtained through social interaction are contingent on social exchange (Emerson, 1981).

However, a basic difference between economic and social exchange theories must be taken into account. Economic exchange theory takes the individual as the unit of analysis and is based on the assumption that each exchange transaction is independent. Thus, economic exchange theory cannot account for long-term relations between exchange partners and the feeling of trust or attachment they develop for one another. In contrast, social exchange theory takes the exchange relationship as the unit of analysis and expands the time frame from a single transaction to a series of transactions. Thus, the value of a reward is defined over time as the exchange relationship evolves. Moreover, because the exchange relationship is assumed to continue over time, the theory is able to deal with feelings of trust, commitment, and equity that develop between exchange partners (Emerson, 1981). This makes social exchange theory more appropriate for studying family relationships.

We do not provide a direct test of social exchange theory in this chapter. As discussed earlier, we did *not* try to provide a test of the predictors that would be suggested by exchange theory. Rather we *assume* greater investment on the part of the parents relative to their children. From the time their children are born, parents, by virtue of their greater resources (e.g., age, education, income, social standing, etc.), "input" or invest more in their children (e.g., time, money, energy, sacrifice, etc.) than their children do in them.

Rossi mistakenly concludes that the basic asymmetry to which we are referring in our discussion of exchange theory is "the finding that at Time-1, parents are closer to children than children are to them" (p. 271). However, the basic asymmetry to which we are referring is the greater *input* or investment of parents relative to children. The intergenerational stake phenomenon is the *output*, the result of this even more basic asymmetry.

Based on the "principle of distributive justice," the ratio of inputs to outputs of Person should equal the ratio of inputs to outputs of Other (Homans, 1974). If they do not, then inequity occurs. The greater input of parents relative to their children motivates parents to distort their perceptions of the output of their relationship in order to restore psychological equity. Parents might say "I've invested a great deal in my child and it has paid off—my child and I have a very close relationship." Rossi's statement that one "does not divorce a parent or a child" (p. 271) is precisely our point: parents might resort to using distortion of perception as a way of restoring equity since the other options for reducing inequity (such as divorcing a parent or a child) are not readily available to them.

We used both developmental theory and exchange theory to explain the "distortion" in the perceptions of parents. (Other cognitive theories such as attribution theory and cognitive dissonance theory would make similar predictions.) However, the rationale given by each theory for the perceptual distortion is different and each has different long-term consequences over the life-course. Thus, we argued that exchange theory seems to provide a better explanation of the intergenerational stake phenomenon than developmental theory because it suggests that the perceptual distortion persists across the life course whereas developmental theory suggests that the perceptual distortion is limited to early and late phases of the family life cycle.

Although we are not the first to apply exchange theory to the study of parents and children (Edwards & Brauberger, 1973; Ihinger, 1975; Mutran & Reitzes, 1984; Richer, 1968; Shehan & Dwyer, 1989), Rossi claims that we are "applying exchange theory from studies of friendship and courting couples to the parent–child relationship" (p. 271). We are not aware of any difference between general exchange theories and those that have been applied to friendship and courting couples. We see exchange theory as providing an explanation of the general principles of social behavior.

Rossi objects to the application of exchange theory to close relationships, saying that she has "seen no evidence to support any notion that asymmetry in intergenerational affection, interaction, or exchange of help is experienced by those involved in the parent–child relationship as lacking in equity or justice". However, the frequency with which children hear parents say the phrase, "After all I've done for you" suggests that parents do experience inequity, and that some expect reciprocation in some form or another from their children. In fact, we found that nearly two-thirds of our G2 parents reported times when they felt their children acted "indifferent" or "ungrateful" for all they had done for them.

RESPONSE TO CRITICISM 5: GENDER OF CHILD

We agree that it is important to consider the gender of the child as well as gender of the parent when investigating parent–child relationships. We recalculated the regression analyses, this time including gender of the child as well as gender interaction terms (parents' gender by children's gender) in the equations. Overall, the results indicate that the gender interaction terms are not significant. This suggests that, for these analyses, it is unnecessary to calculate separate equations for each of the four parent–child gender types (father–son, father–daughter, mother–son, mother–daughter) because these predictors of the intergenerational stake phenomenon are the same for sons and daughters.

REFERENCES

Bengtson, V. L., & Black, K. D. (1973). Solidarity between parents and children: Four perspectives on theory development. Paper presented at the Preconference Workshop on Theory and Methodology, National Council on Family Relations, Toronto, Canada.

Bengtson, V. L., & Kuypers, J. A. (1971). Generational difference and the "developmental stake." *Aging and Human Development, 2,* 249–260.

Edwards, J., & Brauberger, M. (1973). Exchange and parent-youth conflict. *Journal of Marriage and the Family, 35,* 101–107.

Emerson, R. M. (1981). Social exchange theory. In M. Rosenberg & R. Turner (Eds.), *Social psychology: Sociological perspectives.* New York: Basic Books.

Erikson, E. H. (1950). *Childhood and society.* New York: Norton.

Homans, G. (1974). *Social behavior: Its elementary forms.* New York: Harcourt Brace Jovanovich.

Ihinger, M. (1975). The referee role and norms of equity: A contribution toward a theory of sibling conflict. *Journal of Marriage and the Family, 37,* 515–523.

Mangen, D. J., Bengtson, V. L., & Landry, P. H. (1988). Measurement of intergenerational relations. Beverly Hills: Sage.

Mutran, E., & Reitzes, D. (1984). Intergenerational support activities and well-being among the elderly: A convergence of exchange and symbolic interaction perspectives. *American Sociological Review, 49,* 117–130.

Richer, S. (1968). The economics of child rearing. *Journal of Marriage and the Family, 30,* 246–266.

Shehan, C., & Dwyer, J. (1989). Parent-child exchanges in the middle years: Attachment and autonomy in the transition to adulthood. In J. Mancini (Ed.), *Parent-child relationships and the life course.* Lexington, MA: Lexington Books.

AFTERWORD:
Six Controversies in Current Research on Adult Intergenerational Relationships

Vern L. Bengtson

Controversies that reflect problems of aging and intergenerational relations are as old as recorded history (see the account of the aging King David and the murder of his rebellious son Absalom in 2 Sam. 11: 23–56) and as new as today's headlines about the distribution of government benefits ("Are your parents robbing you blind? The coming war between the young and the old," Weisberg, 1992). Such problems of intergenerational relations and aging are central to the analysis of social structures and their change over time: issues of power, position, expectations, and indeed the social contract itself are related to the succession of one age group by another (Bengtson, 1993).

During the past few years social scientists—as well as the mass media and policymakers—seem to have rediscovered the age-old problem of adult intergenerational relationships, and this has led to new controversies. My concern in this afterword is to describe six current controversies in research on intergenerational relationships and aging, and to use this as a means to summarize some of the themes and findings reported in this volume. The controversies, as I see them, are as follows:

1. Have the effects of population aging resulted in significantly more "verticalized" intergenerational family structures than in earlier times; and if so, has this enhanced or weakened family support and interaction patterns?
2. To what extent do historical changes in social structure have direct effects on relations between generations; conversely, to what extent are there stubborn intergenerational continuities that persist despite even massive socioeconomic changes?
3. What kind of assistance can families provide for children of teenaged childbearers? How extensive and adequate is the care; and what are the implications for government assistance?
4. Are there universal norms of cross-generational support across societies, or are these norms culture-specific? Are there universal tensions between kinship/generational norms and individualistic norms; or are these also culture-specific?
5. How important is family environment to intellectual abilities, relative to more intrinsic factors such as behavioral genetic effects; and do these effects persist through later life? To what extent do shared family environments exist, and what are the mechanisms that produce within-family uniformity or variation (between siblings and across generations) in family environment?
6. To what extent is there a "generational bias" in perceptions of parent–child relationships, and does it persist over time and into later adulthood? What accounts for the generational bias in perceptions? Is it so pervasive as to question the validity of surveys that rely only on the report of one generation to characterize family relationships?

THE DEMOGRAPHY OF CHANGING INTERGENERATIONAL RELATIONSHIPS

In the opening chapter Janice Farkas and Dennis Hogan address one of the most visible controversies: Have the effects of population aging in the 20th century resulted in markedly more "verticalized" intergenerational family structures throughout the Western world? If so, has this enhanced or weakened family support and interaction patterns?; do elders gain from having more intergenerational kin? They examine the incidence and consequence of what has been called the "beanpole" family structure of three, four, and even five living generations (Bengtson, Rosenthal, & Burton,

1990) by analyzing recent data on the structure of kin lineages in seven industrialized societies with aging populations. Using data from the 1986–1987 International Social Survey Program (ISSP), Farkas and Hogan organize their analysis in terms of four explicit hypotheses: (1) that families in the seven countries will exhibit a "very vertical" family structure, with many respondents listing several adult generations in their lineage; (2) that the presence of each additional level of adult lineage member (child, grandchild, great-grandchild) will yield increased contact and reliance on generational kin; (3) that a lineage with more generations present will also yield enhanced generational relations in terms of greater support mechanisms; and (4) that older persons will be more likely to rely on generational kin than on friends for support. In addition, they examine cross-national differences and similarities in these data, as well as contrasts by gender.

Their analyses yield several results that readers might find surprising. First, their data do not provide much support for the hypothesis that "verticalized" family structures are now typical in today's industrialized countries. Fewer respondents than expected report membership in a generational lineage of more than three adult links; from this one might infer that great-grandparenthood is still relatively rare in these countries. Second, Farkas and Hogan were surprised (as I was) that national patterns of extended generational lineages did not emerge. In these cross-national comparisons, however, Americans are consistently lower in reported contact with kin than are respondents from other countries, and older Americans expected to rely less on kin for assistance when compared to elderly in other countries. Third, membership in a multigenerational lineage does not necessarily enhance levels of kin contact, or of reliance on kin for support. Rather, it is the size of the kin group (and not their intergenerational relationship) that seems to be related to support.

Peter Uhlenberg, in his discussion of the chapter, highlights some of the controversies in the demography of changing intergenerational relationships. On the one hand, he notes that cross-sectional data from one point in time, such as Farkas and Hogan's, cannot directly provide information about the role of demographic change in altering intergenerational relations over recent time. On the other hand, he argues against uncritically accepting the notion that four- and five-generation families are becoming common under modern demographic conditions: because of the paucity of empirical data concerning intergenerational family structure, it is as yet not possible to confirm or deny such trends.

Judith Treas' commentary (her title, "Beanpole or Beanstalk?," engagingly summarizes one aspect of this controversy) suggests another perspective in the debate. She notes that almost everyone (93%) in the Farkas and Hogan data can count on having some kin up or down the generational ladder. While the authors seem to express surprise that only a few (1%) report a six-generation family and 3% report five generations, this is not the most important finding. What *is* important, Treas argues, is that intergenerational family structures appear far more pervasive and supportive for individuals in industrialized countries than often is acknowledged.

Other surveys appear to support the suggestion that the "beanpole" intergenerational family structure may be creeping up, at least in the United States. In the recently concluded Health and Retirement Survey (Juster & Suzman, 1993), 52% of respondents reported membership in four-generation families (Soldo & Hill, 1994), with an additional 21% reporting membership in three-generation families (no data are available concerning five- and six-generational structures). The 1990 AARP Intergenerational Linkages survey of a cross section of American households suggests similar conclusions (Bengtson & Harootyan, 1994).

In any event, whether the effects of population aging are to be seen in intergenerational family structures that approximate the "beanpole" shape, or whether, as Bengtson, Rosenthal, and Burton (1990) argue, their effects are increasingly "diverse and heterogeneous," the central issue concerns the consequences of intergenerational family structures for support and well-being of their members. Farkas and Hogan deserve praise for examining such consequences in their data with care and thought.

INTERGENERATIONAL CONTINUITY AND CHANGE IN RURAL AMERICA

A second controversy concerns the degree to which macrosocial economic trends have direct effects on primary social group relationships, such as those between generations within families. We now accept, almost as a matter of faith, that historical changes in social structure alter both the individual life-course progression and the nature of kinship relationships (Elder, 1981; Hareven, 1987; Kohli, 1986a,b). But to what degree? And here may be a new controversy: to what extent are there stubborn continuities in family relationships that persist despite even massive socioeconomic changes?

In Chapter 2 Glen Elder, Laura Rudkin, and Rand Conger provide a powerful case study of both changes and continuities across generations in families who have been recent victims or survivors of macroeconomic changes. Their analysis of 451 rural farm families in Iowa provides a unique portrait of elderly individuals who have known both hard times and prosperity and who passed on to their children both values and property reflecting the American ethic of generational mobility—only to see this thwarted by the disastrous farm economy in the 1980s, during which the State of Iowa lost 5% of its population.

In this context, Elder et al. examine the kinship effects of younger generations' life-course decisions to enter into (or leave) farming, as well as the implications of these decisions for proximity, contact, support, and emotional relations with the older generation. They hypothesized that the younger generation's decision to continue a farming career will result in greater proximity, contact, emotional relations, and support for the parent generation. Furthermore, they predicted that men who lost their farms during the 1980s would report more strained relations with parents, compared to those who are still farming.

Their results may provide some surprises to the reader. First, they did not find that displaced farmers have ended up with more negative relations with their fathers and mothers than those who remained on the farm. Second, while there were gender differences in parent–child relationships, these were not in the expected direction; that is, fathers appeared to be more accepting of the farm loss than the mothers. Third, pre-crisis relationships (earlier parent–child relations, as reflected in retrospective accounts of childhood) are correlated with current relationships (post-crisis), suggesting an overall continuity in relationship styles, with or without the loss of the family farm.

In their commentary of Chapter 2 John Myles and Susan Morgan address the central aspect of this controversy: the problem of demonstrating causal linkages between a disruptive historical event and outcomes in the life course and microsocial relationships. They note this is difficult, because it requires several models specifying several outcomes. Moreover, they ask whether the time frame of the Elder et al. analysis is sufficient to assess any hypotheses concerning historical events and individual/family outcomes. They suggest that the finding of little difference between those who lost their farms and those who did not requires a focus on variations *within* these two groups, in addition to *between* them.

Martin Kohli's commentary focuses on the rural farm family as a model for analyses of intergenerational transmission in recent history. He notes that agriculture provides a window on family consequences of modernization, both economically and culturally. Interpreting Elder et al.'s finding that the loss of the farm by the sons has had little impact on intergenerational relations, he suggests that family relations have become highly individualized during past decades, even among farmers. Sons are allowed to have a life of their own, Kohli concludes: their personal well-being and that of their own family of procreation may take precedence over any criteria of lineage or of the farm as a material embodiment of lineage.

INTERGENERATIONAL PATTERNS OF PROVIDING CARE IN AFRICAN-AMERICAN FAMILIES WITH TEENAGED CHILDBEARERS

The controversy over what (if any) public assistance should be provided to teenage or unmarried childbearers is increasingly the subject of partisan political discourse and media commentary. Stereotypes pervade public discussion in this area. For example, it is often assumed that most teen and out-of-wedlock parents are African American (though in fact they are a minority). The image of the "welfare queen" has become an icon for some political conservatives' crusades. To social scientists, the controversy should be located in social structures and their outcomes: how do kin, particularly older kin, provide care for children of teenaged mothers and fathers? How extensive and adequate is this care?, and what are the patterns of care provision?

In Chapter 3 Linda Burton presents a fascinating case study in the negotiation of dependencies and caregiving in contemporary intergenerational relationships. Focusing on lineages in an urban African-American community, she demonstrates that there is striking diversity in patterns of kin providing care in families with teenage mothers (and fathers). She bases her analysis on the premise that we must move beyond a focus on two- or three-generational structures—the grandmother, and the teenage mother and her child—to include other generations and kin if we are to adequately assess supports for teenage childbearing families from minority populations.

The data from her 5-year ethnographic study suggest there is extensive, if frequently unnoticed assistance provided to kin in crisis by poor minority families. Her data also indicate the multiple patterns of intergenerational support networks within this population, seen in the 14 subtypes of intergenerational support networks Burton can identify. Students will find her analysis an excellent example of moving back and forth between concepts and data in research. She concludes that we should no longer talk about "*the* African-American family," any more than we should simplistically attempt to characterize "*the* American family." Her findings represent a more realistic and complex alternative to the too-frequent stereotype of a matricentric African-American family.

Linda Chatters and Rukmalie Jayakody, in their discussion of Burton's chapter, provide a highly useful summary of additional findings from both ethnographic and large nationwide surveys on African-American families. These provide a valuable macrolevel companion to Burton's case-study analysis. Above all, they support her argument that we must consider the diversity of intergenerational structures and support mechanisms in minority families within contemporary American society.

Christine Fry's comments focus on the utility of the qualitative research methodology Burton has employed. Fry suggests that observational methods are precisely what is needed when the topic under investigation is virtually unexplored, such as the case with the negotiation of dependencies and support within family life. She notes that it is not unusual for qualitative research strategies to reveal a world more complicated than we originally thought, and concludes by calling on researchers to incorporate this variance into classifications and theories about families as the first and last sources of support for elders.

KINSHIP AND INDIVIDUATION: CROSS-CULTURAL PERSPECTIVES ON INTERGENERATIONAL RELATIONS

In Chapter 4 Christine Fry presents a review of cross-cultural differences in kinship ideologies and resulting expectations about intergenerational relations. I believe there are two controversies reflected here: (1) Are there universal trends supporting norms of cross-generational support across most cultures and societies? or are these norms culture-specific? and (2) Are there universal tensions between kinship/generational norms and individualistic norms? or are these also culture-specific?

Fry begins her analysis by observing that, as one looks across a variety of cultural contexts, "kinship can be either an asset or a liability or both." She supports this paradoxical theme with data from the AGE Project (conducted with Jennie Keith and other investigators) that examines how different communities shape the experience of aging for their older members. The project involves comparative ethnographic investigation in seven areas across the globe: two in Southern Africa, two in Ireland, two in the United States, and one in Asia.

The results from these cross-cultural investigations are varied, as Fry notes, in terms of any "universals" reflecting norms about elder caregiving or intergenerational reciprocities. What the studies do indicate is that there are a variety of forms in kinship relations, and each involves issues of dependency and support across generations and age groups. She suggests that we must be aware of "our predominately middle-class, middle-aged view of kinship" in presuming to give any order to cross-societal data.

David Kertzer, in his commentary on Fry's chapter, suggests an additional perspective on the universalistic controversy. He notes that Fry begins with the premise that "if we are to understand the way different peoples conceive of and divide up the life course, we cannot impose our own categories" of chronological age, for example, or of families and kinship. But Kertzer suggests that such idiographic distinctions dissolve when social scientists attempt to do more than ethnosemantic ethnography, which locates culture at the level of the individual informant. Rather, he says, the challenge is to develop methods that will best enable us to document cultural diversity while providing conceptual and methodological tools that will enable meaningful comparison. The need is to accommodate both cultural diversity while developing a common language allowing comparison.

Carmi Schooler indicates still another approach to Fry's thesis. In order to construct ideas of how a culture may change, he suggests, we have to pay attention to differences between individuals in different social structural positions *within* a given culture. He cautions that we cannot assume that all the members of a society have the same values any more than we can assume that individuals hold similar levels of status. Furthermore, he suggests that the distinction between individualistic versus collectivistic models of culture may be a useful dimension along which to make such comparisons.

PERCEIVED FAMILY ENVIRONMENTS ACROSS GENERATIONS

An important controversy in life-course studies concerns the effects of early environmental characteristics on long-term individual outcomes. How important is family environment on the maintenance of intellectual competence throughout adulthood—relative to more intrinsic factors, such as behavioral genetics? And how stable are family environments across time, between siblings, or across generations?

In Chapter 5, Warner Schaie and Sherry Willis begin to examine this thorny issue with results from the 35-year-old Seattle Longitudinal Study of intellectual abilities over the life course. This study has by now become a textbook example of longitudinal research design and of aging effects versus cohort effects. Because of the Seattle study (designed when Schaie was still a Berkeley graduate student) we know a great deal about age-related patterns in fundamental dimensions of intelligence. But there still is a great deal to discover about the antecedents of intellectual growth and decline, in particular the role of family contexts.

Schaie and Willis explore the extent to which shared family environments exist and the mechanisms that produce within-family uniformity or variation. Their results are fascinating and sometimes surprising. For example, they find that respondents perceive shifts in the quality of family environment over their own life course: they see their current families as more cohesive and expressive, but also characterized by more conflict than was true for their families of origin. Second, siblings (particularly sisters) are highly similar in the perception of their family of origin, but this similarity does not extend to perceptions of their current (unshared) families. Third, there are substantial correlations between the parents' description of their current family environment and their children's description of the family they grew up in—despite the time gap of several decades in between. Fourth, the intensity (frequency) of contact between parents and offspring has virtually no impact on similarity of reported family environments.

Christopher Hertzog, in his commentary, focuses on the limitations of self-report retrospective data such as that utilized by Schaie and Willis. He also questions the definition of "current family" in their analysis—cohabitation being an important, but not exclusive, criterion. He acknowledges that the findings on generational differences in family environments may indicate, as Schaie and Willis conclude, cultural shifts in the nature of family environments, but he cautions that whether these lead to generational differences in intellectual development is still speculative.

John Henretta reviews the Schaie–Willis results from the standpoint of the life-course perspective that has recently emerged in sociology. He notes that this perspective allows conceptual linkages to be made to other analytic problems and explanations, particularly those involving social structures over time. For example, he suggests that the level of correlation across generations reported by Schaie and Willis may result from the loose coupling of transitions that allows siblings to diverge. Second, he argues that different children in the same family may experience variable environments because historical events mediated by family history produce variability in family environments over time. Third, Henretta notes that perceptions of environments are influenced by processes of "subjective reconstruction" through which individuals construct and interpret the meaning of life events. Each of these explanations is parallel with Schaie and Willis' interpretation of their data, but each provides a wider context for resolving controversies about socioenvironmental effects on individuals' lives.

PARENT–CHILD DIFFERENCES IN PERCEPTIONS OF THEIR RELATIONSHIP: THE "INTERGENERATIONAL STAKE" HYPOTHESIS REVISITED

The sixth controversy has grown out of a finding from a study completed over two decades ago which, if reliable over time, raises the specter of methodological bias in much of family survey research to date. The finding is this: When parents and adolescent children are asked independently about the quality of their joint relationship, their reports often vary; moreover, parents' evaluations are consistently and systematically higher than that of the children's. The controversy has two parts. First, what accounts for such "generational bias" in evaluation, and does it persist into the later life course? Second, since most surveys in the research literature have relied on the report of just one generation to characterize family relationships, is the generational bias so substantial as to question the validity of these surveys?

In Chapter 6 my colleagues Roseann Giarrusso and Mike Stallings and I examine the fate of the "developmental stake" hypothesis proposed many years ago (Bengtson & Kuypers, 1971) to explain why parents tended to overestimate intergenerational solidarity and their children to underestimate it. The original explanation of this phenomenon concerned parents' and children's differential psychosocial involvement (or "stake") in relations down or up the generational ladder, which in turn was a function of parents' and children's different developmental levels in the life course. Since 1971, a number of researchers have used (and modified) the original hypothesis to include sociostructural as well as individual-developmental variables and to focus on generational location itself as an explanatory variable; hence the current term, the "intergenerational stake" hypothesis.

Giarrusso and colleague pose three questions for analysis: (1) does the "intergenerational stake" finding persist over time, across 20 years of the adult life course, for aging parents and their now middle-aged children?; (2) which of two theoretical explanations – individual development or social exchange – provides a better explanation of the phenomenon?; and (3) how do variables of age and gender affect the hypothesis and its explanation? To examine these questions they utilize data from a longitudinal study involving both parents' and children's reports on intergenerational affect between 1971 and 1991. They develop and test four specific hypotheses derived from developmental and exchange theoretical perspectives in order to examine the adequacy of competing explanations.

This is a complex task, involving both empirical and logical–theoretical analyses; and the results (as the authors admit) are somewhat mixed. On the one hand there is empirical support for the "generational bias" hypothesis: when the perceptions of parents and their children concerning quality of their intergenerational relationship are charted over 20 years, the parents consistently report higher affect than the children. On the other hand, the empirical results do not provide compelling support for either of the theoretical explanations – individual development or social exchange – as stated in the hypotheses. However, the authors conclude that the intergenerational stake phenomenon is better explained by variables related to social position (especially lineage generational structure) and social exchange than it is by individuals' psychosocial progression through developmental stages.

In her commentary, Alice Rossi raises a number of concerns about both the empirical and theoretical results presented by Giarrusso et al. She first questions the procedures used in measuring affectual solidarity, the major independent variable, since they appear inconsistent with the previous measurement procedures of the Southern California research group and/or contaminated by other constructs (such as consensual solidarity). Second, she suggests that both the developmental and exchange theories employed by the authors are insufficiently specified or interpreted. She is particularly critical of what she terms "a niggardly exchange model of rational men seeking 'equity'" (p. 275), which presumably is what the USC researchers are advocating. Third, given Rossi's own many contributions to the analysis of gender in social structures, it should be no surprise that she offers several suggestions about the re-analysis of the USC data to reveal the male–female contrasts. She concludes by asking that gerontologists more seriously consider altruism and empathy as primary motivators of family relations—these are the "sentiments that stoke solidarity" in society generally, and nowhere more so than in intergenerational relations. Giarrusso and her colleagues respond to the criticisms of Rossi in their own commentary. They report that, after redoing their analyses following her criticisms, there were very few substantive changes in the empirical results.

Victor Marshall agrees with Rossi in several respects, but says he would not join her in dismissing "such a promising line of inquiry." He says that the intergenerational stake is one of a very small number of original research questions in the social psychology of intergenerational relationships. He suggests that the liveliness of the discussion (between Giarrusso et al., Rossi, and himself) may itself indicate the importance of the research question and the relevance of the resulting controversy. Marshall then gives his version of the issue. First, he argues that the developmental stake hypothesis is really a variation on another empirical theme, the finding of repeatedly high levels of expressed solidarity in both the cross-sectional and longitudinal data: what "leaps from the charts and tables" of the Giarrusso et al. chapter is not the *differences* between generations, he says, but rather the *similarities* in levels of affect over time. Second, he asks what has happened to the "drama" of intergenerational succession noted in the original Bengtson and Kuypers (1971) formulation of the problem—the "fear of loss" by parents if their children reject solidarity with them, or by children if their parents smother their individuality. Third, he argues for a more phenomenological approach to the question—one that would lead away from the usual fixed-question quantitative research designs and toward data-gathering based less on the properties of individuals and more on the properties of families.

I want to add a personal note here. The "developmental stake" hypothesis was published when Joe Kuypers and I were just out of graduate school; some of my co-authors in this volume were in grammar school at the time. If I had any notion it would still be the subject for scholarly debate 25 years later, I would have been astonished—and undoubtedly would have toned down the speculative flavor of the paper. But if I had been less speculative, the paper would not have caused other scholars to stop and think, to explore the utility of this line of explanation on their data, to try to develop better explantions; and I wouldn't have had as much fun. Like Vic Marshall, I find the "drama in the continuing succession of one generation by the other" lacking in most research studies of intergenerational relations today, and I miss it.

CONCLUSIONS

The chapters in this volume present a wealth of information concerning adult intergenerational relations and the effects of social change. Reflected in these findings and interpretations are some important controversies that have relevance to the analysis of social structures over time. In this chapter I have outlined six of these controversies; let me briefly restate them below:

- Are families becoming more "verticalized," and if so, has this weakened support resources?
- How persistent is generational continuity despite disruptive historical events?
- Can older kin provide much help to younger kin—for example, unmarried teenage childbearers?
- Are there universal and cross-cultural norms of intergenerational support, or do such expectations vary by society?
- Do family environments persist over time, and are they related to intellectual competence throughout life?
- Does our generational placement color our social perceptions—especially about other generations?

These are serious and important questions. And as I look through the pages of this volume it occurs to me that the time is ripe for a younger cohort of social scientists to enter the fray with their own perspectives on these controversies. In any event, I believe there will always be problems of aging and intergenerational relations for scholars to puzzle—as long as there is generational succession among scholars.

ACKNOWLEDGMENTS

I would like to thank Elisabeth Burgess, Judith Richlin-Klonsky, Merril Silverstein, Sandra Reynolds, and Maria Schmeeckle for their suggestions about this chapter, and to acknowledge Linda Hall, Chris Hilgeman, David Sharp, Efrain

Trujillo, and Danielle Zucker for applying their considerable skills to preparing this and other chapters in this volume.

REFERENCES

Bengtson, V. L. (1993). Is the "contract across generations" changing? Effects of population aging on obligations and expectations across age groups. In V. L. Bengtson & W. A. Achenbaum (Eds.), *The changing contract across generations*, (pp. 3–24). New York: Aldine de Gruyter.

Bengtson, V. L., & Harootyan, R. (Eds.). (1994). *Intergenerational linkages: Hidden connections in American society.* New York: Springer.

Bengtson, V. L., & Kuypers, J. A. (1971). Gerontological differences and the developmental stake. *Aging and Human Development, 2,* 249–260.

Bengtson, V. L., Rosenthal, C. J., & Burton, L. M. (1990). Families and aging: Diversity and heterogeneity. In R. Binstock & L. George (Eds.), *Handbook of aging and the social sciences* (3rd edition), (pp. 263–287). New York: Academic Press.

Elder, G. H., Jr. (1981). History of the family: The discovery of complexity. *Journal of Marriage and the Family, 43,* 489–519.

Hareven, T. K. (1987). Family history at the crossroads. *Journal of Family History, 12,* ix–xxiii.

Juster, T., & Suzman, R. (1993). *The health and retirement study: An overview.* HRS working paper #94-1001. Ann Arbor, MI: University of Michigan Institute for Social Research.

Kohli, M. (1986a). The world we forgot: A historical review of the life course. In V. Marshall (Ed.), *Later life: The social psychology of aging.* Beverly Hills, CA: Sage.

Kohli, M. (1986b). Social organization and the subjective construction of the life course. In A. B. Sorensen, F. E. Weinert, & L. R. Sherrod (Eds.), *Human development and the life course: Multidisciplinary perspectives*, (pp. 271–292). Hillsdale, NJ: Erlbaum.

Soldo, B., & Hill, M. C. (1994). *Intergenerational transfers and family structure in the health and retirement survey.* Health and Retirement Survey working paper #94-1004. Ann Arbor, MI: University of Michigan Institute for Social Research.

Weisberg, J. (1992). Are your parents robbing you blind? The coming war between the old and the young. *Worth* (June/July): 68–75.

Author Index

311

Subject Index